Legalines

MW01701896

Editorial Advisors:
Gloria A. Aluise
Attorney at Law
Jonathan Neville
Attorney at Law
Robert A. Wyler
Attorney at Law

Authors:
Gloria A. Aluise
Attorney at Law
David H. Barber
Attorney at Law
Daniel O. Bernstine
Attorney at Law
D. Steven Brewster
C.P.A.
Roy L. Brooks
Professor of Law
Frank L. Bruno
Attorney at Law
Scott M. Burbank
C.P.A.
Jonathan C. Carlson
Professor of Law
Charles N. Carnes
Professor of Law
Paul S. Dempsey
Professor of Law
Jerome A. Hoffman
Professor of Law
Mark R. Lee
Professor of Law
Jonathan Neville
Attorney at Law
Laurence C. Nolan
Professor of Law
Arpiar Saunders
Attorney at Law
Robert A. Wyler
Attorney at Law

CORPORATIONS

Adaptable to Ninth Edition* of Hamilton Casebook

*If your casebook is a newer edition, go to www.gilbertlaw.com to see if a supplement is available for this title.

THOMSON
WEST

EDITORIAL OFFICES: 111 W. Jackson Blvd., 7th Floor, Chicago, IL 60604
REGIONAL OFFICES: Chicago, Dallas, Los Angeles, New York, Washington, D.C.

SERIES EDITOR
Linda C. Schneider, J.D.
Attorney at Law

PRODUCTION MANAGER
Elizabeth G. Duke

FIRST PRINTING—2006

SHORT SUMMARY OF CONTENTS

TABLE OF CONTENTS AND SHORT REVIEW OUTLINE

I. INTRODUCTION

A. BASIC BUSINESS FORMS

The subject of "business associations" involves the study of the means and devices by which business is conducted either by a single individual or cooperatively by a few or many individuals. "Business" means all kinds of profitmaking activity.

The subject is broken down into unincorporated associations (agency, partnership, etc.) and corporations. A further basic distinction can be made between "closely held" businesses (ones with a few owners) and "publicly held" businesses (with hundreds or even thousands of owners). The first several chapters in your outline will discuss closely held businesses.

B. ROLE OF AGENCY LAW

1. **Problem.** A and B go into a small business together, with A putting up the capital and B providing the management. A wants to avoid being called on for additional capital and wants veto power over the important decisions affecting the business. Profits are to be divided equally after B is paid a salary. If A and B enter an oral agreement and B starts in, what form of business organization has been formed?

2. **Agency Law.**

    a. **Principal-agent.** An agency is a fiduciary relationship that results from consent between the principal and agent that the agent shall act on the principal's behalf and subject to her control. [Restatement (Second) of Agency §§1, 2]

    b. **Master-servant.** A master is a principal who employs an agent to perform service in her affairs and who controls or has the right to control the physical conduct of the other in the performance of the service.

    c. **Independent contractor.** An independent contractor is a person who contracts with another to do something for her, but who is not controlled by the other nor subject to the other's right to control with respect to his physical conduct in the performance of the undertaking. The independent contractor may or may not be an agent.

    d. **Questions.** In the above situation, has a principal-agent relationship been established? An employer-employee relationship? An independent contractor relationship? Alternatively, are A and B partners? Is A a limited partner? Can A get what she wants if she organizes as a corporation?

II. THE PARTNERSHIP

A. INTRODUCTION

1. **The Basic Nature of a Partnership.** A partnership is an association of two or more persons to carry on a business as co-owners for profit. [Uniform Partnership Act ("UPA") §6] Note that a lawful partnership cannot be formed for nonprofit purposes.

2. **Comparison with Other Forms of Doing Business.**

   a. **Agency.** A partnership is a more complex form of organization than a sole proprietorship—it is really an extension of the sole proprietorship, which incorporates many of the principles of agency law in structuring how the partnership will function.

      1) For example, A, formerly a sole proprietor, takes in B and C as partners. Now an association has been formed, in which all (A, B, and C) will be co-owners.

      2) Each partner is the agent of her copartners, and when any partner acts within the scope of the partnership, her acts will bind the other partners.

   b. **Joint venture.** A joint venture is an association of two or more members, agreeing to share profits. However, a joint venture is usually more limited than a partnership; *i.e.,* it is formed for a single transaction and usually is not the complete business of the individual associated members. However, the rights and liabilities of partners and joint venturers are usually the same, and the courts usually apply the provisions of the UPA to joint ventures.

   c. **Other unincorporated associations.** There are other types of unincorporated associations (such as the business trust) that are not partnerships.

3. **The Uniform Partnership Act.** The UPA has been adopted by most states, so that the provisions governing partnerships are usually a part of state statutory law, rather than the common law.

4. **Entity and Aggregate Characteristics of a Partnership.**

   a. **Both characteristics.** A partnership is treated both as a separate entity from its partners (for some purposes) and as though there is no separate entity but merely an aggregate of separate, individual partners.

b. **Aggregate theory.** For example, the partners are jointly and severally liable for the obligations of the partnership. [*See* UPA §15] And, for federal income tax purposes, the income or losses of the partnership are attributed to the individual partners; the partnership itself does not pay taxes (although it does file an information return).

c. **Entity characteristics.** For other purposes, a partnership is treated as a separate entity apart from its individual partners.

1) **Capacity to sue or be sued.** The jurisdictions vary as to whether a partnership can be sued and/or sue in its own name. For example, if a "federal question" is involved, then a partnership can sue or be sued in its own name in the federal courts. [*See* Fed. R. Civ. P. 17(b)]

2) **Ownership of property.** A partnership can own and convey title to real or personal property in its own name, without all of the partners joining in the conveyance. [UPA §8]

5. **Formation of a Partnership.**

a. **Partnership by contract.** Since a partnership is a voluntary association, there must be an express or implied agreement in order to form a partnership.

1) **Formalities.** If the partnership is to continue beyond one year, the agreement must be in writing since it comes within the Statute of Frauds.

2) **Duration.** If no term is specified, then the partnership is terminable at the will of any partner.

3) **Capacity to become a partner.** Persons must have the capacity to contract. Some states hold that corporations cannot be partners.

4) **Consent of other partners.** A prospective partner must have consent of all of the other partners. [UPA §18(g)]

5) **Intent of the parties.** Where there is any question, the intent of the parties involved is determined from all of the circumstances. [*See* UPA §7 for the factors considered (including the sharing of profits of the business)]

b. **Partnership by estoppel.**

1) **Liability of alleged partner.** One who holds herself out to be a partner, or who expressly or impliedly consents to representations that she is such a partner, is liable to any third person who extends credit in good-faith reliance on such representations. [UPA §16]

a) For example, A represents to C that she has a wealthy partner, B, in order to obtain credit. B knows of the representation and does nothing to inform C that he is not a partner. C makes the loan.

b) For the purposes of the loan, B will be held to be a partner with A, but he has no other rights to participation in A's business.

2) **Liability of partners who represent others to be partners.** In the above example, if A were part of an actual partnership, then she would make B an agent of the partnership by her representation that B was also a partner. As such B could bind A as though they were in fact partners (but only those other partners of A who made or consented to A's representation would be bound).

B. SHARING OF PROFITS AND LOSSES

Each partner, in the absence of agreement, shares profits and losses equally. [UPA §18(a)]

1. Absence of Agreement--

Richert v. Handly, 311 P.2d 417 (Wash. 1957).

Facts. Richert (P) alleged that P and Handly (D) entered into a partnership agreement where P was to contribute the purchase price of timber ($26,842), D was to use his equipment (for a fee) in logging the timber, and profits and losses were to be shared equally. The proceeds of the sale of timber were about $41,000; P had received back $10,000 and D $7,016; but there was no more cash since the project had lost money (when the cost of the timber was included). P sued for an accounting, alleging a partnership loss of $9,800, and indicating that he was entitled to $26,842, less the $10,000 he had received and one-half of the $9,800 loss (or roughly $12,000). D claimed that additional amounts were due for his services in managing the logging operation, that there was no agreement for reimbursement of P's capital contribution, but that there had been a joint venture on the logging operation and each was to share profits and losses only as to this operation. The trial court found that D's version of the facts was correct, and that the $10,000 received by P and the $7,016 by D were unexpended gross revenues of the undertaking, of which total ($17,016) each was entitled to one-half ($8,508). Hence, P had received $1,491 too much, which he owed D. P appeals.

Issue. Do the findings of fact make clear the agreement as to sharing of profits and losses?

Held. No. Judgment reversed and case remanded.

- It is immaterial whether P and D formed a partnership or a joint venture; the issue is what they decided about sharing profits and/or losses.

- There are conflicting findings by the trial court. For example, it decided that P and D had decided to share profits and losses equally, but that D was not to contribute to P's cost of the timber (*i.e.,* that they had not really decided to share losses equally).

- Also, the trial court did not determine whether D was to be paid the additional amounts claimed for his services.

- Profit or loss of a partnership cannot be determined until all expenses are determined, including whether cost of the timber is to be included.

- The findings are inadequate to support the court's conclusions.

---

2. On Appeal--

Richert v. Handly, 330 P.2d 1079 (Wash. 1958).

Facts. Appeal of the preceding *Richert* case by P to the Washington Supreme Court. On remand, the trial court made additional findings of fact: The partners had not made a specific agreement as to how losses were to be shared; there was no agreement about paying D for additional services; and there was no understanding as to how P was to be reimbursed for the cost of the timber.

Issue. When the partners do not specifically agree, are losses to be shared as provided by the UPA?

Held. Yes. Judgment of trial court reversed; case remanded.

- When the partners do not specifically agree on how losses are to be shared, then the provisions of the Uniform Partnership Act control. [*See* UPA §18(a),(f)]

- Gross proceeds less expenses leaves $14,720. If the cost of the trees is considered an expense, then $26,842 less $14,720 leaves a net loss of $12,121. One-half of this to each partner is $6,060. So $26,842, less $10,000 already received, less $6,060, means that P is due $10,781 from D.

C. LAW FIRM PARTNERSHIPS

1. **Partner Compensation.** Law firms have developed partner compensation schemes that differ from partner compensation in true partnerships. In deter-

mining compensation, law firms tend to consider the partner's productivity and billable hours, how much new business a partner brings in, the partner's activities in management, administration, training, and supervision, and what the partner has done towards the firm's marketing advancement. Some firms have also begun implementing pension plans for retiring partners.

2. Pension Plans--

Bane v. Ferguson, 890 F.2d 11 (7th Cir. 1989).

Facts. Bane (P) was an attorney and partner in Isham, Lincoln & Beale, a law firm. In 1985, the firm adopted a retirement plan that entitled every retiring partner to a pension. The plan document indicated that the plan itself and the retirement payments would end if and when the firm dissolved without a successor entity. P retired four months after the plan went into effect and began drawing a pension. Several months later, the firm merged with a larger firm. The merger proved disastrous and the merged firm dissolved in 1988. P filed suit against the members of Isham, Lincoln & Beale's managing council (Ds) alleging that they had acted unreasonably in deciding to merge the firm, and that their negligent mismanagement led to the firm's dissolution. P sought damages representing the present value of his pension. The district court dismissed the complaint for failure to state a cause of action, and P appeals.

Issue. Does P have any common law or statutory claim against Ds for the loss of his pension?

Held. No. Judgment affirmed.

- ♦ While P set forth several arguments in support of his claim, none entitle him to relief. P first alleged that Ds violated section 9(3)(c) of the Uniform Partnership Act ("UPA") by taking an action that would make it impossible to carry on the ordinary business of the partnership. This argument is without merit. The purpose of this section of the UPA is to protect other partners for the unauthorized acts of one partner. P ceased to be a partner when he retired.

- ♦ P's second argument similarly fails. It is true that a partner is a fiduciary of his partners. However, as stated above, P was a ***former*** partner. Thus, Ds had no fiduciary duty to him. We note that even if P had been owed a fiduciary duty, he would still have no cause of action. P's complaint alleges negligence, not fraud or deliberate misconduct. The business judgment rule protects Ds from liability for mere negligent operation of the firm.

- ♦ P also alleged breach of contract. The plan instrument expressly stated that the plan would terminate upon dissolution of the firm. Thus, there was no breach of the contract.

- P's final theory is based on general principles of tort law. P alleges that Ds violated a general duty of care to him. We can find no precedent for imposing tort liability under these circumstances (*i.e.*, holding careless managers responsible for the consequences of a firm's dissolution to all those persons who were hurt by the dissolution). In the absence of misconduct, the act of dissolution of an entity is not in itself a sufficient basis for a tort action.

D. LIMITED LIABILITY PARTNERSHIPS (LLPs)

Nearly all states allow the creation of limited liability partnerships ("LLPs"). An LLP is essentially a general partnership and subject to the UPA; however, the partners in an LLP are ***not personally liable*** for some or all of the partnership debts and obligations. Once an LLP has been formed and properly registered with the state, most state statutes provide that a partner in an LLP is not personally liable for the debts and obligations of the partnership arising from the negligence, wrongful acts, or similar misconduct (*i.e.*, torts) of her copartners. Many states go further and shield a partner from personal liability for any partnership debts and obligations, whether in contract, tort, or otherwise. Note though that in most states, even if a partner in an LLP is not liable for some or all partnership debts and obligations, the partner remains personally liable for her ***own wrongful acts*** and for those committed by someone whom she directly supervises.

E. MANAGEMENT

All partners have equal rights in management (even if sharing of profits is unequal). [UPA §18(e)]

1. One Coequal Partner Cannot Escape Responsibility by Notifying Creditor--

---

National Biscuit Co. v. Stroud, 106 S.E.2d 692 (N.C. 1959).

Facts. Stroud (D) and Freeman entered a partnership to sell groceries under the name Stroud's Food Center. There were no restrictions in the partnership agreement on the management functions or authority of either partner. Several months prior to February 1956, D notified National Biscuit (P) that he would not be responsible for any additional bread delivered to the Food Center. Nevertheless, on Freeman's order P delivered $171 worth of bread over a two-week period in February. At the end of this time, D and Freeman dissolved the partnership, and D was responsible for winding up its affairs. D refused to pay P's bill. The trial court found for P, and D appeals.

Issue. If there are no restrictions in the partnership agreement as to the partners' authority, can an equal partner escape responsibility for partnership obligations by notifying a creditor that he will not be responsible for partnership debts incurred with that creditor?

Held. No. Judgment afirmed.

- ♦ The acts of a partner within the scope of the partnership business bind all partners.
- ♦ A majority of partners can make a decision and inform creditors and will thereafter not be bound by acts of minority partners in contravention of the majority decision. But here there could be no majority decision, as they are equal co-partners.
- ♦ Hence, the partnership is liable for the debt to P.

Comment. Had D dissolved the partnership and given P notice prior to the order by Freeman, then D would not have been personally liable for the partnership debt to P.

2. **Admissions and Representations.** The partnership is charged with the admissions and representations of any partner concerning partnership affairs, when they are made in the scope of her actual, implied, or apparent authority. [UPA §11]

   a. **Apparent authority--**

Smith v. Dixon, 386 S.W.2d 244 (Ark. 1965).

Facts. The Smith family (Ds) entered into a general partnership soon after the purchase of some land. The purpose was for farming. W.R. Smith was the "managing partner." As general partner he had negotiated and signed for the partnership in a few sales and purchases of land. He then entered a contract to sell to Dixon (P), who took possession and began farming. Then Ds refused to close the sale, arguing that W.R. Smith had been given the authority to sell the land for $225,000, not for $200,000. P sued for specific performance or damages; the trial court awarded $11,000 in damages. Ds appeal.

Issue. May one partner have the authority to sign for the partnership in transferring land owned by the partnership?

Held. Yes. Judgment affirmed.

- ♦ A partner may transact land sales if operating with apparent authority. As W.R. Smith had in the past negotiated land transactions for the partnership, he had apparent authority to set the price in this sale, and the partnership must adhere to his bargain.

Comment. A partner has the authority to make a conveyance of partnership land when this is done in the ordinary course of partnership business. [UPA §9(1)] When, however, such transactions are not in the ordinary course of business, the real property represents critical assets of the partnership, and a partner cannot convey such land unless he has been given special authority to bind the partnership. If a partner does exceed his authority in conveying land, the partnership can usually recover the property from the grantee unless the grantee is a bona fide purchaser who had paid the purchase price without knowledge of the lack of authority. [UPA §10(1)]

---

b. **Imputed notice.** Knowledge or notice to one partner of matters pertaining to regular partnership business is imputed to the partnership. [UPA §12] However, there is no imputation of notice or knowledge when the partner is acting fraudulently or adversely to the partnership.

   1) **Fraudulent acts--**

Rouse v. Pollard, 18 A.2d 5, *aff'd,* 21 A.2d 801 (N.J. 1941).

Facts. Fitzsimmons was a partner in a law firm (D), and Rouse (P) was his client. Very early in their relationship Fitzsimmons, on learning that P had some valuable securities, induced P to cash them in, on the representation that the firm would invest the money for her in some good mortgages and pay her interest semiannually. Fitzsimmons embezzled the money but paid P interest for many years (several after the law firm was dissolved). Fitzsimmons was convicted of embezzlement; P sued to recover her money. When Fitzsimmons was found to be insolvent, P sued the members (partners) of the law firm. None of the partners knew of the transaction or that Fitzsimmons had done similar acts many times with clients; nor was it the practice of D to invest clients' money.

Issue. Will D be held liable for the fraudulent acts of a copartner?

Held. No. Judgment for D.

- ♦ In order to hold copartners liable for the fraudulent acts of one of the partners, the acts in connection with which the fraud is committed must have been within the general scope of the partnership business.
- ♦ While the law firm often held the money of clients for investment in mortgages or other investments, these situations were normally part of a transaction the firm was handling for the client. The firm had not had the practice of investing money generally for its clients.

---

3. Vicarious Liability of Law Partnership for Negligent Acts of One Partner Within the Firm's Normal Business--

Roach v. Mead, 722 P.2d 1229 (Or. 1986).

Facts. Mead, a lawyer, had a long relationship of doing work for Roach (P), including representing P in many business transactions. After Mead formed a law partnership with Berentson (D), Mead continued to represent P. P asked Mead's advice in investing $20,000 for him; Mead indicated he would take the $20,000 as a loan and give P 15% interest on it. Mead failed to advise P that he should get independent advice on the loan, it should be secured, and that the interest rate was usurious under state law. Mead had a relationship of trust with P. Mead subsequently borrowed another $1,500 from P, then defaulted on the loans and went bankrupt. P sued D, contending that he was vicariously liable for the negligent acts of his partner, Mead. D defended on the basis that the negligent acts of Mead were outside the scope of the partnership's business. The trial court denied a directed verdict for D and sent the case to the jury, which found for P. The court of appeals affirmed, and D appeals the case to the state supreme court.

Issue. Was D vicariously liable for the negligent acts of his law partner?

Held. Yes. Judgment affirmed.

- ♦ Partners are jointly and severally liable for the acts of copartners based on the principal-agent relationship between the partners and the partnership.
- ♦ Partners are jointly and severally liable for the tortious acts of other partners if they have authorized those acts or if the wrongful acts are committed in the ordinary course of the business of the partnership. [UPA §§13, 15]
- ♦ The reasonableness of P's belief that the service he seeks is within the domain of the profession of law is a question that must be answered on the basis of the particular facts of each case.
- ♦ There is nothing to suggest that the ordinary business of the law firm or of Mead was to solicit personal loans. However, there is enough evidence for the case to go to the jury on the basis that it was part of the normal business of the firm and Mead to give clients advice about business matters, including the advisability of making personal loans, and on what terms these loans should be made. This being the case, it is reasonable for the jury to have found that Mead was negligent in not giving sound legal advice to his client, P, concerning the loan P made to him. Specifically, Mead should have told P that the loan should have been checked out by an independent party, should have been a secured loan, and that the interest rate was usurious.
- ♦ Since Mead was negligent in giving advice to P on a matter within the normal scope of the law firm's business, D can be held vicariously liable for the negligent acts of Mead.

F. DUTIES OF PARTNERS TO EACH OTHER

The duty of one partner to all others is based on a fiduciary relationship.

1. Duty of Loyalty--

Meinhard v. Salmon, 164 N.E. 545 (N.Y. 1928).

Facts. Gerry leased a hotel to Salmon (D) for 20 years; D was obligated to spend $200,000 in improvements. Shortly thereafter D entered a joint venture with Meinhard (P) for P to pay one-half of the money needed to alter and manage the property, receiving 40% of the net profits for five years and 50% thereafter. D had the sole power to manage the property; D's interest in the lease from Gerry was never assigned to P. Gerry owned a substantial amount of adjoining property and near the end of the lease term tried to put together a deal to level all of the property and put up one large building. Failing that, Gerry approached D, and they entered a lease on all of the ground (renewable for a period up to 80 years), eventually calling for the destruction of the hotel and the building of a new, larger building. P found out about the new lease and demanded that it be held in trust as an asset of their joint venture. The lower court held that P was entitled to a half interest in the new lease and must assume responsibility for half of the obligations. D appeals the judgment.

Issue. Does the new lease come within D's fiduciary obligation to his joint venture partner as a joint venture "opportunity"?

Held. Yes. Judgment for P affirmed.

- Joint venture partners have the highest obligation of loyalty to their partners. This includes an obligation not to usurp opportunities that are incidents of the joint venture. The duty is even higher for a managing co-adventurer.

- There was a close nexus between the joint venture and the opportunity that was brought to the manager of the joint venture, since the opportunity was essentially an extension and enlargement of the subject matter of the old one.

- Since D was to control the project, he should receive 51 shares of the corporation that holds the lease on the new project, and P should have 49 shares.

Dissent. This is not a general partnership. It is a joint venture, entered into by D to get financing for his project. There was no expectancy of a renewal of the lease, and no intention that P be part of D's business forever. P, for example, never received an assigned interest in D's lease with Gerry; and P could not have renewed the lease had there been a renewal provision. It was a limited venture for a specific term. So the new opportunity was not an extension of the old one.

G. PARTNERSHIP PROPERTY

A frequent issue involves whether property is partnership property or the individual property of a partner.

1. **Definition of Partnership Property.** All property originally brought into the partnership or subsequently acquired by purchase or otherwise, for the partnership, is partnership property. [UPA §8(1)]

   a. **Proof of intent.** If there is no clear intention expressed as to whether property is partnership property, then courts consider all of the facts related to the acquisition and ownership of the asset in question. Some of the factors considered: (i) how title to the property is held; (ii) whether partnership funds were used in the purchase of the property; (iii) whether partnership funds have been used to improve the property; (iv) how central the property is to the partnership's purposes; (v) how frequent and extensive the partnership use is of the property; and (vi) whether the property is accounted for on the financial records of the partnership.

2. **Individual Partner's Interest in the Partnership.** The property rights of an individual partner in the partnership property are (i) her rights in specific partnership property, (ii) her interest in the partnership, and (iii) her right to participate in the management of the partnership. [UPA §24]

   a. **Rights in specific partnership property.** Each partner is a tenant-in-partnership with her copartners as to each asset of the partnership. [UPA §25(1)] The incidents of this tenancy are as follows: (i) each partner has an equal right to possession for partnership purposes; (ii) the right to possession is not assignable, except when done by all of the partners individually or by the partnership as an entity; (iii) the right is not subject to attachment or execution except on a claim against the partnership (the entity theory); (iv) the right is not community property, hence it is not subject to family allowances, dower, etc.; and (v) on the death of a partner, the right vests in the surviving partners (or in the executor or administrator of the last surviving partner). Hence, partnership property is not part of the estate of a deceased partner but vests in the surviving partner, who is under a duty to account to the deceased partner's estate for the value of the decedent's interest in the partnership. (*See* below.)

   b. **Partner's interest in the partnership.** A partner's interest in the partnership is her share of the profits and surplus, which is ***personal property.*** [UPA §26]

      1) **Consequences of classification as personal property.** A partner's interest is personal property, even if the firm owns real property.

Thus, the partner's rights to any individual property held by the partnership are equitable (the partnership holds title), and this equitable interest is "converted" into a personal property interest. This can be important in inheritance situations where real property may be given to one heir and personal property to another.

2) **Assignments.** A partner may assign her interest in the partnership (unless there is a provision in the partnership agreement to the contrary), and unless the agreement provides otherwise, such an assignment will ***not*** dissolve the partnership. [UPA §27(1)]

a) The assignee has no right to participate in the management of the partnership (*i.e.,* he is not a partner; he only has rights to the assigning partner's share of the profits and capital).

b) But the assignee is liable for all partnership obligations.

3) **Rights of partner's creditor.** A creditor of an individual partner may not attach partnership assets. He must get a judgment against the partner and then proceed against the individual partner's interest (by an assignment of future distributions, a sale of the interest for proceeds, etc.).

c. **Liability to partnership creditors.**

1) **On contracts.** All partners, including silent ones, are jointly liable on all partnership debts and contracts. [UPA §15(b)]

2) **Tort liability.** Each partner is liable for any tortious act committed by a copartner within the scope of the partnership business or within her authority as a copartner. Liability is both joint and several. But if the tort involves a showing of malice or intentional conduct, then it must appear that each partner sought to be held liable possessed such intent.

H. PARTNERSHIP ACCOUNTING

From this point on, much of the material on corporations assumes a basic understanding of accounting. The following is a very short summary.

1. **Definition of Accounting.** Accounting is the recording, classification, summary, and interpretation in money terms of transactions affecting the accounting unit.

2. **Accounting Names.**

a. **Balance sheet.**

1) **Assets.** Assets are things of value owned by the corporation.

2) **Liabilities.** Liabilities are claims on assets by creditors of the corporation.

3) **Net worth.** Net worth is the difference between assets and liabilities (assets - liabilities = net worth). In effect net worth represents the claims of the corporation's owners on the company's assets.

4) **Purpose.** The balance sheet shows the financial condition of the corporation as of some specific moment in time.

5) **Sample balance sheet.**

Assets		**Liabilities**	
Cash	$100	Accounts payable	$ 50
Equipment	100	Bonds	100
Land	100		
		Net Worth	
Total	**$300**	Common stock	$ 50
		Paid-in surplus	50
		Retained earnings	50
		Total Liabilities plus Net Worth =	**$300**

b. **The accounting equation.** The basic accounting equation is:

Assets = Liabilities + Net Worth

c. **Income statement.**

1) **Revenue.** Revenue or income is derived from the sale of things of value (services or goods) for money.

2) **Expenses.** Expenses are costs associated with producing revenue.

3) **Losses.** Losses are costs that do not result in producing revenue, *e.g.*, buying a building for $1,000 and selling it for $500.

4) **Purpose.** The income statement indicates what has happened to the accounting entity over some period of time (*e.g.*, January 1 to December 31)—how much revenue is produced and the expenses associated with producing that revenue. At the end of the accounting period, the net effect of the transactions for the period (either net income or net loss) are transferred to the balance sheet (retained earnings). All accounts making up the income statement are cleared, and the process of tracking income and expenses for a new period begins all over again.

5) **Sample income statement.**

XYZ Corporation
Income Statement
1/1 to 12/31/05

Revenue		$500
Interest		100
Total Income		$600
Cost of Goods Sold	$200	
Marketing Costs	200	
Administrative Costs	150	
Total Expenses		$550
Net Income		$ 50

d. **Capital.** Note the use of the word "capital." It means different things in different contexts. Sometimes it is used to mean "equity" (that is, net worth, or the amount of assets free from the claims of outside, third-party creditors). Sometimes it is used to mean net worth and liabilities, or all of the sources of the corporation's assets.

I. PARTNERSHIP DISSOLUTION

1. **Introduction.** Dissolution of a partnership does not immediately terminate the partnership. The partnership continues until all of its affairs are wound up. [UPA §30]

2. **Causes of Dissolution.** Unless otherwise provided for in the partnership agreement, the following may result in a dissolution:

   a. **Expiration of the partnership term.**

      1) **Fixed term.** Even if the partnership is to last for a fixed term, partners can still terminate at will (but it will be a breach of the agreement by the terminating partner).

      2) **Extension of term.** And partners can extend the partnership by creating a partnership at will on the same terms.

   b. **Express choice of partner.** Any partner can terminate a partnership at will (since a partnership is a personal relationship that no one can be forced to continue in). However, even if it is a partnership at will, if dissolution is motivated by bad faith, then dissolution may be a breach of the agreement.

      1) **Breach of agreement--**

Collins v. Lewis, 283 S.W.2d 258 (Tex. 1955).

Facts. Collins (P) and Lewis (D) entered a partnership agreement for P to put up the money to build and equip a large cafeteria and D to supervise its development and manage it. P and D entered a lease in a building being built. The partnership agreement provided that P was to be paid back from net income, then P and D would share profits equally. Estimated cost to develop was $300,000. The construction of the building was delayed and so was the development of the cafeteria; costs at opening two years later were in excess of $600,000. On opening, the cafeteria operated at a loss; P demanded that it show a profit. D indicated that there were costs of development that were being paid out of operating revenue, rather than by P as promised. Accusations went back and forth. P sued for a receiver, for dissolution, and for foreclosure of a mortgage he held on D's partnership interest. The agreement provided that D was to repay $30,000 of P's investment the first year and $60,000 each year thereafter. D filed a cross-action alleging that P had breached the partnership agreement, and asked for damages if dissolution were granted. The trial court found that D was competent to manage the cafeteria; that without P's conduct there was an expectation of profit; that P had breached his agreement to put up the funds; and that D had earned more than $30,000 in the first year, but due to P's refusal to pay costs of development, that profits had gone to make these payments. The trial court denied the petition for a receiver and also all of the other remedies sought by P. P appeals.

Issue. In these circumstances, does P have the right to dissolve the partnership?

Held. No. Judgment for D affirmed.

- P has the power to dissolve the partnership, but not the right to do so without damages, since his conduct is the source of the partnership problems and amounts to a breach of the partnership agreement.

- P can either continue the partnership and perform on the agreement or dissolve the partnership and subject himself to possible damages for breach of the agreement.

Assignment. Note that an assignment is not an automatic dissolution, nor is the levy of a creditor's charging order against a partner's interest. But the assignee or the creditor can get a dissolution decree on expiration of the partnership term or at any time in a partnership at will. [UPA §§30-32]

---

c. **Death of a partner.** On the death of a partner, the surviving partners are entitled to possession of the partnership assets and are charged with winding up the partnership affairs without delay. [UPA §37] The surviving partners are charged with a fiduciary duty in liquidating the partnership and must account to the estate of the deceased partner for the value of the decedent's interest.

1) **Right of deceased partner's estate to profits--**

Cauble v. Handler, 503 S.W.2d 362 (Tex. 1973).

Facts. Handler (D) and Cauble were equal partners in a retail furniture store. Cauble died in May 1971; D valued the partnership as being worth approximately $80,700 at that date (using cost or book value for the assets, including inventories). D then continued operating the partnership business, without winding up the affairs of the partnership or paying Cauble's administrator (P) the value of Cauble's one-half interest. P then sued D for the value of Cauble's one-half interest plus half of the profits from operation of the partnership from the death of Cauble until the time of suit. The trial court used book value to value the partnership, gave P only interest on the value of the one-half interest used by D in operation of the partnership, and charged P with the entire cost of the court-appointed accountant that audited the partnership. P appeals.

Issue. If the surviving partner continues to operate the partnership after dissolution (without paying the deceased partner his share of the value of the partnership), does the deceased's administrator have a right to a share of the profits subsequently earned by the partnership?

Held. Yes. Judgment for D reversed and case remanded for error.

- ♦ The partnership should be valued as of the time of the deceased's death (dissolution). Market value, rather than cost or book value, should be used to value the assets.
- ♦ If the partnership business is continued by the surviving partner—with or without the consent of the administrator of the deceased partner—then the deceased's administrator has the right to receive a share of the profits from operation of the partnership (equal to the percentage interest that the deceased partner owned in the partnership).
- ♦ The accountant's fee for the audit should be charged to the partnership as an expense, rather than to one partner.

d. **Withdrawal or admission of a partner.** Most partnership agreements provide that admitting or losing a partner will not result in dissolution. New partners may become parties to the preexisting agreement by signing it at the time of admission to the partnership.

1) **Provisions of partnership agreement control--**

Adams v. Jarvis, 127 N.W.2d 400 (Wis. 1964).

Facts. Three doctors entered a partnership; the agreement provided that withdrawal would not terminate the partnership, but that the withdrawing partner was to receive the amount of his capital account at the time of withdrawal (but no part of the partnership's accounts receivable) and a share in the profits earned for the partial year for which he was a partner. Adams (P) withdrew and later sued the partnership on the basis that withdrawal was a dissolution and statutory provisions for dissolution indicated that each partner was to receive his partnership interest in all of the net assets of the partnership (including accounts receivable). The action is for a declaratory judgment; the trial court found for P. Ds appeal.

Issue. Do the provisions of a valid partnership agreement, providing that withdrawal of a partner is not a dissolution of the partnership, control?

Held. Yes. Judgment reversed.

- Under the state statute (partnership law), withdrawal is usually a dissolution of the partnership, but here there is a valid provision in the partnership agreement to the contrary, and since the agreement provides for a way in which the withdrawing partner is to receive payment for his interest in the partnership, the agreement controls.

- UPA section 38(1) indicates the way that distributions are to be made to partners in dissolution, and it is to control "unless otherwise agreed." Here the partners have agreed that no withdrawing partner is to receive an interest in the accounts receivable, each partner was in an equal bargaining position at the time the partnership was formed, and such an agreement is not against public policy. So the provision is valid (it being interpreted to mean patient accounts receivable).

---

2) Liability of withdrawing partners--

8182 Maryland Associates, Limited Partnership v. Sheehan, 14 S.W.3d 576 (Mo. 2000).

Facts. The limited partnership 8182 Maryland Associates (P) leased office space and part of a parking garage to a law firm. At the time of the lease's execution, the law firm had 14 general partners including Sheehan (D). All 14 general partners signed the lease agreement. The lease was for 120 months and included a clause requiring consent by the landlord for assignment. The lease was silent as to the liability of incoming or withdrawing partners from the lessee law firm. After signing the agreement but before the lease commenced, D withdrew from the partnership and assigned his interest in the firm to the remaining partners. The remaining partners created a new partnership. The lease with P was not expressly assigned in writing by the old partnership and the new partnership did not assume the obligations of the lease in writing. Over the next four years the new partnership occupied the space. Within the four years, four new individuals became general partners and later withdrew from the firm. Five years into the lease, the firm defaulted on the lease and filed for bankruptcy. P filed suit and named as defendants all past and present general partners of the firm since the origination of the lease agreement. D and the other four former partners filed motions for summary judgment. The trial court granted the motions and P appeals.

Issues.

(i) Did D's withdrawal before the lease commenced terminate his personal liability?

(ii) Are the four individuals who joined the firm as partners after the lease began personally liable for the lease agreement?

Held. (i) No. (ii) No. Judgment affirmed in part and reversed in part.

- ♦ D became personally liable for the lease at the moment it was executed. His withdrawal before the commencement of the lease period and before the breach of the lease occurred does not relieve him of his liability on the contract.

- ♦ The four individuals who became partners after the lease was signed and left before the breach occurred never expressly assumed the lease. However, the firm's occupation of the leased space creates a presumed assignment. The firm was in privity of estate with P as a result of its occupation of the premises. Each succeeding partnership became jointly and severally liable for rent payments, but only during the period the partnership was in privity of estate with P. When each partner withdrew from the partnership, the privity of estate ended and the withdrawing partner could not be held liable for rent arising subsequent to the time of the withdrawal.

- ♦ Therefore, granting the motion for summary judgment for D was improper. We affirm the entry of summary judgment on behalf of the other four individuals.

3) Forbidden restriction on withdrawing partner--

Lampert, Hausler & Rodman PC v. John F. Gallant, 2004 WL 3120801 (Mass. Super. 2004).

Facts. John F. Gallant (D) was a partner/shareholder in the law firm of Lampert, Hausler & Rodman (P), formerly Gallant, Hausler & Lampert. The firm was established as a closely held corporation, but the parties never created a written agreement addressing the dissolution of the firm or the division of any unfinished business. D resigned from P, and some of D's clients followed him to his new firm. A lawsuit was filed over unfinished contingent fees from those clients. P seeks a partial summary judgment against D on the issue of liability for breach of fiduciary duty.

Issue. Does a lawyer who is a partner and shareholder in a law firm, which is a closely held corporation, have a fiduciary duty not to compete with the firm after the lawyer leaves the firm?

Held. No. P's motion for partial summary judgment allowed in part.

- Because D is still a shareholder of P, P argues that D must abide by his fiduciary duties to P, specifically the duty not to compete with the business.
- Rule 5.6 of the Massachusetts Rules of Professional Conduct states that a lawyer may not make an agreement restricting the lawyer's right to practice as part of a settlement. There is a strong public interest in allowing clients to retain counsel of their choice. [Meehan v. Shaughnessy, 535 N.E.2d 1255 (Mass. 1989)]
- Similarly, the Rule does not permit the enforcement of a "fiduciary duty" that restricts the right of a lawyer to practice after termination of the relationship. Although here D remains a shareholder of P, and thus technically the relationship has not been terminated, the strong public policy behind the disciplinary rule trumps what otherwise would be a valid fiduciary duty. Thus, this court will enforce the fiduciary duties between and among the shareholders of P, except insofar as any such fiduciary duties may prohibit D from practicing law.

Comment. This case is important because it illustrates that an attorney's ethical duties to his clients can override his fiduciary duties to his fellow attorneys.

---

4) Withdrawing partners removing employees from firm--

Gibbs v. Breed, Abbott & Morgan, 271 A.D.2d 180 (N.Y. 2000).

Facts. Gibbs and Sheehan (Ps) were both partners in the law firm of Breed, Abbott & Morgan (D). Gibbs was the head of D's trusts and estates department, and he and Sheehan were the only partners in that department. In June of 1991, Ps informed the other firm partners that they had accepted offers to join another firm. D's presiding partner asked them not to discuss their departure with any of the associates in the trusts and estates department. Prior to leaving D, Ps sent their new employer, Chadbourne, a memo listing the names of D's trusts and estates department personnel, as well as confidential employee information including salaries, background information (such as where they attended school), annual billable hours, and the rate at which D billed the employees out to clients. When Ps left D, they took their "chronology" files, which included client information. Using his chronology file, Gibbs began to contact former clients two days after leaving D. In the following weeks, 92 of D's 201 trusts and estates clients moved their business to Chadbourne. Chadbourne interviewed and made employment offers to four employees that Gibbs indicated that he wanted to bring to work with him. All four accepted. Ps brought suit for monies due under the D partnership agreement. D counterclaimed, asserting that Ps had breached their fiduciary duties to D in the planning and implementing of their withdrawal from the partnership. The trial court found that Gibbs breached his duty of loyalty to D in persuading Sheehan to leave D, and that both Ps breached their fiduciary duties by sending Chadbourne the memo containing personnel information, and by taking their chronology files for use in soliciting clients. The court held that Ps were entitled to recover their share of partnership profits accruing until they left the firm, but that D was entitled to recover lost profits for a reasonable period following Ps' departure because their actions had crippled D's trusts and estates department. Ps appeal.

Issues.

(i) Did Gibbs breach any duty to D by discussing a joint move to Chadbourne with Sheehan?

(ii) Did Ps breach any duty to D by supplying confidential employee information to Chadbourne?

(iii) Did Ps breach any duty to D by improperly soliciting D's clients?

Held. (i) No. (ii) Yes. (iii) No. Judgment affirmed in part, reversed and remanded in part.

- Members of a partnership owe each other a duty of loyalty and good faith. The manner in which a partner plans for and implements withdrawal from the partnership is subject to the constraints imposed by virtue of his status as a fiduciary. D has not established that Gibbs violated any duty by discussing with Sheehan a joint move to Chadbourne. It does not appear from the evidence that Sheehan's decision to leave was based on anything other than his own personal interests. In addition, we find no breach of duty in Ps taking their chronology files, and no evidence of improper client solicitation.

- However, both partners breached their fiduciary duties to D by supplying Chadbourne with confidential personnel information. Pre-withdrawal recruitment of employees has generally been allowed after the firm has been given notice of a partner's intent to withdraw. However, because of the nature of the confidential information Ps gave to Chadbourne, Chadbourne was given an unfair advantage in recruiting certain employees from D. While partners may not be restrained from inviting qualified personnel to move with them, Ps began recruiting while still members of the firm and prior to giving notice of their intent to withdraw.

- The dissent argues that the information Ps provided Chadbourne is generally known to "headhunters" and therefore is not confidential information. We disagree. Ps had unique access to the data in D's personnel files by virtue of their being partners. While the employees' salaries may have been known, the memo contained much more than a list of salaries. It contained information regarding bonuses, billable hours, and the rates at which D billed these employees out to their clients. Such information is highly individualized and privileged, and is certainly not available to the public. The memo provided Chadbourne with information it could not have obtained through independent research, and gave it the upper hand in negotiating employees away from D.

- ♦ The case is remanded for a determination of the financial loss D incurred through Ps' disloyal act of supplying competitors with D's confidential employee information.

Concurrence and dissent. I concur with the court's findings with the exception that I find no breach of duty in connection with the memo Ps sent to Chadbourne. The information Ps provided Chadbourne could easily have been obtained elsewhere. The salary levels and bonuses paid to associates at large firms is regularly published in professional publications, billing rates are well known by professional "headhunters," and an associate attorney's background information is available from sources such as the Martindale-Hubbell directory. I therefore find no breach of any fiduciary duty in Ps providing this information to Chadbourne.

---

e. **Illegality.** Dissolution results from any event making it unlawful for the partnership to continue in business.

f. **Death or bankruptcy.** Without an agreement to the contrary, the partnership is dissolved on the death or bankruptcy of any partner. [UPA §31(4),(5)]

g. **Dissolution by court decree.** A court, in its discretion, may in certain circumstances dissolve a partnership. These circumstances include insanity of a partner, incapacity, improper conduct, inevitable loss, and/or wherever it is equitable. [UPA §32]

h. **Expulsion of a partner.** UPA section 31(1)(d) describes rules regarding expulsion of a partner.

1) **Involuntary expulsion.** A partnership agreement may provide for involuntary expulsion of a partner by majority vote of the other partners. Absent bad faith, the provision will be enforced by the courts. The expelled partner has the burden of proving that the other partners acted in bad faith. [*See* Gelder Medical Group v. Webber, 363 N.E.2d 573 (N.Y. 1977)]

2) **Expulsion for whistleblowing--**

Bohatch v. Butler & Binion, 977 S.W.2d 543 (Tex. 1998).

Facts. Bohatch (P) was an attorney at the law firm of Butler and Binion and became a partner in 1990. After reviewing internal firm reports, P became concerned that another attorney, McDonald, was overbilling Pennzoil, one of the firm's largest clients. P discussed her concerns with various supervisors and the firm's management committee and was told that the matter would be investigated. P was later told that the firm's investigation revealed no basis for her concerns about McDonald, and that she should begin looking for other employment. The firm denied P's year-end partnership distribution for 1990 and reduced her tentative distribution share for 1991 to zero. The firm paid P her monthly draw in June and told her it would be her last. She was to vacate her office by November. P filed suit against Butler and Binion and several of its partners (Ds) for wrongful discharge, breach of the fiduciary duty of good faith and fair dealing, and breach of contract. The trial court granted Ds summary judgment on the wrongful discharge claim, and the remaining claims were tried to a jury. The jury trial found that the firm breached the partnership agreement and its fiduciary duty and awarded P damages for lost wages, mental anguish, punitive damages, and attorneys' fees. The trial court disallowed the attorneys' fees and reduced the punitive damages award. All parties appealed. The court of appeals found that the firm's only duty to P was not to expel her in bad faith (*i.e.*, for self-gain). Finding no evidence that P was fired for the self-gain of the firm, the court held that P could not recover for breach of fiduciary duty. However, the appellate court found that Ds had breached the partnership agreement when they reduced P's tentative distribution to zero without notice, and when it terminated her draw three months before she left. Ds appeal.

Issue. Is there a fiduciary duty among partners not to expel a partner who reports suspected unethical conduct by another partner?

Held. No. Judgment affirmed.

- ♦ Partners have a fiduciary relationship and are obligated to exercise good faith, fairness, and honesty in their dealing with each other with respect to matters concerning the partnership. However, a partnership is a voluntary association. Partners may choose with whom they wish to associate, and they have no obligation to remain partners.
- ♦ The partnership agreement contains procedures to be followed in expelling a partner. It in no way specifies or limits the grounds for expulsion. Thus P's claim that she was expelled from the partnership in an improper manner is governed by the agreement. Her claim that she was expelled for an improper reason is not.
- ♦ Courts have held that a partnership may expel a partner for purely business reasons. (*See* St. Joseph's Regional Health Center v. Munos, 934 S.W.2d 192 (1996).) P urges us to create an exception to the at-will nature of partnerships and, based on public policy reasons, to recognize a duty not to expel a partner who is a "whistleblower" acting in good faith.
- ♦ While this argument has merit, we must reject it. We hold that a partner can be expelled for accusing another partner of overbilling without a breach of any common law duty, and without subjecting the partnership to tort damages. Such allegations, once made, will have a profound effect on the personal confidence and trust essential to the partnership relationship. Partners may find it impossible to work together once such accusations are made.
- ♦ Our refusal to create an exception to the at-will nature of partnerships does not obviate the ethical duties of lawyers as the dissent suggests. The fact that the

ethical duty to report may create an irreparable schism between partners and result in a partner's expulsion does not excuse the failure to report unethical behavior.

♦ We do find, however, that the firm breached the partnership agreement. The agreement requires that a partner be given notice before reduction of her tentative annual distribution. The firm does not dispute that P was not given this notice. Thus, the lower court's finding that Ds breached the agreement is affirmed. Additionally, we affirm the award of attorneys' fees to P.

Concurrence. Permitting a law firm to retaliate against a partner who in good faith reports suspected overbilling would discourage compliance with the rules of professional conduct and thereby hurt clients. An extension of a partner's fiduciary duty is necessary. I would hold that a whistleblower be protected if her allegations are proven to be correct.

Dissent. I would hold that partners violate their fiduciary duty to one another by punishing compliance with the rules of professional conduct. The partners in this case retaliated against P for her good faith effort to alert her partners to the possible overbilling of a client.

---

3. **Distribution of Assets.**

   a. **Partnership debts.** The debts of the partnership must first be paid.

   b. **Capital accounts.** Then amounts are applied to pay the partners their capital accounts (capital contributions plus accumulated earnings and less accumulated losses).

   c. **Current earnings.** Finally, if there is anything left over, the partners receive their agreed share of current partnership earnings. [*See* UPA §40]

   d. **Distributions in kind.** If there are no partnership debts, or if the debts can be handled from the cash account, partnership assets may not be sold, but they may be distributed in kind to the partners.

   e. **Partnership losses.** If liabilities exceed assets, the partners must contribute their agreed shares to make up the difference. [UPA §18(a)]

4. **Rights of the Partners.**

   a. **No violation of agreement.** If the dissolution does not violate the partnership agreement, the partnership assets are distributed as set forth above, and no partner has any cause of action against any other partner.

b. **Dissolution violates agreement.** If dissolution does violate the partnership agreement (for example, the fixed term of the agreement), the innocent partners have rights in addition to those listed above.

1) **Right to damages.** Innocent partners have a right to damages (*e.g.,* lost profits due to dissolution, etc.) against the offending partner. [UPA §38(2)]

2) **Right to continue the business.** The innocent partners also have the right to continue the partnership business (*i.e.,* not sell off and distribute the assets) by purchasing the offending partner's interest in the partnership. [UPA §38(2)(b)—provision for posting bond and beginning court proceedings] Alternatively, of course, the innocent partners may simply dissolve and wind up the business, paying the offending partner her share (less damages).

5. **Effects of Dissolution.**

a. **Liability of partners for existing partnership debts remains until they are discharged.**

b. **New partnership remains liable for old debts.** When there has been a dissolution due to death, withdrawal, or admission of a new partner, and the partnership business is continued, the new partnership remains liable for all the debts of the previous partnership. [UPA §41]

c. **Retiring partner's liability for debt incurred by partners continuing the business.** Dissolution ends the power of a partner to bind the partnership except to the extent necessary to wind up its affairs. [UPA §33] However, if third parties do not know of the dissolution, contracts entered into with a partner bind the partnership.

1) Hence, a retiring partner must make sure that prescribed procedures are followed to terminate any possible liability for partnership obligations. The UPA provides that notice of withdrawal or dissolution may be published in a newspaper of general circulation. [UPA §35(1)]

J. INADVERTENT PARTNERSHIPS

A partnership may be formed inadvertently (*i.e.,* not by express mutual consent, but by implication). *See* the discussion of formation, *supra.*

1. **Profit-Sharing Arrangement--**

Martin v. Peyton, 158 N.E. 77 (N.Y. 1927).

Facts. Knauth, Nachod & Kuhne ("KNK"), a partnership in the securities business, was in financial difficulty. Hall, a partner, arranged for a loan of some securities from

Peyton and some other friends (Ds), which were to be used as collateral for a bank loan to KNK. The "loan" agreement provided that no partnership was intended; until the loan was repaid, Ds were to receive 40% of the profits of the firm; collateral was given to Ds in the form of speculative securities owned by the firm; all dividends on the securities loaned by Ds were to be paid to Ds; Ds were to be advised of and consulted on all important matters affecting the firm; they could inspect the books and ask for any information they wanted; they could veto any of the firm's business deemed "speculative"; all partners assigned their interest in the firm to Ds as security for the loan; Ds had an option to buy half of the firm; each partner submitted his resignation, which could be accepted at any time by Ds on paying the firm member the value of his interest. But Ds could not initiate any actions for the firm or bind the firm by their actions. Creditors of KNK (Ps) claimed that Ds had entered the partnership and therefore sought to hold Ds for the partnership's debts. The trial court found that the transaction was a loan; Ps appeal.

Issue. Has a partnership been formed?

Held. No. Judgment affirmed.

- A partnership is an association of two or more persons to carry on a business for profit. Creation is by express or implied agreement. Ps claim that the written agreement of the firm with Ds constitutes the formation of an express partnership.
- Sharing of profits is considered as an element of a partnership; but not all profit-sharing arrangements constitute those participating as partners. Nor is the language saying that no partnership is intended conclusive. The entire agreement will be looked at in making this determination.
- All of the features of the agreement are consistent with a loan agreement, so no partnership has been formed.

2. Intention of Parties Controls--

Smith v. Kelley, 465 S.W.2d 39 (Ky. 1971).

Facts. Kelley and Galloway (Ds) were partners in an accounting firm; they hired Smith (P) and paid him $1,000 per month, plus expenses, and at year-end a bonus out of the profits of the business. There was no agreement that P would share in the profits; he made no contribution of capital to the firm; he took no part in management, had no authority to hire and fire employees, sign notes, or borrow money; and he was not responsible for losses. However, Ds had represented on partnership tax returns that P was a partner, as well as in a major contract, a lawsuit, and a statement filed with the state board of accountancy. After three years P left the firm and sued for an accounting on the basis that he was a partner and was due 20% of the profits of the firm. The trial court found for Ds. P appeals.

Issue. Do the facts establish an intention among the parties that P was to be a partner?

Held. No. Judgment affirmed.

- It is the intention of the parties among themselves that establishes a partnership, and here the intention was not to make P a partner. While a partnership as to third parties may arise by estoppel from Ds' conduct, that is irrelevant as to the relationship between the parties.

---

3. **Partnership by Estoppel.** According to UPA section 16, a person who represents himself, or permits another to represent him, to anyone as a partner in an existing partnership or with others who are not actual partners, is liable to any such person to whom a representation is made who has, on the faith of the representation, given credit to the actual or apparent partnership. This is an exception to the rule that persons who are not actual partners as to each other are not partners as to third persons. However, at least one court has interpreted section 16 narrowly and held that it only creates liability to third persons who "give credit" to the partnership. [*See* Young v. Jones, 816 F. Supp. 1070 (D.S.C. 1992)] In *Young*, the plaintiffs invested in a company based on an unqualified report prepared by Price Waterhouse-Bahamas ("PW-Bahamas"). Price Waterhouse-U.S. ("PW-U.S."), a United States partnership, allowed PW-Bahamas, its foreign affiliate, to use its name and trademark, and made no distinction in its advertising between itself and the foreign affiliate. In fact, Price Waterhouse advertised in a brochure that it was a worldwide organization with 400 offices throughout the world. When the plaintiffs learned that the company they had invested in had falsified its financial statements, they sued both PW-Bahamas and PW-U.S. arguing that the two firms were partners by estoppel. The court held that the firms' advertising practices were not enough to create a partnership by estoppel.

III. THE LIMITED PARTNERSHIP

A. CHOICE OF BUSINESS FORM

The following factors are considered when making a determination of which form to use in conducting a business:

1. **Legal Restrictions.** The law requires that certain businesses be conducted in certain forms (*e.g.,* for a long time professions, such as the practice of law, could not be conducted in the corporate form).

2. **Liability.** A crucial issue concerns the exposure of the participants to liability. For example, in a corporation the shareholders (owners) are liable only to the extent of their contributions to the corporation. If the corporation goes bankrupt, creditors cannot sue the shareholders for the corporate debts (*i.e.,* the shareholders' other assets are not at risk in the business). This is not true for partners in a partnership (*i.e.,* they risk all of their assets—those committed to use in the business, and their other personal assets).

3 **Taxation.** A major motivation is the saving of taxes. Corporations are taxed once on their net income, and the shareholders are taxed again on the dividends they receive. In a partnership the net income or loss is allocated to the member partners, so that there is only one taxation.

4. **Informality, Flexibility, Cost.** A partnership is easier to form and administer than a corporation, and less expensive (fewer forms to file with the state, less formal management structure—meetings, etc.—that must be adhered to).

5. **Continuity of Life.** A corporation goes on forever, unless dissolved by the shareholders or by order of the courts. If the president dies, this does not automatically dissolve the business. On the other hand, the Uniform Partnership Act provides that on certain events (such as the death of a partner) a partnership is dissolved. However, legal continuity and economic continuity are two different things. For example, partners may provide that the partnership will not dissolve on the death of a partner, but will continue, with the partnership paying the dead partner's estate the value of her share in the partnership. On the other hand, the death of the president of the corporation might necessitate the economic termination of the business (*e.g.,* if there were no one else capable of running the business).

6. **Centralization of Management.** Corporate law generally indicates that the business shall be managed by the board of directors, although recent changes have allowed more flexibility than this (*i.e.,* in small corporations the shareholders may manage the business). While all partners are generally responsible for management, partners may agree among themselves as to other arrangements (*i.e.,* they might decide on a managing partner, etc.).

B. THE MODERN LIMITED PARTNERSHIP

Limited partnerships are entities created by modern statutes. They were developed to facilitate commercial investments by those who want a financial interest in a business but do not want all the responsibilities and liabilities of partners. Prior to 1976, most states had adopted the Uniform Limited Partnership Act ("ULPA"). In 1976 the ULPA was revised to make it applicable to large partnerships and to reflect new business practices. Most states have now adopted the Revised Uniform Limited Partnership Act ("RULPA"). Another revision in 1985 is only slightly different from the 1976 Act.

1. In General.

a. **Definition.** A limited partnership is a partnership formed by two or more persons and having as its members one or more general partners and one or more limited partners.

1) The "general partner" assumes management responsibilities and full personal liability for the debts of the partnership.

2) The "limited partner" makes a contribution of cash, other property, or services rendered to the partnership and obtains an interest in the partnership in return—but is not active in management and has limited liability for partnership debts. [RULPA §303(b)]

3) A person may be ***both*** a general and a limited partner in the same partnership at the same time. In such a case, the partner has, with respect to her contribution as a limited partner, all the rights that she would have if she were not also a general partner. [ULPA §12]

b. **Purposes.** A limited partnership may carry on any business that a partnership could carry on. [ULPA §3]

c. **Liability.** As noted above, the general partner is personally liable for all obligations of the partnership. A limited partner, however, has no personal liability for partnership debts, and her maximum loss is the amount of her investment in the limited partnership. [ULPA §1]

1) **Exception.** However, when a limited partner ***takes part in the management and control of the business,*** she becomes liable as a general partner. [RULPA §303(b)]

d. **Rights of limited partners.** The rights of a limited partner are substantially the same as those of a partner in an ordinary partnership, except that she has no rights with regard to management. Hence, she has rights of access to the partnership books, to an accounting as to the partnership business, and to a dissolution and winding up by decree of court. [ULPA §10]

1) A limited partner may lend money to, or transact business with, the partnership. [ULPA §13]

2) A limited partner's interest is assignable, unless the agreement provides otherwise. The assignment vests in the assignee all rights to income or distribution of assets of the partnership, but unless and until the certificate of limited partnership is amended with the consent of all other partners, the assignee is ***not*** entitled to inspect partnership books, obtain an accounting, etc. [RULPA §702]

2. **Formation of Limited Partnership.** While formalities are usually not required to create a partnership, there are certain requirements for the formation of a limited partnership: (i) The partners must execute a certificate setting forth the name of the partnership, the character of the business and the location of the principal office, the name and address of each of the partners and their capital contributions, a designation of which partners are "general" and which are "limited," and the respective rights and priorities (if any) of the partners; and (ii) a copy of the certificate must be recorded in the county of the principal place of business. [ULPA §2] The certificate may be amended or canceled by following similar formalities. [ULPA §25]

a. If the certificate contains false statements, anyone who suffers a loss by reliance thereon can hold all of the partners (general and limited) liable. [ULPA §6]

b. The purpose of the certificate is to give all potential creditors notice of the limited liability of the limited partners.

c. The ULPA requires at least "substantial compliance in good faith" with these requirements. If there has been no substantial compliance, the purported limited partner may be held liable as a general partner.

1) However, a purported limited partner can escape liability as a general partner if—upon ascertaining the mistake—she "promptly renounces her interest in the profits of the business or other compensation by way of income." [ULPA §11]

3. **Corporate General Partners.**

a. **Duty of corporate general partner--**

In re **USACafes, L.P. Litigation,** 600 A.2d 43 (Del. Ch. 1991).

Facts. Metsa Acquisition Corp. ("Metsa") purchased all of the assets of USACafes, L.P. USACafes, Inc. was the corporate general partner of the limited partnership. Ps are holders of limited partnership units. Following the sale, Ps filed suit against the corporate general partner, the partnership, and several members of the board of directors of the general partner (Ds). Ps' complaint contained a variety of allegations of wrongdoing concerning the sale, including breach of the duty of loyalty. Specifically, Ps alleged that the sale was at a very low price, favorable to Metsa, because the directors of the general partner all received substantial side payments that induced them to sell at a low price. Ds moved to dismiss the breach of duty claims, arguing that the complaint failed to state a claim upon which relief can be granted. Ds argue that while a general partner owes fiduciary duties of loyalty and care to the limited partners of a limited partnership, the ***directors*** of the general partner owe no such duties to those persons.

Issue. Do the directors of a corporate general partner owe fiduciary duties to the partnership and to its limited partners?

Held. Yes. Motion to dismiss denied.

- While there is no precedent on this issue, the general principles of corporate law, as well as analogy to trust law, seem to indicate the existence of such duty. Fiduciary duty, in essence, dictates that one who controls the property of another may not intentionally use that property in a way that benefits the holder of the control to the detriment of the property or the beneficial owner. The core aspect of the concept is fidelity with respect to the control of property for the benefit of another.

- Fiduciary duty arose from trust law, but was quickly extended to achieve substantial justice in a variety of circumstances. For example, corporate directors, while not strictly trustees, were early on regarded as fiduciaries for corporate shareholders. Other courts have extended the fiduciary duty of a general partner to a controlling shareholder. In light of the foregoing, it seems appropriate to extend such duties to the directors of a general partner who, even more so than a controlling shareholder, are in control of the partnership's property.

- I do not undertake to determine the scope of the duty here as such an undertaking is not necessary to rule on this motion. I am confident that the scope includes the duty not to use control over the partnerships' property to the advantage of the corporate director, at the expense of the partnership. That is exactly what is alleged in this case.

---

b. Fiduciary duty regarding confidential material--

In Re **Spree.com Corp.,** 2001 WL 1518242 (E.D.P.A. 2001).

Facts. Cashback Liquidation Company (P) was a new Internet company that hired Technology Crossover Ventures, L.P. ("TCV"), a venture capital fund, to help it choose managers, find investors, handle accounting, and assist with marketing and development of the business. Technology Crossover Ventures, Inc., was the corporate general partner of TCV. Tesler served as a member of P's board of directors as the representative, agent, and/or employee of the TCV investors. The TCV investors and Tesler (Ds) allegedly made damaging statements about P's financial status to a reporter for the Wall Street Journal. The statements appeared in an article in the paper on August 24, 2000, and included statements such as "The cash runs out soon," "They're going to be looking at us for more capital, aren't they?" and "I don't want to be supporting them until who knows when." P alleges that these statements violated the parties' agreement and their duties of confidentiality, loyalty, and due care, and had a chilling effect on P's existing and future ability to attract investors and raise capital. P ultimately filed for bankruptcy. Ds filed a motion to dismiss the complaint.

Issues.

(i) Did the statements made to the reporter and thereafter published constitute a wrongful disclosure of "confidential material" as defined by the parties' agreement?

(ii) Did the statements breach any of Ds' fiduciary duties to P?

Held. (i) No. (ii) Maybe. Complaint dismissed in part.

- The parties' confidentiality agreement provided that the investors agree to keep information furnished to them by the company or on behalf of the company confidential. P claims that the statements about its need for cash were wrongful disclosures of information unavailable to the public. However, the facts indicate that in July and August, prior to the article's publication, P had embarked on a fundraising campaign to solicit additional third-party investors. In the course of this activity, P obviously would have been forced to make a complete disclosure of its financial condition to prospective investors. Since any information that becomes publicly available is no longer "confidential information," the statements indicating that P is "running out of cash" do not provide the basis for a claim of breach of contract.

- While we find no breach of the confidentiality agreement, an issue remains as to whether Tesler breached a fiduciary duty of care by making statements to the press that he knew would injure the corporation by interfering with prospective financing agreements. P's complaint alleges certain capital investors had made verbal commitments to contribute funds to P, but did not honor those agreements as a result of Ds' statements. P has pled facts which, if proven, would establish lack of privilege or justification as to Tesler. Thus, this part of the complaint will not be dismissed.

---

4. **The Master Limited Partnership.** The term "master limited partnership" applies to a large partnership that is widely held and whose ownership interest

(*i.e.*, limited partnership interests) is frequently traded. A provision in the Revenue Act of 1987 clarified that certain "publicly traded partnerships" will be taxed as corporations if they "more nearly resemble a corporation than a partnership."

5. **Dissolution of Limited Partnership.** A limited partnership may be dissolved in any of the ways provided for dissolution of a partnership (*see* discussion *supra*).

   a. Unless otherwise provided in the agreement, the retirement, death, or insanity of a general partner dissolves the partnership. [ULPA §20]

   b. However, the death of a limited partner does ***not*** dissolve the partnership. Instead, the decedent's executor or administrator is given all the rights of a limited partner for purposes of settling the estate. [ULPA §21]

C. OTHER FORMS OF BUSINESS ORGANIZATION

1. **Varied Forms.** There are many other forms of business organization: the business trust, the joint stock company, etc. Also, the Internal Revenue Code allows the formation of a Subchapter S Corporation (formed like a corporation, with limited liability of the shareholders, but taxed like a partnership—*i.e.,* corporate net income is distributed to the shareholders and taxed to the shareholders).

2. **The Professional Corporation.** Most states have enacted legislation permitting professionals to do business under the corporate form. This has raised many questions—whether shareholders are limited in liability to their contributions of capital, etc.

   a. **Motivation to form.** The principal motivation for the formulation of such corporations was the desire to qualify for many tax saving plans (pension, profit-sharing, etc.) that the Internal Revenue Code permitted corporations and their employees but that were not permitted to the sole proprietor (or partnerships). Recently, due to abuses, Congress limited most of these benefits.

      1) **Abuses.** Senior members of professional corporations, usually high-income taxpayers, abused pension plan benefits by making very large, deductible contributions to defined benefit plans and then borrowing money for living expenses and deducting the interest on these loans. Another abuse was the practice of creating corporations of one professional, effectively creating a one-person retirement plan and excluding lower-paid employees from coverage.

      2) **TEFRA.** In 1982, Congress passed the Tax Equity and Fiscal Responsibility Act ("TEFRA"), which has eliminated the professional corporation tax abuses by eliminating its pension plan advantages over unincorporated businesses.

IV. LIMITED LIABILITY COMPANIES

A. INTRODUCTION

Limited liability companies ("LLCs") are unincorporated business entities that combine the tax advantages of a partnership with the limited liability protection of a corporation. State statutes generally set out the requirements for formation and operation of an LLC. Some issues, however, have not been settled by statute and continue to be the subject of debate. For example, the scope of fiduciary duties of members of an LLC have not been clearly defined. It also remains unclear whether corporate principles of law, such as piercing the corporate veil, will be applied to LLCs. The Uniform Limited Liability Company Act ("ULLCA") was promulgated in 1996. The ULLCA attempts to provide uniformity and consistency to disparate state legislation. It has had limited acceptance, however, in part because it contains more partnership concepts than most existing state LLC statutes.

B. CONTRACTUAL ASPECTS OF LIMITED LIABILITY COMPANIES

1. Freedom of Contract--

Elf Atochem North America, Inc. v. Jaffari and Malek LLC, 727 A.2d 286 (Del. 1999).

Facts. Elf Atochem North America, Inc., (P) manufactured a solvent-based product that was used in the aviation and aerospace industries. Jaffari was the president of Malek, Inc., and had developed a water-based, more environmentally friendly product. When the Environmental Protection Agency ("EPA") began to regulate solvent-based products as hazardous chemicals, P and Jaffari agreed to undertake a joint venture to market Jaffari's product. The parties formed Malek LLC, a Delaware limited liability company. P contributed capital to the project in exchange for a 30% interest in Malek LLC, and Malek, Inc. contributed its rights to the new product in exchange for a 70% interest in Malek LLC. P, Jaffari, and Malek, Inc. entered into an agreement ("the Agreement") providing for the governance and operation of the LLC. The Agreement contained an arbitration clause covering all disputes arising out of the Agreement, and a forum selection clause providing for exclusive jurisdiction of the state and federal courts sitting in California. Two years later, P filed suit in Delaware against Jaffari and Malek LLC (Ds), individually and derivatively on behalf of Malek LLC. P claimed that Jaffari breached his fiduciary duty to the LLC, used LLC funds for personal use, interfered with prospective business opportunities, failed to make disclosures to P, and breached their contract. Ds filed a motion to dismiss due to lack of subject matter jurisdiction. The court of chancery held that P's claims arose under the Agreement, and that therefore, the Agreement controlled the question of jurisdiction. Because the Agreement states that only a court of law or arbitrator in California may decide claims arising under it, the court granted Ds' motion and dismissed P's complaint. P appeals.

Issue. May the members of a limited liability company, through the use of a forum selection clause in their membership agreement, vest jurisdiction in a particular forum?

Held. Yes. Judgment affirmed.

- The Delaware Limited Liability Company Act provides broad discretion in drafting the LLC agreement and furnishes default provisions only when the members' agreement is silent. It is designed to give maximum effect to the freedom to contract and to the enforceability of limited liability company agreements. Only when the agreement is inconsistent with mandatory statutory provisions will the members' agreement be invalidated.

- P argues that the dispute resolution provision in the Agreement is invalid under the Delaware Limited Liability Company Act because the Act prohibits the parties from vesting exclusive jurisdiction in a forum outside of Delaware. We find nothing in the Act or elsewhere to indicate that members cannot alter the default jurisdiction provisions of the statute and contract away their right to file suit in Delaware. The policy of the Act is to give maximum effect to the members' freedom of contract to govern their relationship provided that they do not violate any mandatory provisions of the Act. Thus, we find that members may contract to vest jurisdiction where they please. In this case, the Agreement clearly states that no action based on any claim arising out of this Agreement may be brought except in California, and then only to enforce arbitration in California.

- Finally, P argues that Malek LLC, although in existence when the Agreement was executed, did not sign the Agreement and, thus, never assented to the arbitration and forum selection clauses within it. Therefore, P argues, it is suing derivatively on behalf of Malek LLC. We disagree. Malek, Inc. and P, the members of the limited liability company, executed the agreement. P's claims are subject to the arbitration and forum selection provisions notwithstanding Malek LLC's failure to sign the Agreement.

C. LEGAL ASPECTS OF LLCs

Limited liability companies have been held to be distinct, artificial entities, a legal status similar to that of corporations.

1. Legal Representation Required--

Poore v. Fox Hollow Enterprises, 1994 WL 150872 (Del. 1994).

Facts. Poore (P) was suing Fox Hollow Enterprises (D). Campbell, who is not an attorney, filed an answering brief that he had drafted himself on behalf of D. P filed a motion to strike D's answering brief for failure to properly file an answer through counsel. Campbell argued that because D is a limited liability company and not a corporation, he could represent the company in court himself.

Issue. Must an LLC be represented in court proceedings by counsel?

Held. Yes. P's motion to strike granted.

- A partnership may represent itself in court. A corporation is regarded as an artificial entity and not a natural person, and cannot appear or conduct business in court without representation by counsel. The issue then is if a limited liability company more closely resembles a partnership or a corporation.

- The Delaware Limited Liability Company Act ("DLLCA") treats an LLC as a partnership for tax purposes. However, the DLLCA considers an LLC a separate legal entity, and treats the interest of a member as analogous to shareholders of a corporation. In addition, a member or manager of an LLC cannot be held personally liable for the company's debts above his contribution. We find that these factors make an LLC a distinct, artificial entity under Delaware law. Thus, Campbell cannot represent the LLC and representation by counsel is required.

V. THE DEVELOPMENT OF CORPORATION LAW IN THE UNITED STATES

A. HISTORICAL BACKGROUND AND PERSPECTIVE

1. **Historical Perspective.** The law of corporations has a long history. Its beginnings trace back to the Middle Ages and the guild system, when only the government gave out business charters (as a means of controlling wealth and as a means of limiting the growth of power in private hands). Since that time there have been many major conceptual developments in the law of corporations: *e.g.,* the development of general state incorporation laws; the enactment of laws to regulate the issuance and trading of corporate securities; and the development of the antitrust laws to regulate competition.

2. **Economic Perspective.** In terms of the control of economic resources, corporations dominate the economy. Obviously, therefore, the condition of the markets that corporations operate in are of critical importance to the economy as a whole—*e.g.,* the capital markets and the markets for goods and services.

3. **Sociological Perspective.** Another possible perspective is to view the corporation as an organization of people. As such it has been studied by sociologists, business administration experts, psychologists, and decision theorists (to name a few). One of the questions most frequently asked, and not really answered, is: "What are the real goals of corporate management?"

4. **Accounting Perspective.** Accounting is very important to the corporate entity, to those who relate to it externally, and to the law of corporations. For example, corporate performance is measured in accounting terms; accounting reports are given to regulatory bodies; capital is attracted to corporations on the basis of their accounting results; and many legal rules depend directly on accounting concepts (*e.g.*, the legal term "insolvency" is based on an accounting concept).

5. **Legal Perspective.** The laws of many diverse fields affect corporations—labor law, administrative law, contract law, tax law, etc. In some sense, the law of corporations incorporates all of these. However, in a special, limited sense the law of corporations is the basic body of law concerning the relationships among all of those "inside" the corporation; *i.e.,* shareholders, management, the board of directors, etc.

B. DEPARTURE OF RESTRICTIONS ON CORPORATE ACTIVITY

1. **The Modern Trend.** The trend from the late 1800s until recently has generally been away from restrictions on corporate activity—in terms of the purposes

for which corporations may incorporate and in terms of the types of transactions and activities in which they may engage. However, many significant limitations still remain (most of which will be examined in the sections that follow), and in many areas the limitations are now growing and expanding.

2. **Tax on Retail Stores--**

Louis K. Liggett Co. v. Lee, 288 U.S. 517 (1933).

Facts. Louis K. Liggett Co. (P) was owner of a chain of retail stores in Florida. A Florida statute imposed a tax on retail stores in the state but exempted gas stations. The tax gradually increased per store, based on the total number of stores in the chain and depending on whether the stores were located in the same county or spread among many counties. The Florida Supreme Court upheld the statute against P's challenge. P appeals.

Issue. Does the statute represent an unreasonable regulation of corporations, offending the Equal Protection Clause of the United States Constitution?

Held. Yes. Judgment reversed.

- ♦ The statute is an unconstitutional violation of Fourteenth Amendment equal protection. There is no reasonable classification for discriminating in the tax amount between chain stores and single retail stores.

Dissent (Brandeis, J.). The state ought to be able to impose restrictions on the size and scope of corporate activity in the public interest.

- ♦ Historically, corporations were so limited in order to limit the political and economic power in the hands of the few and provide equal opportunity for all.

- ♦ General incorporation laws do not signal an abandonment of the regulation of corporations in the public interest. They were simply to take the granting of corporate charters away from a discretionary practice subject to fraud and abuse and make it a process subject to the rule of law.

- ♦ Many restrictions in general corporation laws remain which limit corporate powers (restrictions on capital structure, etc.).

- ♦ Here, equal protection is not violated if the state wants to deter intrastate monopoly by imposing on corporations a discriminatory license fee based on the number and location of stores owned by a chain of stores.

---

3. **Modern Incorporation Statutes.** Each state has an incorporation statute that sets forth the basic law governing the corporation and its affairs. Generally,

the law of Delaware has been the most liberal (*i.e.,* sympathetic to management in allowing it to do most of the things it wants to do in managing the affairs of the corporation). Other states are more restrictive; California takes a position of limiting management in favor of protecting the rights of the shareholders and corporate creditors. One influence in the liberalization of state law has always been the desire by the states to attract incorporation in the state in order to increase state economic growth.

C. FEDERAL CORPORATION LAW

There is no specific federal corporation law, but so much federal law affects the affairs of a corporation that it is fair to say that federal law is equally (if not more) important than state corporate law. For example, federal securities laws influence every issuance of corporate securities, and there are many federal laws that regulate specific industries (Federal Communications Act, Interstate Commerce Act, etc.).

D. PUBLIC AND CLOSE CORPORATIONS

A "public" company is generally a large corporation that has its securities owned by a large number of people and traded in interstate commerce over a stock exchange or between brokerage firms (in the "over-the-counter" market). A "close corporation" is a company owned by relatively few shareholders; the stock of such a company is not traded in public markets. A close corporation may be very small (and typically is) or it may be a large company in terms of assets and sales. Most states have only one corporations statute; but a few are beginning to recognize that the situation of a close corporation is sufficiently different that special provisions should be applicable to it.

1. **Stock Ownership.** In the close corporation the objective is to limit the transfer and trading of the corporation's stock to the few owners.

2. **Control and Management.** In a close corporation normally the owners wish to retain control, and each owner has veto power over important decisions. In public corporations, effective control is centralized in the management (principally the officers).

3. **Financing.** Close corporations normally get funds through borrowing and pledging the corporation's and the owners' personal assets as security. Public corporations use the public securities markets to get financing.

4. **Fiduciary Duties.** The owners of close corporations may often treat the corporation as a partnership and thus violate the delineation of legal duties set up by corporation law, or they may arrange the affairs of the corporation to their personal benefit (such as distributing all corporate profits in the form of salary in order to avoid the double taxation involved in the receipt of dividends—*i.e.,* income taxed first to the corporation and then taxed again as a dividend to the shareholders).

VI. THE FORMATION OF A CLOSELY HELD CORPORATION

A. PROCESS OF INCORPORATION

1. General Characteristics of the Corporation.

a. **Separate legal entity.** A corporation is a separate legal entity (created by the law of a specific state), apart from the individuals that may own it (shareholders) or manage it (directors, officers, etc.). Thus, the corporation has legal "rights" and "duties" as a separate legal entity.

b. **Limited liability.** The owners (shareholders) have limited liability; debts and liabilities incurred by the corporation belong to the corporation and not to the shareholders.

c. **Continuity of existence.** The death of the owners (shareholders) does not terminate the entity since shares can be transferred.

d. **Management and control.** Management is centralized with the officers and directors. Each is charged by law with specific duties to the corporation and its shareholders. The rights of the corporate owners (shareholders) are spelled out by corporate law.

e. **Corporate powers.** As a legal entity, a corporation can sue or be sued, contract, own property, etc.

2. Constitutional Status of Corporations.

Constitutional Status of Corporations. In *Wheeling Steel Corp. v. Glander,* 337 U.S. 562 (1949), the United States Supreme Court specifically held that corporations were "persons" under the Due Process and Equal Protection Clauses of the Fourteenth Amendment. However, it has also been held that corporations are not "citizens" within the meaning of the Privileges and Immunities Clauses of the Fourteenth Amendment or Article IV.

B. REQUIREMENTS FOR FORMATION: ARTICLES OF INCORPORATION

A corporation is a legal entity; it comes into existence by compliance with the statutory requirements of the state where it is incorporated. Incorporation begins by filing articles of incorporation.

1. **Mandatory Provisions of the Articles of Incorporation.** Normally the articles must state:

   a. **Corporate name.**

b. **Corporate purpose.** Typically, most state laws say that a corporation may be formed for any "lawful" purpose. This clause normally sets forth the types of activities engaged in by the corporation.

c. **Specific business.** Normally, the articles must also state the specific business in which the corporation will engage. Note that while formerly many states did not allow professionals (lawyers, doctors, etc.) to incorporate, most now do.

d. **Location of principal office and the corporation's agent for service of process.**

e. **Number of directors.** Normally, a minimum number is required. The original directors of the corporation must be named.

f. **Capital structure.** Types of shares (voting, nonvoting, common, preferred, etc.); par or no par value for each share; number of shares authorized of each class must be specified. If there is more than one class, there must be a statement of the preferences, privileges, and restrictions of each class. Note that some states require that a corporation begin with a minimum amount of capital.

2. **Optional Provisions in the Articles.** In addition, the articles may also contain many other provisions, such as:

   a. **Preemptive rights.** Existing shareholders have the right to subscribe to any additional shares offered.

   b. **Power of assessment.** Board of directors may assess additional amounts to be paid in by shareholders.

   c. **Other.** Any other regulating provision that is not against state law.

3. **Execution.** The original directors (called "incorporators") must sign and acknowledge the articles.

4. **Filing.** The articles must be filed with the secretary of state. Some states provide that a copy of the articles must also be filed in other locations (county of principal office, etc.).

5. **Corporate Existence.** Most state laws provide that a corporation's existence begins when the articles are stamped as filed in the secretary of state's office.

C. COMPLETION OF CORPORATE ORGANIZATION

1. **Organizational Meeting.** As soon as the articles are filed, the corporation must hold an organizational meeting of the new board of directors to complete all

of the steps necessary to its organizational structure so that the corporation may begin to operate.

2. **Matters to Be Decided.**

a. **Resignation of incorporators and election of directors.** Often the incorporators are simply persons used to file the articles (such as the attorney who is preparing the articles). Thus, the incorporators propose and elect the first directors and then resign after the end of the first meeting.

b. **Election of officers.**

c. **Adoption of the bylaws.** The bylaws indicate the duties of the officers, the meetings to be held by the directors and shareholders, where the corporate records are to be kept, regulations for issuing shares, and other matters regulating the conduct of the corporation. The bylaws may contain any provision not contrary to the provisions of the articles. The directors or the shareholders may amend the bylaws.

d. **Authorization to issue shares and other matters.** Also covered in this meeting is the adoption of a corporate seal, authorization to open a bank account, authorization to qualify to do business in other states, leases of property, and authorization to issue the first shares of stock.

D. CORPORATE PURPOSES AND POWERS AND THE DECLINING ROLE OF ULTRA VIRES

1. **Corporate Purposes.** Both business and legal theory agree that a corporation must have a purpose or goal. They tend to disagree about what this purpose should be.

a. **Business theory.** When business theory talks about "corporate purposes" it tends to talk in terms of "strategy." Strategy is the determination of the basic long-term goals and objectives of the company and the adoption of courses of action and the allocation of resources necessary to carry out the basic goals. Strategy includes:

1) Selection of target markets, definition of basic products to address markets, and determination of the distribution systems (all from among many alternatives).

2) Matching corporate resources and capabilities with necessary resources and capabilities for possible market alternatives. Once alternatives have been selected, planning the necessary resources and their allocation.

3) Selection of alternatives in terms of management's personal preferences and values.

4) Selection of alternatives according to perceived obligations by management to segments of society other than the stockholders.

b. **Legal theory.** In the law the issue is what purposes are within those bounds set by the articles and the statutory law under which the corporation was formed. In effect, the articles are a contract between the state and the incorporators.

1) Originally the issue was whether a corporation had exceeded the powers granted under a state-given charter.

2) More recently, with general incorporation laws, the issue is whether the corporation has remained within the purposes set by the incorporators and the state law.

3) Closely related to the issue of proper purposes is the issue of proper "powers." State law often sets forth the acts that a corporation may legally perform. These acts should be in aid of a proper corporate purpose.

4) If the corporation engages in an improper purpose or uses an improper power, then the purpose or act is said to be "ultra vires" (beyond the corporation's powers).

2. **Distinction Between Purposes and Powers.** There is a distinction in meaning. A "purpose" means the end or objective and usually is a statement of the type of business that the corporation will engage in. A "power" means the kind of acts (such as mortgaging property) in which a corporation may engage in pursuit of corporate purposes. Discussions involving purposes or powers often confuse these terms.

3. **Powers of a Corporation.**

a. **Express powers.** A corporation has express power to perform any act authorized by the general corporation laws of the state and those acts authorized by the articles of incorporation.

1) **General powers.** Most states have express statutory provisions allowing corporations to sue and be sued, own property, make gifts to charity, borrow money, acquire stock in other companies, redeem or purchase corporate stock, etc.

2) **Limitations.** Most states also have some express limitations on corporate powers. For example, a transfer of substantially all of a corporation's assets normally requires the approval of a majority of the voting power of the shareholders.

b. **Implied powers.** In most states corporations also have implied powers to do whatever is "reasonably necessary" for the purpose of promoting their express purposes and in aid of their express powers, unless such acts are expressly prohibited by common or statutory law. The trend is to construe broadly what is reasonably necessary.

1) Some states limit the right of a corporation to enter into partnerships, since a partner may bind the corporate partner (removing management responsibility from the corporation's board). Shareholders may give this power in the articles, however.

2) Some states have continued the common law prohibition of corpoations practicing a profession (law, etc.).

c. **Constructive notice.** All parties dealing with a corporation are held to have constructive notice of the corporation's articles and of state corporation law.

4. Ultra Vires Acts by a Corporation.

a. **Definition.** Any act that is beyond the purposes or powers (express or implied) of a corporation is an ultra vires act. Such acts may arise because the corporation acts outside the powers granted in its articles or beyond the powers granted by the state corporation law.

b. **Consequences of an ultra vires act.** The state may bring a quo warranto action to cancel the corporation's charter or to oust the corporation from operating illegally, or an equity action for an injunction. Alternatively, a shareholder may bring an injunctive action to prevent the corporation from acting outside its authority.

c. **Specific instances of ultra vires acts.**

1) **Torts.** Generally, ultra vires is no defense to a tort action brought against a corporation for the act of one of its employees acting within the scope of his employment.

2) **Criminal acts.** The rule for criminal acts is similar to torts.

3) **Contracts.** In certain situations, the common law permitted a claim of ultra vires to corporate contracts, *e.g.,* where the contract was purely executory. But the claim was not favored since it threatened the security of commercial transactions. Now most states have passed statutes severely limiting the claim of ultra vires acts.

a) For example, ultra vires generally may not be claimed once the contract is executed (performed) or is executed on one side. The basis for so holding may be "estoppel."

b) Ultra vires contracts may generally be "ratified" by the unanimous vote of the shareholders, which validates the contract.

And when there is a benefit to the corporation from the ultra vires act, ratification by a majority of the shareholders is sufficient. However, the corporation (or the shareholders in a derivative suit) may sue the directors for damages on the basis that they undertook an unauthorized action.

c) The state may always raise the issue, however.

4) **Illegal acts.** Note that illegal acts are not merely ultra vires; the corporation may always be held liable for such acts.

d. **Executory contracts--**

---

711 Kings Highway Corp. v. F.I.M.'s Marine Repair Service, Inc., 273 N.Y.S.2d 299 (1966).

Facts. 711 Kings Highway Corporation (P) entered into an agreement to lease property to F.I.M.'s Marine Repair (D) for use as a motion picture theater. P later sued (before performance under the lease had begun) for declaratory judgment declaring the lease to be invalid on grounds that a motion picture theater business falls completely outside the scope of the powers and authorities conferred by D's corporate charter. D moved to dismiss the complaint for legal insufficiency or in the alternative for summary judgment.

Issue. May the lease be declared invalid on grounds that the intended use of the premises falls completely outside the scope of the powers and authorities conferred by D's corporate charter?

Held. No. D's motion to dismiss granted.

- ♦ Section 203 of the New York Business Corporation Law states that "no act of a corporation and no transfer of property to or by a corporation, otherwise lawful, shall be invalid by reason of the fact that the corporation was without capacity or power to do such act or engage in such transfer. . . ." Three exceptions are cited that do not apply to this case.
- ♦ The fact that ultra vires is raised in the complaint and not in the defense will not bar application of section 203.
- ♦ P's contention that the ultra vires doctrine still applies fully to executory contracts is rejected.

---

e. **Charitable contributions.** In the early days, corporate charters were granted by the government on the theory that the corporation would contribute to the public interest as well as making money for shareholders only. In the 1930s, a debate began about the responsibility of corporations. Some argued that a corporation's objective should be to produce the best goods and service, that no other legal standard is enforceable, and that any other standard allows an unhealthy divorce between management (making such decisions) and ownership. Others argued that corporations have a "social responsibility" and that they must balance the interests of stockholders, employees, customers, and the public at large.

1) Gifts must be reasonable--

Sullivan v. Hammer, 1990 WL 114223 (Del. Ch. 1990).

Facts. Occidental Petroleum Corporation (D) mailed its stockholders a proxy statement for the company's 1989 annual meeting. The statement reported that a special committee of D had approved a proposal to provide financial support to an art museum named after Dr. Armand Hammer, D's founder and chairman of the board. Certain shareholders (Ps) filed class and derivative claims, alleging that this was a waste of corporate assets and that Dr. Hammer had breached his duty of loyalty by causing D to make these expenditures for his personal benefit. The parties reached a settlement agreement proposing, among other things, that the museum would be named the "Occidental Petroleum Cultural Center Building", that D would be publicly acknowledged as the corporate sponsor of the museum, and that there would be certain financial limits as to the amount of support D would give to the museum. The proposed settlement is before the court for approval.

Issue. May a court approve a settlement of a shareholder derivative and class action, alleging that the funding of an art museum was a waste of corporate assets, if the claims asserted fall within the ambit of the business judgment rule and the settlement provides adequate benefit to the class?

Held. Yes. Settlement approved.

♦ In ruling on a proposed settlement such as this, a court must look to the facts and circumstances upon which the claim is based, and the possible defenses thereto, and must then exercise its own business judgment and determine the overall reasonableness of the settlement. The factors to be considered include: (i) the probable validity of the claims; (ii) the apparent difficulties in enforcing the claims through the courts; (iii) the collectibility of any judgment recovered; (iv) the delay, expense, and trouble of litigation; (v) the amount of compromise as compared with the amount and collectibility of the judgment; and (vi) the views of the parties involved.

♦ Ps' potential for success in this case is very poor. Ps have not shown that D's directors have any self-interest in the transaction. It is highly probable that a court would find that the decision is entitled to the presumption of propriety afforded by the business judgment rule.

- The museum qualifies as a charity. The test of whether a corporation may make a charitable gift is its reasonableness. The gift as now limited is clearly within the range of reasonableness.

- D will receive goodwill from this transaction and will be able to utilize the museum in the promotion of its business purposes. Therefore, the benefit to D's stockholders is sufficient to support the settlement, particularly when compared to the weakness of Ps' claims.

---

f. **Summary.** Many states have dealt with the ultra vires problem by statute. These statutes tend to take the approach that the state may bring an action against the corporation for ultra vires acts and so may a shareholder (in order to enjoin unauthorized activities and to sue directors and officers for damages to the corporation). But the statutes generally limit the right of the corporation or parties external to the corporation to claim ultra vires as a basis for rescinding a commercial transaction.

E. PREMATURE COMMENCEMENT OF BUSINESS

1. Problems Connected with Preincorporation Transactions by Promoters.

a. **Introduction.** The word "promoter" has a precise definition—*i.e.,* one who takes part in the formation of a new corporation. Problems connected with promoters at the preincorporation stage are considered at this point (as part of the problems of formation), although many of the problems relate very closely to the financing of the corporation (considered *infra*).

b. **Fiduciary responsibilities.** Promoters are said to have certain fiduciary responsibilities to their copromoters and to the corporation and its other shareholders.

1) **Duty to copromoters.** Prior to incorporation, promoters owe a fiduciary responsibility to each other. In effect, they are partners in the formation of the corporation. In this regard they must disclose all relevant matters and deal fairly with each other. So, for example, one promoter may not take for himself a "business opportunity" that was intended for the corporation.

2) **Duty to the corporation.** The promoters also owe a fiduciary duty to the corporation. So, for example, when a promoter has a personal interest in property to be sold to the corporation, the promoter must

make a full disclosure of all material factors that might affect the corporation's investment decision (*e.g.*, ownership interest, profit to the promoter, etc.). For disclosure to be effective it must be made to an independent board of directors or the shareholders.

c. **Preincorporation promoter contracts.** In the course of forming the corporation, promoters often contract for products or services on behalf of the corporation (not yet formed).

1) **Promoter liability.**

a) **General rule.** If the promoter contracts in the name of, and solely on behalf of, the corporation to be, then the promoter cannot be held liable if the corporation is never formed. Of course, if the promoter contracts in his own name, then the promoter may be held liable and may enforce the contract. The tough cases are the ones where both the promoter's name and the name of the corporation appear.

b) **Promoter liable--**

Stanley J. How & Associates, Inc. v. Boss, 222 F. Supp. 936 (S.D. Iowa 1963).

Facts. At the time the contract for architectural services was signed, Boss (D) signed as follows: "Edwin A. Boss, agent for a Minnesota corporation to be formed who will be the obligor." How (P) performed services worth $38,250 under the contract but was paid only $14,500. The corporation was never formed. P sued D to recover the balance due on the contract.

Issue. Is the person signing for the nonexistent corporation liable under the contract if the corporation subsequently does not materialize?

Held. Yes. Judgment for P.

♦ The Restatement (Second) of Agency, section 326 comment b, states that when a promoter makes an agreement on behalf of a nonexistent corporation, the following alternatives may represent the intent of the parties:

(i) The other party is making a revocable offer to the corporation, which will result in a contract if the corporation is formed and accepts the offer prior to withdrawal.

(ii) The other party is making an irrevocable offer for a limited time. Consideration to support the promise to keep the offer open can be found in an express or limited promise by the promoter to organize the corporation and use his best efforts to cause it to accept the offer.

(iii) A present contract binds the promoter, with an agreement that his liability terminates if the corporation is formed and manifests its willingness to become a party.

(iv) A present contract is made on which, even though the corporation becomes a party, the promoter remains liable either primarily or as surety for the performance of the corporation's obligation.

- The ***general rule*** is that the person signing for the nonexistent corporation is to be held personally liable, unless the intent is clearly expressed otherwise. Hence, D is liable here.

---

2) **Corporate liability.** If the corporation ratifies or accepts the contract after incorporation, then the corporation may be held liable on the preincorporation promoter contract (and may enforce the contract). Ratification may be express or implied from adoptive conduct of the corporation.

a) **Quasi-contractual recovery.** If the corporation repudiates the contract, it is still liable for the value of anything that it makes use of (in quasi-contract).

b) **Adoption by implication.** While a corporation generally is not bound by contracts made on its behalf by promoters before its organization, adoption may be inferred from acts of acquiescence by the corporation or its authorized agents. In *McArthur v. Times Printing Co.,* 51 N.W. 216 (Minn. 1892), the court found an employment contract that had been made by a promoter, although not ratified, had been adopted by implication because the directors of the corporation knew of the contract, did not object to it, and paid a salary under it for six months. Most jurisdictions recognize that adoption may be by implication. Note that adoption by implication generally is not held to be a novation (although some argue that it should be), and thus the promoter is not relieved of personal liability by the adoption.

c) **Relation back.** The general rule is that ratification is retroactive and adoption is not. When a contract is adopted, the date of adoption does not relate back to the original date when the contract was made, but relates to the date of the actual adoption. Relation back only occurs when there is a ratification. Ratification implies that the principal existed at the time the contract was made and gave authority to its agent to make the contract, which it then ratified.

2. **Defective Incorporation.**

a. **Introduction.** Once there has been an attempt to incorporate, the first issue is whether a corporation has actually been formed, and if not, what the consequences are. For example, any one of a number of the formal requirements for incorporation may have been omitted or improperly performed. Or, even though the articles have been properly filed, the steps necessary to complete the company's internal organization (adoption of bylaws, etc.) may not have been completed. What is the effect? The question normally arises when an outside party (such as a creditor) wants to disregard the corporate shield against liability and hold one or more of the shareholders personally liable for "corporate" debts. Note also the relationship of this topic to that of "piercing the corporate veil," discussed *infra.*

b. **"De jure" corporation.** A corporation that has complied strictly with all of the mandatory provisions for incorporation cannot be attacked by any party (even the state). What is mandatory and what is "directive" is a matter of judicial construction of the state's incorporating laws.

c. **"De facto" corporation.** There is a body of common law that indicates that even when a corporation has not complied with all of the mandatory requirements to obtain de jure status, it may have complied sufficiently to be given corporate status vis-a-vis third parties (although not against the state).

1) **Requirements for de facto status.** De facto incorporation is accomplished by (i) a good faith attempt to comply with the provision of the incorporation law, and (ii) a good faith actual use or conduct of business as though a corporation existed.

2) **Examples.** A corporation may have only de facto status if it fails to put a seal on articles, as required by law, or its incorporator gives an incorrect address in the articles. Note that if a corporation has de facto status, all parties must treat it as a corporation, except that the state may bring a quo warranto action to declare the corporation invalid.

3) **Legislation.** A number of states have eliminated the de jure or de facto question altogether. Legislation has specified that if the corporation's articles have been stamped as "filed" with the secretary of state, they will be conclusively presumed to form a valid corporation, except in actions brought by the state.

d. **Corporation by estoppel.** When a corporation is not given de jure or even de facto status, its existence as a corporation may be attacked by any third party. However, there are situations where courts will hold that the attacking party is "estopped" to treat the entity as other than a corporation. The relevant questions to determine whether the estoppel doctrine will apply are:

(i) To what degree did the corporation attempt to comply with the requirements of incorporation?

(ii) Did the plaintiff deal with the entity as a corporation and how much knowledge did the plaintiff have about the entity's legal posture?

(iii) Did the defendants whom the plaintiff seeks to hold personally liable know that no corporate entity existed?

Estoppel may apply when a third party deals with a corporation before it has actually become a corporate entity. For example, in *Cranson v. International Business Machines Corp.,* 200 A.2d 33 (Md. 1964), International Business Machines Corp. ("IBM") sold typewriters to a company through its agent, Cranson. At the time of the sale, the company's articles of incorporation had not yet been filed. When IBM later sought to hold Cranson personally responsible for the cost of the typewriters, the court applied the doctrine of estoppel to prevent recovery against him. The court found that IBM did business with the company as if it were a corporation and relied on the company's credit, not on Cranson's, in making the sale.

1) MBCA provisions--

Robertson v. Levy, 197 A.2d 443 (D.C. 1964).

Facts. Levy (D) submitted articles of incorporation to the state to organize a business. He bought out Robertson's (P's) business in the corporation's name even though no certificate of incorporation had been issued. The certificate of incorporation was issued one month later, and six months later the corporation ceased doing business. P sued D personally for the balance due on the note he received from the corporation and for additional damages. The trial court held that the Model Business Corporation Act ("MBCA"), section 146, did not apply and that therefore P was estopped to deny the existence of the corporation. He therefore could not recover directly from D.

Issue. Can the president of an "association" that filed its articles of incorporation (which were first rejected but later accepted) be held personally liable on an obligation entered into by the association before the certificate of incorporation has been issued?

Held. Yes. Judgment reversed.

♦ Historically, the following types of corporations have been recognized:

(i) ***De jure***: results when there has been compliance with the mandatory conditions precedent to formation (as opposed to merely directive conditions). It is not subject to direct or collateral attack.

(ii) *De facto*: a defective incorporation with the following requisites: (i) a valid law under which such a corporation can be lawfully organized; (ii) an attempt to organize thereunder; (iii) actual user of the corporate franchise; and (in some jurisdictions) (iv) good faith in claiming to be a corporation.

(iii) ***Corporation by estoppel***: generated by the reliance interest of a third party.

- ♦ To avoid the problems listed above, MBCA section 56 provides that the corporation comes into existence only when the certificate has actually been issued.

- ♦ Also, MBCA section 146 provides that if an individual or group of individuals assume to act as a corporation before the certificate of incorporation has been issued, joint and several liability attaches. This section is applicable to D's conduct.

2) Partner liability versus investor liability--

Frontier Refining Company v. Kunkel's, Inc., 407 P.2d 880 (Wyo. 1965).

Facts. Frontier Refining Company (P) filed suit against Kunkel's, Inc., as a partnership, and against George Fairfield, Clifford Kunkel, and Harlan Beach as individual members of the partnership (Ds). P claimed that Ds operated a service station and truck terminal as a partnership under the name Kunkel's, Inc. P sold gasoline to the partnership and was not paid. Kunkel was never served and the suit proceeded against Fairfield and Beach, both of whom denied the existence of any partnership. Fairfield and Beach indicated that Kunkel operated the business as an individual without their involvement, and that they were merely investors in the business. After a trial, the lower court held that Kunkel's, Inc. was not a partnership and found for Ds. P appeals.

Issue. Will an individual who did not hold himself out as a partner be held personally liable for a partnership debt if he merely provided capital and equipment for the company?

Held. No. Judgment affirmed.

- ♦ P relies on a state statute in effect at the time of these events that provided that "all persons who assume to act as a corporation without authority so to do shall be jointly and severally liable for all debts and liabilities incurred or arising as a result thereof." However, in this case, the facts fail to indicate that Fairfield and Beach held themselves out as partners or as a corporation.

- ♦ Trial testimony indicates that Kunkel became interested in taking over a filling station and truck stop owned by P. Kunkel spoke to Warren, zone manager of P, about acquiring a lease. Kunkel told Warren that he did not have the money for the venture, but that he would speak to Fairfield to see "if he could raise the money." Fairfield and Beach were associates in a mining venture. Fairfield testified that Kunkel asked him for a loan, which he refused. However, Fairfield told Kunkel that he and Beach may be interested in the venture, but only if Kunkel incorporated the business. Kunkel was to be responsible for incorporating and for managing the business of the corporation. Once the business was incorporated, Fairfield and Beach would purchase the necessary equipment to run the service station, and, in return, they would each take one-third of the stock of the new corporation.

- During the contract negotiations, Warren submitted Kunkel's financial statement to P and advised P that the business was to be incorporated under the name of Kunkel's Incorporated, and would be financed by Fairfield and Beach. It is important to note that no financial statement of Fairfield or Beach was ever sought or obtained by P. P entered into a lease agreement for the station with Kunkel signing the lease document as "Clifford D. Kunkel DBA Kunkel's Inc." On other agreements signed at the same time, Kunkel signed "C.D. Kunkel" with no reference to the purported corporation.

- The facts indicate that P, with full knowledge that a corporation had not yet been formed, chose to contract with Kunkel as an individual. The court should therefore not go out of its way to discover grounds for compelling payment by parties who did not contract the debt, who had no knowledge of its existence until a suit was filed, and who gave no authority to borrow money on their account. This is especially the case when, as here, the lender did not rely upon their credit in entering into the agreement.

- There was conflicting testimony as to whether Fairfield ever met with or spoke to Warren. From the facts presented, the trial court was entitled to infer that Kunkel was the only source of the information given to P about a proposed corporation or partnership, and that neither Fairfield nor Beach held themselves out as partners but instead were merely investors.

VII. DISREGARD OF THE CORPORATE ENTITY

A. CORPORATION AS SEPARATE ENTITY FROM ITS SHAREHOLDERS

Since a corporation is held to be a separate legal entity, the corporation normally incurs in its own name debts and obligations that are not the responsibility of the owners (shareholders). At the same time, the corporation is not responsible for the debts and obligations of its owners (shareholders).

B. PIERCING THE CORPORATE VEIL

There are exceptions to the rule of limited liability. In these exceptional situations, a court is said to "pierce the corporate veil" and to dissolve the distinction between the corporate entity and its shareholders so that the shareholders may be held liable as individuals despite the existence of the corporation.

1. Situations Where "Corporate Veil" May Be Pierced.

a. **Fraud or injustice.** When the maintenance of the corporation as a separate entity results in fraud or injustice to outside parties (such as creditors).

b. **Disregard of corporate requirements.** When the shareholders do not maintain the corporation as a separate entity but use it for personal purposes (*e.g.,* corporate records are not maintained, required meetings are not held, money is transferred back and forth between personal and corporate accounts and commingled, etc.). The rationale is that if the shareholders have disregarded the corporate form, by "estoppel" they cannot complain if the courts do likewise. This is most likely to occur with close corporations.

c. **Undercapitalization.** When the corporation is undercapitalized (given the liabilities, debts, and risks it reasonably could be expected to incur).

d. **Requirements of fairness.** In any situation where it is only "fair" that the corporate form be disregarded.

2. Contract Liability.

a. **Introduction.** The major difference between contract cases and tort cases (discussed *infra*) is that in contract cases the plaintiff has had an opportunity in advance to investigate the financial resources of the corporation and has chosen to do business with it. Thus, the intention of the parties and knowledge of the risks assumed in entering a contract are factors in assessing the facts of each situation and making a determination as to whether the corporate veil should be pierced. Note that one test purportedly used in the contracts area is whether the corporation was the mere "agent" or "instrumentality" of its shareholder(s). But this test is not very meaningful. It is better to analyze the facts of each case and make a determination whether it is fair in each instance to pierce the veil. One factor looked at here, as in the tort cases, is adequate capitalization.

b. **Public companies.** Usually, the situations of piercing the corporate veil arise in close corporations, where there is approximate identity of the corporate entity and a few people. This is simply a fact, not a theoretical necessity; courts find it easier to somehow equate the idea of piercing the veil with holding a few controlling people liable. There are situations, however, where there are many shareholders and the courts still look through the corporate entity to the shareholders. Normally there must be a showing of actual fraud or violation of an important public policy before this is done.

c. **Parent not responsible--**

Bartle v. Home Owners Cooperative, 127 N.E.2d 832 (N.Y. 1955).

Facts. Home Owners Cooperative (D) was a cooperative corporation composed mainly of veterans. It attempted to build low-cost housing for its members. It formed Westerlea Corporation to act as the builder of 26 homes. Costs turned out to be higher than anticipated, and Westerlea's contract creditors took over the corporation. Westerlea then went bankrupt. D had provided the original $50,000 capital for Westerlea; Westerlea's officers and directors were the same as D's. Each corporation kept separate and correct corporate records. Bartle (P) is the trustee in bankruptcy.

Issue. In the absence of fraud, if a parent corporation and its subsidiary do not mingle their affairs together, will the parent be responsible for the contract debts of the subsidiary?

Held. No. Judgment for D affirmed.

- The law allows incorporation for the purpose of limiting liability. The corporate veil will be pierced only when there is fraudulent use of the subsidiary by the parent or when the parent has committed acts with the subsidiary to its benefit and to the detriment of the creditors. There were no such acts in this instance.

- Here the creditors had the opportunity to investigate the financial standing of Westerlea before extending credit.

Dissent. D's business was done on a basis that Westerlea could not make a profit from the building it did. The homes were sold to D's members at cost. Westerlea was the mere agent of D.

Comment. Note that no claim was made about undercapitalization in this case. The majority is probably right in this instance, as long as there was no fraud and the creditors had the chance to assess the situation before making the extension of credit (along with the fact that on the front end of the deal the capitalization of Westerlea appeared to be adequate to the creditors).

---

d. Fraud not necessary--

DeWitt Truck Brokers v. W. Ray Flemming Fruit Co., 540 F.2d 681 (4th Cir. 1976).

Facts. A creditor, Flemming Fruit Co. (P), brought an action to impose individual liability on the president of the debtor corporation, DeWitt Truck Brokers (D). There was a complete disregard of corporate formalities in the operation of D, which functioned only for the financial advantage of its president; D was undercapitalized; the president withdrew from D funds that he had collected as due P; and the president had stated to P that he would take care of payment of P's charges if the corporation failed to do so. The lower court pierced the corporate veil, and D's president appeals.

Issue. Can the corporate veil be pierced and the corporation and its stockholders be treated as identical, without fraud being alleged?

Held. Yes. Judgment affirmed.

- In applying the "instrumentality" or "alter ego" doctrine, courts are concerned with reality and not form, with how the corporation operated and the individual defendant's relationship to that operation.

- Factors to be considered in applying the "instrumentality" doctrine are whether the corporation was grossly undercapitalized for the purpose of the corporate undertaking, the failure to observe corporate formalities, nonpayment of dividends, insolvency of the debtor corporation at the time, siphoning funds of the corporation by the dominant stockholder, nonfunctioning of other officers or directors, absence of corporate records, and that the corporation is merely a facade for the operations of the dominant stockholder or stockholders.

- The mere fact that all or almost all of the corporate stock is owned by one individual or a few individuals will not afford sufficient grounds for disregarding corporateness.

- The conclusion to disregard the corporate entity may not rest on a single factor, whether undercapitalization, disregard of corporation's formalities, or whatnot, but must involve a number of such factors. In addition, it must present an element of injustice or fundamental unfairness.

- Finding that the corporate entity should be disregarded in an action on a debt wherein the creditor sought, by piercing the corporate veil, to impose individual liability on the president of the corporation, was not clearly erroneous under these facts.

---

3. Tort Liability.

a. Piercing the veil for dram shop liability--

Baatz v. Arrow Bar, 452 N.W.2d 138 (S.D. 1990).

Facts. Edmond and LaVella Neuroth formed Arrow Bar, Inc. to own and operate a bar. Edmond served as president of the corporation, and Jacquette Neuroth was the manager of the business. All three Neuroths were corporate shareholders. Kenny and Peggy Baatz (Ps) were seriously injured when their motorcycle was struck by a car driven by McBride, who was intoxicated and had crossed the center line of traffic. Prior to the accident, McBride had been drinking at Arrow Bar. Arrow Bar corporation did not maintain dram shop liability insurance at the time of the accident. Ps filed suit against Arrow Bar, Inc. and Edmond, LaVella, and Jacquette Neuroth (Ds) as individuals. Ps alleged that Arrow Bar continued to serve drinks to McBride after he was already intoxicated, and that Arrow Bar's negligence contributed to the injuries they sustained in the accident. The individual defendants motioned for and were granted summary judgment. Ps appeal, arguing that the corporate veil of the corporation should be pierced to hold the individual defendants responsible.

Issue. May a court disregard the corporate entity if the evidence fails to indicate injustice and inequitable consequences?

Held. No. Judgment affirmed.

- A corporation will be treated as a separate legal entity unless such treatment would result in injustice or inequitable consequences. Factors that indicate injustice and inequitable consequences include fraudulent representation by corporate directors, undercapitalization, failure to observe corporate formalities, absence of corporate records, payment of individual obligations from corporate funds, or use of the corporation to promote fraud, injustice, or illegalities.

- Ps advance several arguments to support their request to pierce Arrow Bar's corporate veil, but fail to provide facts or evidence in support of their allegations. For example, Ps argue that the corporation is simply the alter ego of the Neuroths. However, they present no evidence to support this conclusion. In fact, the evidence presented indicates that the Neuroths treated the corporation separately from their individual financial affairs.

- Similarly, Ps argue that the corporation is undercapitalized because it was started with only $5,000, but do not explain how that amount failed to equip the corporation with a reasonable amount of capital.

- Finally, Ps allege that Arrow Bar failed to observe corporate formalities because none of the business's signs or advertising indicated it was a corporation, in violation of state law. Failure upon occasion to follow all corporate formalities will not justify piercing the corporate veil. This is especially so in the case where, as here, there is no relationship between the resulting harm and the alleged defect in form.

- Ps have failed to present any facts or evidence to justify piercing the corporate veil. We therefore affirm the grant of summary judgment dismissing the Neuroths as individual defendants.

Dissent. The incorporators are using the corporate form to escape liability for wrongs they perpetrated in their individual capacities. The corporation here has no separate existence and was created to shield the Neuroths from individual liability in a dram shop action.

---

b. Liability insurance as a basis for adequate capitalization--

---

Radaszewski v. Telecom Corp., 981 F.2d 305 (8th Cir. 1992).

Facts. Radaszewski (P) suffered serious injuries in an automobile accident with a truck driven by an employee of Contrux, Inc., a common carrier. P brought a tort claim for damages against Contrux and Telecom (D). Contrux was a wholly owned subsidiary of D, which was not incorporated in Missouri, where the case was brought. The district court held that it lacked personal jurisdiction over D. P appeals.

Issue. Is a subsidiary corporation undercapitalized for purposes of piercing the corporate veil (*i.e.,* created by its parent without adequate funds to pay its bills and satisfy judgments against it) if the subsidiary has adequate liability insurance?

Held. No. Judgment affirmed.

- The district court did not have jurisdiction over D; the corporate veil of Contrux may not be pierced to hold D liable. Generally, a person injured by the conduct of a corporation or one of its employees can only look to the assets of the employee or of the employer corporation for recovery. The shareholders of the corporation (including a parent corporation) are not liable.

- There is an exception where the law allows a plaintiff to pierce the veil of the subsidiary to make a parent-shareholder liable. Under Missouri law, in a tort case, a plaintiff must show three things:

  (i) Control beyond stock control; *i.e.,* complete domination of finances, policy, and business practice, with regard to the transaction that is attacked so that the subsidiary had no mind of its own;

  (ii) Control must be used by the defendant to commit a fraud or wrong of some kind (*i.e.,* there is a breach of a duty to plaintiff); and

  (iii) The control and breach of duty must proximately cause the injury to the plaintiff.

- D had no contact with Missouri. The district court has jurisdiction over D only if the corporate veil of Contrux can be pierced to bring D into the case.

- At issue is the second element of the three-pronged test. Missouri courts have held that undercapitalization of the subsidiary by the parent is a basis for a breach of duty. This allows an inference that the parent is either deliberately or recklessly creating a business that cannot pay its bills or satisfy judgments against it.

- The district court found, and we assume, that Contrux was undercapitalized in an accounting sense. The only equity capital put in by D was $25,000. The remainder of the capital was periodic loans made by D to Contrux, secured by a lien on Contrux equipment. In addition, D controlled all of Contrux's major decisions.

- However, Contrux took out a $1 million basic liability insurance policy and a $10 million excess coverage policy. They were in effect at the time of P's accident. Unfortunately, the excess liability insurance carrier became insolvent two years after the accident and is now in receivership. However, this is not the fault of D.

- We hold that there is no breach of duty by D here. Contrux, at the time of the accident, was "financially responsible" through having adequate insurance (it met the test of federal law for the amount of its liability insurance by a common carrier). It is not necessary for Contrux to have had sufficient equity capital to meet such liability claims.

Dissent. There was sufficient evidence to send the issue of "undercapitalization" to the fact finder in the trial court for a decision. It may have found, after a trial, that having insurance is not sufficient by itself to avoid the charge of being undercapitalized.

c. Alter ego theory and subsidiary corporations--

Fletcher v. Atex, Inc., 68 F.3d 1451 (2d Cir. 1995).

Facts. Two computer users (Ps) filed suit against Atex, Inc. ("Atex") and its parent company Eastman Kodak Company ("Kodak") alleging repetitive stress injuries resulting from their use of keyboards manufactured by Atex. At all times relevant to the litigation, Atex participated in Kodak's cash management system, and Kodak exercised control over Atex's major expenditures, stock sales, and asset sales. There was some overlap between the members of the board of directors of both companies. Atex's promotional literature bore the Kodak logo, and some of Kodak's literature described Atex as "a Kodak company." Based on these facts, Ps argued that Atex was merely the alter ego of Kodak and that therefore, it was proper to pierce the corporate veil and hold Kodak liable for their injuries. The district court granted Kodak's motion for summary judgment, stating that there was no genuine issue of material fact as to Kodak's liability. The court noted that Kodak and Atex had at all times observed all corporate formalities and maintained separate existences. Ps appeal, arguing that there is a genuine issue of material fact as to whether Atex is Kodak's alter ego and completely dominated and controlled by Kodak.

Issue. Is summary judgment proper when no evidence has been presented to indicate that a company is merely the alter ego of its parent company?

Held. Yes. Judgment affirmed.

- To prevail on an alter ego theory, Ps must show that the two corporations operated as a single economic entity. Some factors to be considered in this analysis are whether the subsidiary corporation was adequately capitalized and solvent, whether corporate formalities (such as regular directors' meetings and recordkeeping requirements) were observed, and whether the dominant shareholder siphoned corporate funds.

- Kodak has shown that Atex followed all corporate formalities, and there was no evidence presented to contradict this assertion. Nor was there evidence of undue domination or control of Atex. The fact that Atex participated in Kodak's cash management system is consistent with sound business practice and courts have declined to find alter ego liability based on this practice. The fact that Atex was required to seek approval from Kodak for major expenses and sale of its assets does not raise a material issue of material fact as to whether the companies were a single economic entity. This type of oversight is also typical of a parent corporation.

- Parent and subsidiary corporations often have overlapping boards of directors, while maintaining separate business. In this case, between 1981 and 1988 only one director sat on both boards. From 1989 to 1992, there were no directors who sat on both boards. In addition, the use of the Kodak logo and the phrase "a Kodak company," even when viewed in the light most favorable to the plaintiffs, are simply not enough to show that the two companies operated as a single economic entity. It is not uncommon for parent companies to refer to their subsidiaries in such terms (such as "family" companies).

♦ Finally, while no showing of fraud is necessary under an alter ego theory, Ps must show some evidence of unfairness in upholding a legal distinction between the two companies. In this case, Ps have presented no evidence whatsoever of injustice or unfairness that would justify a court in disregarding the separate legal identities of these companies.

C. THE PIERCING DOCTRINE IN FEDERAL/STATE RELATIONS

1. CERCLA Liability for Polluting Facility's Parent--

United States v. Bestfoods, 524 U.S. 51 (1998).

Facts. Ott Chemical Company ("Ott I") manufactured chemicals at its Michigan plant from 1957-1965. In 1965, CPC International Inc. ("CPC") incorporated a wholly owned subsidiary to buy out Ott I in exchange for CPC stock. The new company, Ott II, continued to manufacture chemicals on the site until 1972, when CPC sold Ott II to Story Chemical Company ("Story"). Story operated the facility until 1997 when it declared bankruptcy. Aerojet General Corp. ("Aerojet") purchased the site from Story's bankruptcy trustee and created a wholly owned subsidiary, Cordova Chemical Company ("Cordova/California"), to purchase the property. Cordova/California then created a wholly owned Michigan subsidiary, Cordova Chemical Company of Michigan ("Cordova/Michigan"), which manufactured chemicals on the site until 1986. In 1977, the Michigan Department of Natural Resources began investigating the site and found the soil and water heavily contaminated with hazardous substances. The federal Environmental Protection Agency ("EPA") declared the site a "Superfund site," and began implementation of a remediation plan that would cost tens of millions of dollars. To recover the costs of the cleanup, the EPA filed suit under the Comprehensive Environmental Response, Compensation, and Liability Act of 1980 ("CERCLA") against CPC (now known as Bestfoods), Aerojet, Cordova/California, and Cordova/ Michigan. Ott I and Ott II no longer existed. Section 107 of CERCLA allows recovery of cleanup costs against any person who owned or operated a facility at the time of disposal of hazardous substances. CERCLA defines the term "owner or operator" as "any person owning or operating" a facility. The EPA argued that CPC and Aerojet, as the parent companies of the Ott and Cordova companies, had owned or operated the facility within the meaning of section 107(a)(2). The district court held that both CPC and Aerojet were liable as operators under section 107(a)(2). The appellate court reversed, stating that a parent corporation may only be held liable as an operator when the requirements necessary under state law to pierce the corporate veil are met. In this case, the court explained, the parent and subsidiary corporations maintained separate identities, and the parents did not use the subsidiaries to perpetrate fraud or subvert justice. The United States Supreme Court granted certiorari.

Issue. May a parent corporation that actively participated in, and exercised control over, the operations of a subsidiary, without more, be held directly liable under CERCLA as an operator of a polluting facility owned or operated by the subsidiary?

Held. No. Judgment vacated and case remanded.

- It is a fundamental principle of corporate law that a parent corporation is not liable for the acts of its subsidiaries. However, there is an equally fundamental principle of corporate law allowing the corporate veil to be pierced and the parent corporation held liable if the corporate form is misused to accomplish wrongful purposes. Nothing in CERCLA expands or restricts either of these fundamental rules.

- Under the plain language of CERCLA, any person who operates a polluting facility is directly liable for the cost of cleanup. This is so regardless of whether that person is the facility's owner or the owner's parent corporation. The difficulty arises due to CERCLA's failure to adequately define the term "operator." We note that in the context of a business, the word operate ordinarily means to conduct the affairs of or manage. So under CERCLA, an operator is someone who directs the workings of, manages, or conducts the affairs of a facility. We find further that the operator must manage, direct, or conduct operations specifically related to pollution. In situations in which piercing the corporate veil is appropriate, a parent corporation may be charged with derivative liability under CERCLA for its subsidiary's actions.

- The district court found CPC directly liable under section 107(a)(2) as an operator because CPC actively participated in and exerted significant control over Ott II's business and decisionmaking. In finding CPC ***directly*** liable as an operator, the district court erroneously applied the actual control test (that is, whether the parent actually operated the business of its subsidiary). Under CERCLA, the question is not whether the parent operates the ***subsidiary***, but rather whether the parent operates the ***facility***. That operation is evidenced by participation in the activities of the facility itself, not the subsidiary corporation. As stated above, if parental control of the subsidiary is extensive enough, it gives rise to ***indirect*** liability under the piercing the corporate veil doctrine, not direct liability under the statutory language.

- The district court also erred in its analysis of the relationship between Ott II and CPC. The court found that because high-ranking CPC officers served in Ott II management positions and on the board of directors, CPC actively participated in and controlled the policy-making decisions of Ott II. In imposing direct liability on these grounds, the court failed to recognize that it is entirely appropriate for directors of a parent company to serve as directors of a subsidiary. Common corporate personnel acting at management and directorial levels is insufficient to expose the parent corporation to liability for the acts of its subsidiary. Courts will presume that the directors are wearing their "subsidiary hats" and not their "parent hats" when acting on behalf of the subsidiary unless evidence is presented to the contrary. The district court automatically, and erroneously, attributed the actions of dual officers and directors to the corporate parent.

- There is, however, some evidence that an agent of the parent alone may have played a conspicuous part in the management of environmental matters at the plant. The evidence indicates that Williams, CPC's governmental and environmental affairs director, was actively involved in and exerted control over Ott II environmental matters, and issued directives regarding Ott's responses to regulatory inquiries. This evidence is enough to raise an issue of CPC's operation of the facility through Williams's actions, and we remand the case for evaluation of his role, and the role of any other CPC agent who might have had a role in operating the facility. Direct liability may be found if the evidence proves that Williams, as an agent of CPC alone, controlled the environmental practices at the facility.

2. Other Situations.

a. Social Security payments--

Stark v. Flemming, 283 F.2d 410 (9th Cir. 1960).

Facts. Stark (P) placed her assets (a farm and a duplex) in a corporation for which she worked for a monthly wage of $400. Her purpose in forming the corporation was to qualify for old-age benefits under Social Security. The secretary of Health, Education, and Welfare ("HEW") (D) ruled that P was not entitled to such benefits, and the district court affirmed. P appeals.

Issue. When a plaintiff established a corporation for the purpose of qualifying for old-age benefits, may those benefits be withheld on grounds that the corporation is a mere sham?

Held. No. Judgment reversed.

- Congress could have provided that the motivation to obtain Social Security by organizing a corporation would defeat the end. It did not. Since the corporation is extant for all other purposes, the secretary of HEW must also recognize it for Social Security purposes.

- However, the secretary may challenge P's salary as to whether it was unreasonable and excessive. The district court decision is vacated, and the case is remanded for further proceedings.

b. Unemployment benefits--

Roccograndi v. Unemployment Compensation Board of Review, 178 A.2d 786 (Pa. 1962).

Facts. Roccograndi (P) was a member of a family involved as shareholders and employees in an incorporated family-run wrecking business. During periods of insufficient work, some members of the family were laid off. Their applications for unemployment benefits were denied by the Bureau of Employment Security on the basis that they were not really employees but were self-employed. A referee reversed. The Board of Review (D) reversed the referee.

Issue. May the Bureau of Employment Security in this case ignore the corporation in determining whether to grant benefits to Ps?

Held. Yes. Board of Review affirmed.

- The corporate entity may be ignored in this case in determining whether the claimants were, in fact, unemployed under the act, or were self-employed persons whose business merely proved to be unremunerative during the period for which the claim was made.

- In this situation P was able to exert sufficient control over the employer (the corporation) to determine when he would be "laid off" and when he would be "rehired." Hence, in essence, he was self-employed.

D. "REVERSE" PIERCING

1. Corporation Formed to Avoid Creditors--

Sweeney v. Kane, 773 N.Y.S.2d 420 (N.Y. App. Div. 2004).

Facts. Husband and wife, George and Amy Kane (Ds), incorporated Gin Properties, Inc. ("Gin") in Florida. One week later, Ds purchased a house in New York, which they assigned to the corporation. The house was purchased from Ds' own funds. Amy Kane owes attorneys' fees to two law firms (Ps) in an unrelated case. Ps contend that Gin is merely an alter ego of Ds and that the house should be sold to pay Ps' judgments. The lower court dismissed the complaint. Ps appeal.

Issue. May reverse piercing be applied where a corporation was formed to purchase a residence as part of a scheme to avoid obligations to creditors?

Held. Yes. Judgment reversed and case remanded.

- Florida law applies to this case because the state of incorporation has the greatest interest in determining the extent of insulation that will be afforded to shareholders of corporations incorporated under its laws.

- Piercing the corporate veil allows a creditor to disregard a corporation and hold the shareholders personally liable for corporate debt. Reverse piercing is the opposite and makes the corporation liable for the debt of the shareholders. Under Florida law, to pierce the corporate veil, the plaintiff must show improper conduct such as to mislead creditors or to work a fraud on them or to use the corporation as a means of evading liability with respect to a transaction that was personal and not corporate.

- When Ds purchased the property, they were to trying to avoid Amy Kane's obligations to Ps by purchasing the property through a Florida corporation. Ds are residents of New York. They reside in and are in complete control of the property in question. They have been paying real property taxes and mortgage principal and interest for the property and taking the income tax deductions for the taxes and interest on their own tax returns. They have improved the property for their own use with their own funds by installing a home theater and a putting green. Gin is merely an alter ego of Ds and thus is subject to the claims of Ds' creditors.

- Although George Kane was not a judgment debtor of Ps, he acted in concert with his wife to avoid her creditors and thus may be held jointly and severally liable for the fraud of her creditors. This case is remanded for the purpose of appointing a receiver to sell the corporate real property and distribute the proceeds.

---

2. **Subordination of Shareholder Debts ("Deep Rock" Doctrine).** In an area related to the "piercing the corporate veil" cases, courts will sometimes subordinate the debts of the corporation's shareholders to the claims of its creditors.

   a. **Bankruptcy.** The setting for such actions is bankruptcy proceedings, when the trustee in bankruptcy argues that the claims of the shareholders (even when they are secured) should be subordinated to the claims of the creditors (even when they are not secured).

   b. **Bad faith.** The rationale is usually that the shareholder-creditors have been guilty of some sort of bad faith toward other creditors of the corporation (*i.e.,* fraud in establishing their creditor claims, mismanagement, etc.).

   c. **No personal liability.** Note that this is a form of disregard of the corporate entity, since it is a refusal to recognize the corporation as a separate entity from its shareholders when the corporation has presumably negotiated the creditor arrangements with these shareholders. The difference is that in these cases the shareholder-creditors are not held personally liable for corporate debts—only the capital that is represented by their creditor position with the corporation is put at risk. Note also the relationship of this area to that of preincorporation promoter transactions with the corporation.

d. **Salary claims--**

Pepper v. Litton, 308 U.S. 295 (1939).

Facts. Litton (P) was the sole shareholder of Dixie Splint Coal Company. When Dixie Splint found itself in financial trouble, Pepper sued for an accounting of royalties due under a lease with the corporation. Meanwhile, P caused Dixie Splint to confess judgment in favor of himself for alleged back salary, then he caused execution to be issued on his judgment and purchased the corporate assets at the resulting sale. The corporation then filed for bankruptcy. The trustee in bankruptcy (D) brought suit to have the judgment obtained by P set aside, but the trustee lost. P filed in district court based on the portion of his judgment not satisfied. The district court disallowed the claim. The court of appeals reversed. D appeals.

Issue. May the bankruptcy court disallow either as a secured or as a general or unsecured claim a judgment obtained by the dominant and controlling shareholder of the bankrupt corporation on an alleged salary claim?

Held. Yes. Judgment of the court of appeals reversed.

- There is ample evidence to indicate that the salary claim was fraudulent and may be disregarded. But even if it were not, the district court in a bankruptcy proceeding may disregard it, even where it is evidenced by a previous court judgment.
- Directors and majority shareholders of corporations are fiduciaries to their corporations. Their dealings with the corporation are subject to rigorous scrutiny; they have the burden to justify their dealings with their corporations as to their good faith and the fairness of such dealings from the standpoint of the creditors of the corporation.
- Here, the salary claim was not the result of arm's length dealings by the sole shareholder with the corporation. The claim was not equitable in relationship to the corporate creditors. The bankruptcy court has the power to determine all claims, and to disregard those that are not fair, even when they have previously been reduced to court judgments. Here, P's claims must be subordinated to other creditors.

Comment. Other bases for subordination of shareholder-creditor claims are that the shareholder-creditor disregarded the corporate vehicle and treated the corporation as his alter ego, or that the corporation was undercapitalized (in essence, the shareholder put up part of the needed equity capital in the form of debt). These are familiar claims in piercing the corporate veil cases.

E. SUCCESSOR LIABILITY

1. **Introduction.** The doctrine of successor liability is unsettled. When a corporation is acquired by another company or goes out of business, courts are split on the issue of whether it is fair to impose liability on the successor company. The general rule is that a corporation that acquires all or part of the assets of another corporation does ***not*** acquire the liabilities and debts of the predecessor unless: (i) there is an express or implied agreement to assume the liabilities; (ii) the transaction is a consolidation or merger; (iii) the successor entity is a mere continuation of the predecessor entity; or (iv) the transaction was fraudulent, not made in good faith, or made without sufficient consideration. [American Law of Products Liability 3d §7:1]

2. **Arguments For and Against Imposition of Successor Liability.** Courts that refuse to impose liability do so because they find it unfair and against public policy to hold another entity responsible for the actions of its predecessor. They argue that the doctrine would provide no deterrent effect, and that imposition of liability would make it more difficult to transfer assets. In addition, the doctrine fails to respect the corporate form. Other courts argue that imposition of the doctrine is necessary to prevent fraud and to impose liability on the party most able to bear it. The successor company may be the only party available to compensate an injured plaintiff.

3. **Continuity of Enterprise Theory Rejected--**

Nissen Corp. v. Miller, 594 A.2d 564 (Md. 1991).

Facts. American Tradex Corporation manufactured treadmills. In July of 1981, Nissen Corporation agreed to purchase American Tradex and its trade name, patents, inventory, and assets. Nissen assumed some of American Tradex's liabilities, but expressly excluded assumption of liability for personal injury claims arising from any product previously sold by the company. Under the agreement, American Tradex would continue for five years and would be known as AT Corporation. AT Corporation was administratively dissolved on December 31, 1987. On January 31, 1981, Brandt (P) purchased a treadmill from Atlantic Fitness Products that had been designed, manufactured, and marketed by American Tradex. On October 18, 1986, P was injured while trying to adjust the treadmill. In September of 1988, P filed suit against American Tradex, AT Corporation, Nissen, and Atlantic Fitness Products (Ds). Nissen filed a motion for summary judgment, which was granted. The Court of Special Appeals reversed the dismissal, and Nissen petitioned for a writ of certiorari to the Maryland Court of Appeals.

Issue. As a successor corporation, is Nissen liable to P for his injuries?

Held. No. Judgment reversed.

- All parties agree that this court should adopt the general rule of nonliability of successor companies with the four traditional exceptions. Clearly, the instant case does not fall into any of the exceptions that would allow imposition of liability on Nissen. P argues that we should also adopt a fifth exception, known as the "continuity of enterprise" exception, in products liability cases. The continuity of enterprise theory focuses on the continuation of the business operation or enterprise when there is no continuation in ownership.

- P argues that public policy demands the adoption of this exception because courts have traditionally prevented the evasion of liability by any party in the manufacturing or selling chain in a products liability case. P further argues that a corporation should not be allowed to purchase only the benefits of another company, such as its goodwill, in an asset purchase transaction without assuming its liabilities. Nissen argues that it was not part of the manufacturing and selling chain and that it only purchased American Tradex's assets. Also, Nissen argues that it did not simply purchase the benefits of the corporation. Nissen too will suffer a loss, if American Tradex's products do cause injuries, in the form of a decline in the goodwill of the company it purchased. The price Nissen paid for the business was based on a total contract, which included the provision that American Tradex would retain all liability for injuries caused by defective products it sold before the asset purchase. P purchased his treadmill prior to the asset purchase transaction.

- Strict products liability is based on the concept that sellers who place defective products on the market are at fault and must bear responsibility when a user is injured. A corporate successor is not a seller, and it seems unfair to require a successor corporation to assume liability simply because it is still in business when the party actually at fault is not. We therefore reject the continuity of enterprise theory of successor liability and adhere to the traditional rule of nonliability of successor corporations.

Dissent. We agree with the adoption of the general rule of nonliability of corporate successors, together with its four exceptions. We would, however, allow the continuity of enterprise exception for defective products cases.

VIII. FINANCIAL MATTERS AND THE CLOSELY HELD CORPORATION

A. INTRODUCTION

Usually there are three sources of assets for the beginning corporation: contributions in exchange for stock in the corporation, loans by the shareholders, and loans from other sources, such as banks.

B. TYPES OF SECURITIES

A shareholder is one who owns an "equity" security (that is, he is an owner of the corporation as opposed to a creditor). In addition to equity securities issued to owners, the corporation issues debt securities to creditors.

1. **Creation of Rights of Shareholders.** Typically the rights of shareholders are created (as a matter of contract) in the articles of incorporation. In addition, state corporation law provides shareholders with certain rights (such as the right to obtain a shareholders' list, etc.), and the board (where permitted by law) may set certain terms and conditions in issuing equity securities.

   a. All shares have the same rights, except as otherwise set forth specifically (as in the articles). Thus, when the corporation wishes to make distinctions between the shares, it must create classes of shares (where shares of the same class have the same rights). At least one class of shares must have voting rights.

   b. Typical classes of equity securities are common shares and preferred shares.

2. **Debt Securities.** Debt securities are evidences of the borrowing of the corporation. Those owning the debt securities are creditors of the corporation.

3. **Purpose of Classifying Securities.** The purpose in having various types and classes of securities is to allocate:

   (i) The risk of loss if the corporation does poorly;

   (ii) The power of control (through voting); and

   (iii) Participation rights in the proceeds of the corporation (either through profits or in liquidation).

   The distribution of risk is worked out through fixing the terms of the various classes of securities.

4. **Classes of Equity Shares.**

a. **Common stock.** There must be at least one class of equity shares in a corporation (if there is only one, it is common stock), and at least one class must have voting rights.

1) Common stock is entitled to receive dividends, but it has no priority over any other class of security issued by the corporation.

2) Also, common stock participates in the distribution of assets when the corporation liquidates, but it is normally without any preference over any other class of security.

b. **Preferred stock.** Another common form of equity security is preferred stock. It generally has certain preferences over common stock (generally as to dividends and liquidation rights). However, it is still considered to be part of the ownership (equity) of the corporation (it is not debt of the corporation).

1) **Reasons for issuing preferred stock.** Some of the characteristics of preferred stock make it attractive to the management of the corporation.

a) **Contingent voting rights.** Normally preferred stock carries only contingent voting rights (*i.e.,* voting rights accrue only when dividends are not paid or on major corporate transactions, such as a sale of substantially all of the corporation's assets). This means that preferred stock does not dilute the voting control that resides in the common shareholders.

b) **No required, fixed repayment.** Normally there is no requirement for fixed repayments of principal (however, some preferred issues do require such repayments, and the corporation must set up a sinking fund to periodically pay off part of the principal invested by preferred shareholders). Nearly all preferred stock issues do permit management to "call" the preferred stock (*i.e.*, redeem it) at its discretion.

c) **Fixed percentage annual dividend.** The disadvantage to preferred stock is that this interest (dividend) paid on the preferred is not tax deductible to the corporation. In addition, since the risk to the preferred shareholder is greater (that he will not receive the dividend interest) than to the holder of debt securities (which carry a prior right to interest payments), the rate of interest that must be paid on preferred stock is normally higher than on most forms of debt securities.

2) **Implied preferences.** At common law the courts would sometimes imply terms in preferred stock (*i.e.,* if the stock was called

"preferred," then the courts would imply certain preferences, whether these preferences were specifically provided for in the articles or not). Now most state law provides that all terms and conditions of classes of stock must be specifically stated in the articles.

3) **Specific preferences.**

a) **Dividends.** Normally preferred stock is paid a dividend before other classes of stock. For example, the dividend rate might be 6%; this 6% must be paid before any dividend on the common stock.

(1) **Noncumulative preferred.** On noncumulative shares dividends are paid only if declared by the board, and if not paid in one year, the amount does not accumulate to future years. Sometimes the articles provide that a dividend must be paid if sufficient funds are earned by the corporation.

(2) **Cumulative.** If dividends are cumulative and dividends are not paid in one year, they are accumulated for payment in future years (until they are paid). No amount of dividends may be paid on common stock until all accrued dividends on the preferred are paid.

(3) **Participating preferred.** Preferred may also have a participating right (to participate in dividends paid after the preferred and the common shares have received a certain percentage dividend). Thus, if $100,000 is available for dividends, and $25,000 is used to pay the dividend on preferred shares and $50,000 is used to pay a dividend to the common stock, then both preferred and common shares may "participate" in the remaining $25,000. How participation rights work depends on state law and on what is said in the articles.

b) **Liquidation rights.** Normally, preferred shares have priority (after corporate creditors) to the assets of the corporation in liquidation. Typically, preferred shares receive par value (plus accumulated dividends), the common receive par, and then the preferred and the common share any remainder.

4) **Preferences set by the board.** The corporation law of most states indicates that the articles may give authority to the board to issue the preferred shares in different series and to set certain terms with respect to each series (such as the dividend rate, redemption prices, and liquidation amounts and priorities).

c. **Warrants or options.** The corporation may also issue warrants or options to purchase shares of common or preferred stock.

5. **Corporate Borrowing.** The corporation may also issue debt securities (such as promissory notes or bonds).

a. **Authorization.** All corporate borrowing (and its terms) must be authorized by the board (or the responsibility delegated by the board to the officers). Normally, shareholder approval is not required. Shareholder approval may be required, however, when assets of the corporation are pledged as security for the debt.

b. **Thin capitalization.** When the corporation is "thinly capitalized," the debt may sometimes be treated as equity (particularly when the debt is contributed by the promoters of the corporation). Thus, debt securities might be treated as common stock so that other creditors are given preference to the holders of the debt securities.

c. **Characteristics of debt securities.**

1) Debt securities are normally issued with a maturity date on which the principal amount is to be repaid. Also, there is normally a fixed interest rate on the principal amount borrowed. Holders of debt securities are paid interest due before any dividends may be paid to shareholders (and principal before anything is paid to shareholders in liquidations).

2) There is normally no voting right in the election of directors, but some states provide that voting rights may be given to debt securities by provision in the articles.

3) Debt securities are normally redeemable at the option of the corporation. Occasionally reduction in the amount outstanding is mandatory (and the corporation may be required to maintain a sinking fund for this purpose).

4) Debt securities are often issued pursuant to an indenture (a contract between the corporation and a trustee appointed to act on behalf of the holders of the debt securities). When debt securities of $1 million or more are offered to the public, they must be issued pursuant to an indenture. [*See* Trust Indenture Act of 1939]

5) Interest paid on debt securities is normally tax deductible, which is one of the motivations of issuing it.

d. **Types of debt securities.** There are many types of debt securities. Two examples are:

1) **Mortgage bonds.** A mortgage on corporate property is given to secure the debt incurred by the corporation.

2) **Debentures.** There is no property pledged for the security of debentures. They are issued on the general credit of the corporation.

e. **Convertible debt securities.** Note that debt securities (and preferred stock) may be convertible into shares of common stock.

f. **Determining the mix of debt and equity.** The corporation must not only decide what kind of debt securities to issue, but also in what manner to finance the corporation (*i.e.,* what percentage of debt and what percentage of equity to issue). The factors to consider are:

1) **Risk.** The higher the debt percentage of total capitalization (which debt carries with it a fixed interest rate), the higher the risk to the corporation. That is, if the corporation cannot pay the interest, it is placed in the position of insolvency or bankruptcy (and inevitably, the equity must end up contributing to pay off the debt holders). Thus, creditors carefully examine what "cushion" of equity financing the corporation has before they issue credit (or buy debt securities).

2) **Rate of return.** If the corporation can borrow funds at a lower rate than it can earn on its assets, this borrowing increases the profitability of the corporation (a practice known as "leverage"). Thus, if it borrows at 8% and can earn 10%, the margin of 2% flows through the earnings of the corporation.

3) **Industry ratios.** Typically industries have debt-equity ratios, which financial managers have learned by experience as appropriate risk-return tradeoff positions.

C. PAR VALUE AND WATERED STOCK

1. **Consideration Received for Corporation's Securities.** The common law and state and federal securities laws require that the corporation receive the stated value or the par value of its equity shares when they are issued in exchange for cash or other property.

a. **Par value shares.** Thus, when the corporation's shares have a par value (such as $1 per share), the shares must be sold for at least this par value unless the board of directors finds in good faith that they cannot be sold for par value.

b. **Stated value.** When the corporation's shares are no par, they may be sold for a reasonable value set by the board. This value is called the "stated value." What is "reasonable" depends on the company's financial condition and future prospects: *i.e.,* the company's net worth, its earnings per share, etc. The board's determination is upheld as long as it is in good faith.

2. **Forms of Consideration.** Most state laws prescribe the types of consideration for which stock may be issued. Normally, exchanges for property, services, etc. (as well as for cash), are permissible.

   a. **Services.** Sometimes there are limitations on exchanges for services, such as for services rendered prior to incorporation.

   b. **Executory consideration.** In most states, an executory promise to pay (such as an unsecured promissory note) is not lawful consideration for the issuance of stock. The same is true for an executory promise to transfer assets or to render services in the future. The rationale is that stock should not be issued as "fully paid" until the corporation receives the assets in exchange for the stock.

   c. **Property.** Normally, the state law indicates that shares may be issued only for some form of property. Sometimes there is an issue as to whether promoters have transferred property to the corporation in exchange for their shares.

      1) For example, it has been held that a plan for doing business, where it was not novel or unique, was not property and was not a proper basis for issuing shares.

      2) By holding certain items not to be property the courts have avoided difficult valuation problems and made the issues concerning "stock watering" easier to solve.

3. **Inadequate Consideration.**

   a. **Introduction.** It is an unauthorized act for the corporation to issue stock for inadequate consideration. When inadequate consideration is received, the stock is called by several names:

      1) **Watered stock.** Watered stock is stock of a certain value (say $100,000 in par value) that is issued for property or services said to be worth the same amount ($100,000) but that is actually overvalued and worth less (say $50,000).

      2) **Discount stock.** Discount stock (worth $100,000) is issued for a lesser amount of cash (say $50,000).

      3) **Bonus stock.** Bonus stock is given for no consideration.

   b. **Issue of valuation.** Problems of valuation arise only in the context of watered stock. With discount stock or bonus stock, there is simply a disparity between the par or stated value of the shares and the cash received by the corporation. With watered stock, the issue concerns the proper valuation of the property or services rendered by the corporation for the stock it issued.

c. **Theories of liability.**

1) **Misrepresentation.** Most courts have based liability for inadequate consideration on a theory of misrepresentation to creditors. When this is the theory, the cause of action is not in the corporation but in the creditors. (*See* the discussion below.)

2) **Statutory liability.** Other jurisdictions simply base liability on the theory that there is a statutory obligation to issue shares for the full consideration required by law. Here courts have permitted creditors or a receiver or trustee in bankruptcy to sue, or on some occasions a cause of action has been given to the corporation itself.

3) **Measure of damages.** The recovery under either theory is measured by the difference between the par value (or stated value) of the shares issued and the amount that was paid for them.

d. **Remedies.**

1) **By the corporation.** Normally, the corporation (or a shareholder in a derivative suit) cannot complain that the assets received by the corporation were overvalued. If it received the assets and issued fully paid shares, it in effect agreed to the price and is barred from an action against the subscriber to the shares.

a) However, when the subscriber-shareholder has been guilty of ***fraud or misrepresentation*** to the corporation, the corporation may bring an action for damages or to rescind the transaction.

b) In addition, many courts have held that where the shares issued are bonus shares (*i.e.*, the corporation received no consideration for them) or the consideration received was illegal, the corporation may bring an action to set aside the transaction.

c) Also, if the corporation is about to issue the shares but has not actually done so (or has only recently done so), the shareholders may bring a derivative suit asking for an injunction against issuance.

d) Even though the corporation does not normally have an action (and shareholders do not have a derivative suit against the shareholders receiving watered stock), shareholders may bring an action against the directors or officers for breach of their fiduciary duty in issuing the shares. Also, when the subscriber is also a promoter, there may be an action against the promoter for breach of his fiduciary duty (*see* above), in addition to theories of liability based on watered stock.

2) **By creditors.**

a) **Introduction.** The problem of watered stock normally arises when the corporation has become insolvent and the creditors try to hold some of the shareholders personally liable for amounts by which their shares have been watered.

(1) When there are post-incorporation stock subscriptions that have not been paid, the creditors may force the subscribers to pay the remaining amounts due.

(2) When there are shares that have been issued but not fully paid for, creditors may sue to have the remaining amount due paid.

(3) In the case of watered stock, the shares are supposed to be fully paid. The creditors, however, are suing to collect the difference between the real worth of what was transferred to the corporation and the par value (or stated value) of the shares issued.

b) **Theories of action.** The issue is whether all creditors may sue, or whether only the creditors that extended credit after the stock was issued may sue. The answer depends on which theory the court applies (there are several):

(1) **Misrepresentation theory.**

(a) **Subsequent creditors only.** Most courts regard issuance of stock as an implied representation that the corporation has received assets equivalent in value to the par or stated value of the shares issued. Therefore, those creditors who extended credit after the shares were issued may bring an action against shareholders who received watered or bonus stock.

(b) **Reliance requirement.** Most courts have indicated that the creditors must have actually relied on the valuation of the assets transferred to the corporation by the shareholders receiving watered stock.

Thus, if the creditors had knowledge of the overvaluation, there could be no recovery. However, many of the cases seem to presume this reliance by the subsequent creditors.

(2) **Statutory obligation theory.** Some states have statutes under which a shareholder having received watered stock is liable for the par or stated value of the shares to any creditor, prior or subsequent, with or without notice and independent of reliance.

(a) **Criticism.** This theory may produce unwarranted results in some cases. For example, suppose that the corporation operates for a substantial period of time after the issuance of watered stock. It may be difficult to ascribe the cause of the company's insolvency to the watered stock. Also, the creditors have a chance to look at the balance sheet of the corporation and decide whether to extend credit—why hold shareholders who previously received watered stock liable?

(3) **Trust fund theory.** Courts sometimes refer to an additional theory of liability, the trust fund theory. This theory implies that the capital stock of a corporation is a trust fund for payment of its debts.

e. **Valuation of property and services.** Determining what constitutes adequate consideration involves the problem of valuing the consideration (when it is property or services) given for the corporation's shares.

1) **Measures of value.**

a) **Fair market value.** Fair market value is what property will bring in a nonforced sale between a willing buyer and a willing seller (normally established by comparing other sales of comparable properties).

b) **Book value.** Book value, an accounting concept, is the net worth of a company. Since assets are recorded on the books at cost (and then depreciated), book value may not be an accurate indication of value, since assets at market value may differ substantially from cost.

c) **Liquidation value.** What property will bring when it must be liquidated (normally less than market value, since the sale is forced) is liquidation value.

d) **Replacement value.** Replacement value is the cost to replace property (at current prices, less the amount of depreciation the property has been subject to).

e) **Capitalized value.** Capitalized value is determined by projecting the net cash flow from an asset over its life and discounting this cash flow to a present value amount. The discount factor is determined by the riskiness of the stream of cash flow and the opportunity costs of other investments (*i.e.,* what an investor can receive from competing investments).

2) **Methods used by the courts.** Essentially the courts have established two tests in valuing property or services.

a) **Minority rule—true value.** The decider of fact is asked the question: "Was the property transferred equal or nearly equal in value to the par value or stated value of the shares issued?" Thus, the fair market value of the property transferred must be equal to the value of the shares. It makes no difference whether the board of directors acted in good faith or without fraudulent intent.

b) **Majority rule—good faith.** The majority rule is that an exchange of property for stock is presumed to be valid and made in good faith by the directors. There can be a mistake (between the actual fair market value and the valuation given by the board) as long as the mistake was made in good faith and not as a result of intentional fraud.

(1) Thus, only fraud or intentional misrepresentation by the transferor (giving the corporation a cause of action) or a lack of good faith by the corporation's board of directors results in a cause of action against the shareholders.

(2) This is the best rule since the question of value is often difficult to settle (reasonable minds can differ on the issue) and the "true value" rule allows anyone to question the transaction if he disagrees with the value set by the board.

c) **Misrepresentation under the good faith test.** The shareholder has no duty to disclose what he paid for the property (unless he is also a director, majority shareholder, or a promoter with a fiduciary duty); nor has he a duty not to bargain for all he can get (if it is an arm's length transaction). Probably only collusion with the management of the corporation would be fraud. Under the good faith test, if there is no collusion, the courts are liberal in finding that good faith is satisfied.

4. **Analysis of Par and No-Par Stock.**

a. **Purposes of par value stock.** Originally there were two reasons for the use of par value stock:

(i) In the start-up phase of the corporation, issuing stock for par value was a representation to creditors that assets worth par value had been contributed to the corporation. This set up the opportunity to obtain credit.

(ii) Also, shareholders receiving shares presumably knew that they were contributing the same worth as other shareholders that were receiving shares.

Of course, creative promoters destroyed these assumptions by making an end run around the assumptions—overvaluing the property and services contributed to the corporation.

b. **Exception to the general rule.** There are situations in which exceptions are necessary, such as where the stock of the company was not currently worth its par value. In this case the courts held that the shares could be issued for what the directors, in their good faith judgment, felt the shares were worth. [*See* Handley v. Stutz, 130 U.S. 417 (1891)]

c. **Ramifications of the law.** The issue now concerns what purpose the par value requirement, or the stated value requirement in the case of no-par stock, serves.

1) **Scope of original purpose.** Originally the law was applied only to require that shareholders contribute property or services worth at least par value or stated value of the shares. A way around this requirement was simply to create low par or low stated value shares and, when the stock was worth much more than the low values, to contribute property worth at least the par or stated value but not worth as much as the stock itself was reasonably worth (*i.e.,* the property value would not cover what is stated in the capital account plus the paid-in capital account).

2) **State of the law.** No cases seem to hold shareholders in these circumstances. And most state statutes were not drafted with this intent. But there is no reason conceptually that shareholders in such circumstances could not be held for the overvaluation.

5. **Personal Liability of Shareholders Who Fail to Pay Consideration for Stock--**

Hanewald v. Bryan's, Inc., 429 N.W.2d 414 (N.D. 1988).

Facts. In 1984, Keith and Joan Bryan incorporated Bryan's, Inc. (D), elected themselves officers, and designated George Bryan as manager of a retail store. The articles authorized 100 shares of $1,000 par value stock; D issued 50 shares each to the Bryans. They did not pay the corporation any compensation. Instead, they loaned the corporation $10,000 and personally guaranteed a bank loan of $55,000. They then purchased the assets of a retail store from Hanewald (P) for cash and a $5,000 promissory note, and leased a store from P for five years. The business closed after four months. The corporation paid back the loan of $10,000 to the Bryans and paid back the bank; it defaulted on the lease to P and on the promissory note. P was awarded a judgment against D, the corporation, but the trial court refused to hold the Bryans personally liable. P appeals.

Issues. Can a creditor sue shareholders of a corporation directly because they did not pay anything for their par value stock in the corporation?

Held. Yes. Judgment reversed in part and affirmed in part.

- ♦ P can sue the Bryans directly for the amount of the debt, since the Bryans did not pay the par value required for the stock they received in the corporation. The Bryans had a statutory duty to pay for the shares that were issued to them by the corporation. [MBCA (1969), §25] The kinds of consideration that may be paid for shares is set forth in Article XII, section 9 of the state constitution (*i.e.*, money, labor, property). Failure to pay par value for the shares makes the Bryans personally liable to P for the corporation's debt, at least in the amount of consideration they should have paid into the corporation.
- ♦ When a statute does not say whether the plaintiff can sue the shareholder directly, courts have differed (*i.e.*, some have said the creditor can sue directly, some say the corporation must sue, and some say that the creditor can sue on behalf of the corporation). We hold that the plaintiff can sue the shareholders directly.

6. Par Value Irrelevant in Subsequent Stock Transactions--

Torres v. Speiser, 268 A.D.2d 253 (N.Y. App. Div. 2000).

Facts. The plaintiff (P) sold stock to the individual defendant (D). P later claimed that the sale of his minority interest in the corporation to D was invalid because the price of the stock was less than its par value. The court denied P's motion for summary judgment on this issue, and P appeals.

Issue. Was the sale of P's stock invalid because the price was less than its par value?

Held. No. Judgment affirmed.

- Business Corporation Law section 504 prohibits an initial issuance of stock in a new corporation for less than par value or before the full purchase price is paid. However, section 504's prohibition has no bearing on a resale of issued shares. Shares may be bought or sold at any mutually acceptable price.

D. DEBT FINANCING

1. **Tax Advantages of Debt Securities.** There are several tax advantages in issuing debt securities rather than common stock:

   (i) Interest paid is deductible to the corporation;

   (ii) Repayment of principal is not a taxable event (whereas redemption of common stock is); and

   (iii) If the corporation fails, there may be greater tax benefits from taking a bad debt deduction than a capital loss from worthless stock.

2. **Nontax Advantages of Debt.** Debt has the advantage of increasing the return to the common shareholders. That is, if the corporation can earn a greater percentage on the capital it invests than the cost of borrowing, the increment goes to the common shareholders and increases the return on their invested capital. Of course, the other side is that debt increases the risk; if the corporation cannot earn the money to repay the debt, the common shareholders may have to issue common stock to repay the debt (and possibly lose control of the corporation), or have to liquidate to repay the debt and interest.

E. PLANNING THE CAPITAL STRUCTURE: SHARE SUBSCRIPTIONS AND AGREEMENTS TO PURCHASE SECURITIES

1. **Definition.** A subscription agreement is an agreement between a corporation in existence or to be formed (made on its behalf by incorporators, agents, or trustees) and a subscriber, when the corporation agrees to create and to issue shares and the subscriber agrees to pay for them.

2. **State Law.** State law may regulate shareholder subscriptions (requiring that they be in writing, etc.).

3. **Preincorporation Subscription Agreements.**

   a. **When liability attaches.** There are several theories as to when the subscriber becomes liable on the subscription agreement.

      1) **Continuing offer theory.** Here, the courts have held that the preincorporation subscription is a "continuing offer" to a proposed corporation and that a timely withdrawal or revocation by the subscriber (prior to actual formation of the corporation and acceptance

by the newly formed corporation) will defeat any liability under the agreement.

2) **Agreement among the subscribers.** Other courts hold that when there is a group of subscribers, they have made promises to each other and that there exists a contract among the members of the group to become shareholders when the corporation is formed; thus, the subscriptions are binding and irrevocable from the date of subscription.

3) **Statutory solutions.** Statutes in some states specify that subscriptions are enforceable for some specific period of time (*i.e.,* may not be withdrawn), giving those forming the corporation sufficient time in most cases to incorporate and formally accept the subscriptions.

b. **Other devices to prevent withdrawal.** When state law provides for revocation until acceptance, other devices have been used to prevent revocation, such as by having all of the subscribers give an irrevocable power of attorney to a trustee who can subscribe for the shares for some stated period of time.

4. **Postincorporation Subscriptions.** When a subscription agreement is entered into between a corporation in existence and a subscriber, it is a binding obligation. Thus, when the subscriber has not fully paid the subscription price, creditors (such as in an otherwise bankrupt company) could bring an action to force the subscriber to pay the remainder of the subscription price into the corporation.

5. **Remedies for Breach of the Subscription Contract.**

a. **Suit by the corporation.** Once having tendered the certificates, the corporation can recover the full subscription price.

b. **Suit by corporate creditors.** If the corporation becomes insolvent, the creditors of the corporation may enforce the existing subscription agreements against the shareholders. And, at least when the creditors existed prior to the release, it is no defense by the subscriber that the corporation released him from liability (unless the release is based on fair consideration).

c. **Suit by the shareholder.** When the corporation refuses to issue shares, the subscriber may either purchase other shares and sue for damages, or if other shares are not available, sue for specific performance.

6. **Modern Use of Subscriptions.** Subscription agreements are seldom used today, since the federal securities law and the securities laws of the states typically treat such agreements as "securities" and require that they be registered prior to issuance, which is expensive. Hence, issuers now simply register the securities they wish to issue, and when they have qualified them with the regulatory authorities they offer the securities and enter contracts to sell them.

F. PUBLIC OFFERINGS

This section discusses the Securities Act of 1933 (hereinafter referred to as the "1933 Act" or the "Act"). This Act regulates the original distribution of securities from the issuer (usually a corporation) to the public. A number of exemptions exist for limited offerings of securities, depending on the manner in which the offering is made.

1. **Objectives of the 1933 Act.** The 1933 Act grew out of the stock market crash of the late 1920s. Congressional inquiry into the crash discovered that securities were often sold to investors without any disclosure by the issuer of facts in its possession that were relevant to the investor's investment decision, and that remedies provided by state law for fraudulent practices in connection with these securities transactions were inadequate to protect the investing public. Therefore, the 1933 Act was passed with two objectives in mind.

    a. **To provide full disclosure to potential investors.** The first objective of the 1933 Act is to provide investors with full disclosure of all material investment information in connection with the original interstate issuance of securities from the issuer to the public. To accomplish this, the issuer must file a "registration statement" with the Securities and Exchange Commission ("S.E.C.") prior to issuing its securities. This registration statement must contain all material investment information about the issuer and the issuer's securities. Also, the issuer must prepare a "prospectus"—a digest of the most important information contained in the registration statement—and give this prospectus to investors prior to the sale or delivery of the issuer's securities.

    b. **To prevent fraud and misrepresentation in the interstate sale of securities generally.** The second objective is to prevent fraud and misrepresentation in the interstate sale of securities. To accomplish this, the 1933 Act includes several liability provisions providing remedies to defrauded purchasers on a more lenient basis than formerly available under the common law.

2. **Jurisdiction and Interstate Commerce.** The provisions of the 1933 Act apply only when interstate commerce is involved. As one would expect, the S.E.C. and the courts have adopted a broad interpretation of what constitutes "interstate commerce." It is involved whenever the "means" of doing interstate commerce are used—such as the telephone or the mails—in any part of the securities transaction.

3. **Underwriting Process.** The process of distributing securities from the original issuer to the ultimate retail purchasers is called an "underwriting." Firms that contract with the issuer to market the issuer's securities are known as "underwriters." The firms that buy from the underwriters and resell to the public are "dealers."

4. **Persons Covered by the 1933 Act.**

a. **Introduction.** The requirement of the 1933 Act that a public distribution of securities be registered with the S.E.C. applies to all "persons" selling securities through the use of the facilities of interstate commerce. [*See* Securities Act ("SA") §5] However, the Act exempts from the registration requirement securities transactions by "persons" other than issuers, underwriters, or dealers. [*See* SA §4(1)] Thus, the registration and prospectus requirements are really only applicable to issuers, underwriters, and dealers. These terms are defined below.

b. **Definition of an issuer.** An "issuer" is defined to include every person who issues or proposes to issue any security. [*See* SA §2(4)]

c. **Underwriters.** "Underwriters" also must comply with the registration requirements of section 5 of the Act. The Act defines three classes of persons to be "underwriters." [*See* SA §2(11)]

1) **Persons who purchase securities from the issuer with a view to a public distribution.** An "underwriter" is one who purchases securities from an issuer with a view to distribution. [*See* SA §2(11)] "Distribution" means essentially a public offering (*i.e.,* an offering to a substantial number of people who do not purchase the securities to hold them for a long time as an investment).

2) **Persons who offer or sell for an issuer in connection with a distribution.**

a) **In general.** The second definition of an "underwriter" covers those persons who actually "offer or sell securities for an issuer" in connection with the issuer's public distribution.

b) **Persons who purchase from control persons.** Note that for the purpose of determining those persons who are underwriters, the term "issuer" includes any person directly or indirectly controlling or controlled by the issuer. [*See* SA §2(11)]

(1) This section makes an underwriter out of a person who purchases securities from a "controlling person" for the purpose of a public distribution, or who offers or sells securities for such a controlling person in connection with a public distribution.

(2) The Act defines a "control person" as one having the "power to direct or cause the direction of the management and policies of a company." [*See* SA Rule 405] This may occur through stock ownership, a position in management, influence with the management, or any combination of these factors.

3) **A person who participates in a distribution.** The third definition of an underwriter is one who "participates" in a distribution. Obviously, this makes the definition of an underwriter under section 2(11) very broad.

d. **Dealers.** Dealers also appear to be covered by the Act (because section 4(1) seems to include them in the registration and prospectus requirements); however, a specific exemption is included in the Act for dealers. [*See* SA §4(3)]

5. **Definition of Security.** In order to come within the registration requirement of section 5 of the 1933 Act, the offer or sale of a property interest must constitute the offer or sale of a security.

a. **Categories of securities.** The Act defines three categories of securities. [*See* SA §2(1)]

1) **Any interest or instrument commonly known as a security.** These would include bonds, stocks, debentures, warrants, etc.

2) **Types of securities specifically mentioned in the Act.** For example, the Act specifically mentions the following as being "securities":

(i) Preorganization subscriptions for securities; and

(ii) Fractional, undivided interests in oil, gas, or other mineral rights.

3) **Investment contracts and certificates of participation.** The two most important clauses of section 2(1) are its broad, catch-all phrases—securities are "investment contracts" and "certificates of interest or participation in any profit-sharing agreement." The S.E.C. and the courts have defined these phrases so as to apply to a wide variety of financial schemes.

b. **The traditional test for a security.** The traditional test for whether a property interest constitutes a security under these two broad phrases is known as the "*Howey* test" (set forth by the Supreme Court in *Securities and Exchange Commission v. W.J. Howey Co.,* 328 U.S. 293 (1946)). The Court held that an investment contract is any contract or scheme whereby a person invests his money in a common enterprise and expects to make a profit solely from the efforts of the promoter or a third party who is responsible for management. Thus, the elements of the test are: (i) Is it a profit-making venture? (ii) Is the investor passive in management?

c. **The trend of decisions.** The trend of decisions is toward expanding the scope of what is regulated as a "security." Whereas, originally under the *Howey* test the scheme had to have a profit objective and the investor had to be totally passive in management, the S.E.C. and the courts have expanded the test to cover situations in which investors do participate in management and the form of benefit derived by the investor may be something other than cash profits.

6. **Registration Statements.** Prior to the original public issuance of securities, the issuer must file a registration statement with the S.E.C. The purpose of the registration statement is to disclose all of the information needed to determine whether the securities offered are a good investment. The most important information in the registration statement is digested into a shorter document—the prospectus—which is the document actually given to a purchaser prior to purchase or at the same time as the purchased securities are delivered.

7. **Regulation of Offers and Sales of Securities.** Section 5 of the Act (which sets forth the registration requirement for newly issued securities) divides the underwriting process into three time periods and states the rules concerning making offers and sales of securities in these periods (*i.e.,* the prefiling period, the waiting period, and the posteffective period).

8. **Exemptions from the Registration Requirements of the Act.** The 1933 Act provides for certain exemptions from the registration requirements of section 5.

    a. **Exempted securities.** Certain types of securities are exempt from the registration requirements of section 5. Such an exemption means that the security may be sold and resold and never be subject to the registration or prospectus requirements of the Act.

    b. **Exempted security transactions.** The Act contains certain exemptions for security transactions. [*See* SA §§3, 4]

        1) **Distinction between exempted securities and exempted transactions.** The distinctions between security transactions and exempted securities is an important one. If the security itself is exempted, it can be sold and resold and never be subject to the requirements of section 5. However, if only the security transaction is exempt, then the initial sale may be exempt from section 5, but a later resale may not be.

        2) **Transactions by persons other than issuers, underwriters, or dealers.** As discussed above, transactions by persons other than issuers, underwriters, or dealers are exempted. [*See* SA §4(1)]

        3) **Private offering exemption.** Transactions by an issuer not involving a public offering (*i.e.,* a private offering of securities) are exempted from registration. [*See* SA §4(2)]

a) **Two alternatives—basic exemption and regulation D.** The basis for the private offering exemption is section 4(2) of the 1933 Act. However, since the standard of what constituted a private offering was vague, the S.E.C. adopted regulation D as special instances of the private offering exemption; *i.e.,* it sets forth objective criteria that an issuer can rely on to qualify for the exemption. However, regulation D is not exclusive; issuers may also still rely on section 4(2) if they cannot qualify. Section 4(2) will be discussed first and then regulation D.

b) **Private offerings under section 4(2) of the Act.**

(1) **Fact question.** Whether an offering is a "private offering" or a "public offering" is a question of fact. In order for the transaction to be exempt from registration under the Act, the offering must be "private."

(2) **Primary factors considered.** The following are the primary factors considered by the courts in making the determination whether an offering is a public or a private one.

(a) **Need for the protection of the Act.** Many courts have stated that the primary question is whether there appears in the circumstances of the offering of securities the need for the protection of the Act to be given to the purchasers.

1] Presumably, if the offer of securities is made to those able to "fend for themselves," the transaction does not involve a public offering.

2] This means that the basic issue concerns the level of sophistication of the persons (offerees) to whom the securities are offered for sale. In other words, are they knowledgeable enough to ask the right questions, to demand and get the information they need to make an intelligent investment decision, to appreciate the risk of making securities investments, etc.?

(b) **Access to investment information.** Allied with the idea of the level of sophistication of the offerees is the idea of the investor's access to information material to an investment decision.

1] Courts have indicated that for the private offering exemption to apply, it must be shown that the offerees were given or had access to the same kind of information that would have been contained in a registration statement.

2] Allied with the concept of access to information is the concept that the offerees must be in or have a close relationship to the issuer and its management.

(c) **Distribution of material information.** Some courts have implied that the mere access to material information is not enough.

1] The issuer may have to actually distribute to its offerees the same type of material information as would be contained in a formal registration statement.

2] Also, the issuer may have to give the offerees access to any additional information that they request.

(d) **Number of offerees.** A private offering also seems to imply that the number of offerees will be few in number.

1] The Supreme Court has indicated that the number of offerees is not a major factor. [*See* Securities and Exchange Commission v. Ralston Purina Co., *infra*] However, the Court did suggest that the S.E.C. might adopt a rule of thumb for the purposes of administrative decisions. At one time, this rule of thumb was 25 persons (*i.e.*, if the offering was to more than 25 persons, it was a public offering).

2] But other courts and the S.E.C. have emphasized the aspect of the number of offerees. When they do, it is clear that the rationale is that the more offerees there are, the more the offering looks like a public offering.

3] On the basis of this rationale, when the number of offerees gets very large, no matter how sophisticated the investors might be, or how much information they might have, the offering would be a public one and registration would be required.

(3) **Other important factors.** In addition to the primary factors considered above, there are several other factors that courts have indicated are important when determining whether the offering is a public or private one. Most of these factors are based on the rationale that if an offering looks like a public offering (*i.e.*, a large, dispersed offering), then it is one for the purposes of the 1933 Act.

(a) **The size (amount) of the offering.** The bigger the dollar amount of the offering, the more public it looks.

(b) **The marketability of the securities.** If the issuer has created the type of security that tends to be readily marketable (such as many small units in small denominations; *i.e.,* $1 per share), there is more reason to believe that the issue is made with the intent to distribute the securities to the public rather than to a few private persons.

(c) **Diverse group rule.** The more unrelated to each other (*i.e.,* without knowledge of or relationship to each other) and diverse the group of investors is, the more the offering appears to be a public offering.

(d) **Manner of offering.** The manner in which the offering is made (*i.e.,* was public advertising used?) may also be important.

(4) **Offering made to "key employees"--**

Securities and Exchange Commission v. Ralston Purina Co., 346 U.S. 119 (1953).

Facts. Between 1947 and 1951, Ralston Purina (D) sold nearly $2 million of its stock to employees from all levels of the company without registration and, in doing so, made use of the mails. In each of these years, a corporate resolution authorized the sale of common stock to employees who, without solicitation by D, inquired as to the manner in which common stock could be purchased from D. Sales in each year were to approximately 400 employees. D classified all offerees as "key employees" in the organization. D claimed the private offering exemption. The trial court dismissed the action by the S.E.C., which sought to enjoin D's activities. The court of appeals affirmed. The Supreme Court granted certiorari.

Issue. Was D's offering of stock to "key employees" a public offering?

Held. Yes. Judgment reversed.

- To be public, an offer need not be open to the whole world.
- The design of the Act was to protect investors by promoting full disclosure of information thought to be necessary to informed investment decisions. Thus, the private offering exemption is available only where the protection of the Act is not needed (*i.e.*, an offering to those able to fend for themselves). Absent a showing of special circumstances, a corporation's employees are as much in need of protection as any members of the investing public.
- The burden of proof is on the issuer, who would plead the exemption.
- Since the employees here were not shown to have access to the kind of information that registration would disclose, D was not entitled to the exemption.
- The exemption applies whether the offering is made to few or many investors. However, it may be that offerings to a substantial number of persons would rarely be exempt, and the S.E.C. may adopt a numerical test in deciding when to investigate private offering exemption claims.

---

(5) **Two-step distributions.**

(a) **Introduction.** The issuer may intend a private offering, and the offering may be that way after the initial sales of securities (*e.g.,* in the first step in the distribution a corporation issues its common stock to 10 investors), only to eventually have the offering turn into a public offering (*e.g.,* in the second step the original 10 investors immediately turn around and sell their stock to 50 additional investors). That is, a distribution of securities encompasses the entire process by which a block of securities is dispersed and ultimately comes to rest in the hands of a group of purchasers.

(b) **Purchasers' investment intent.** Thus, the intent of the original purchasers (the 10 purchasers in the example above) in buying the securities is very important.

1] **Purchasers as underwriters.** If the original purchasers buy the securities with a view to distribution (*i.e.,* resale to the public), they are "underwriters." [*See* SA §2(11)] And if the end result is that a public distribution actually takes place, there is a violation of the registration requirements of section 5 of the Act.

2] **Investment intent.** The opposite of taking for resale is purchasing for investment (to keep or hold for a significant period of time).

(c) **Elements showing investment intent.** The intent of the original purchaser (whether for investment or for distribution) is a question of fact—what was the purchaser's subjective intent at the time of purchase? Objective facts are looked at to determine this subjective intent.

1] **Investment letters.** In order to show an investor's investment intent, it is a common practice to require that purchasers give the issuer a letter indicating that they are buying for investment purposes rather than with a view toward resale. However, since the purchaser's intention is a question of fact, his own statement on the matter is not conclusive evidence. Therefore, it is the responsibility of an issuer or underwriter to go beyond the investor's letter and make a reasonable investigation into each investor's circumstances in order to determine his real intent.

2] **Restrictive legends on stock certificates.** In order to show that it has taken all reasonable precautions and has made a reasonable investigation of the investor's intent, and also to make unlawful secondary transfers difficult, the issuer claiming the private offering exemption may place a legend on the stock certificates that states that transfer without the issuer's permission is impossible. The issuer will also normally require that the person wishing to transfer privately offered stock get the opinion of the issuer's lawyer that a transfer will not violate the securities laws.

3] **Length of the required holding period.** The longer the securities are held by the original purchasers before resale, the more likely is a factual finding that the original purchase was for investment. At one time, the S.E.C. would give opinion letters that a one-year holding period was sufficient to show investment intent; then it went to two years, then three, and finally the S.E.C. would not issue an opinion.

4] **Objective criteria.** Due to the confusion and ambiguity involved in making determinations concerning whether an investor has satisfied "investment intent," the S.E.C. adopted Rule 144. This rule defines when and under what circumstances purchasers in a private offering of securities may resell without violating the Act, essentially establishing a two-year holding requirement. The purpose of Rule 144 is to set forth objective criteria by which a purchaser's investment intent may be established.

(6) Distributions by control persons.

(a) **Control persons as issuers.** For the purpose of determining those who are underwriters, control persons are defined by the Act as "issuers." [*See* SA §2(11)]

1] Thus, when a person or persons purchase securities from a control person with the intent of making a public distribution of these securities, the control person becomes an "issuer" and the purchasers are "underwriters." For example, if A is a control person of XYZ Corporation and sells securities of XYZ to B, C, and D, who then resell to 50 other unsophisticated investors, then B, C, and D are underwriters; A is an issuer.

2] In looking for an exemption from the registration requirements, a control person would ordinarily look to section 4(1) (which says that section 5 only applies to issuers, underwriters, and dealers). But in the circumstances of this hypothetical, the control person (A) cannot use section 4(1) (*i.e.*, the control person is an "issuer" when a public offering of her securities occurs).

3] This means that control persons cannot make a public offering of their stock without registration. If, however, those taking from the control person do not intend a public distribution (*i.e.,* they take with investment intent), the sale by the control person is exempt under section 4(1). This means that for control persons to sell their shares without registration, they must sell only in private offerings. The criteria for determining whether a private offering is involved in this context are the same as in the context of section 4(2).

(b) Application of Rule 144 to sales by control persons. In connection with the discussion above concerning two-step distributions and the buyer's investment intent, it was mentioned that the S.E.C. has adopted Rule 144, which gives objective criteria for establishing when an original purchaser who has bought stock in a private offering has established her investment intent and thus can resell the stock without violating the securities laws. Rule 144 also applies to sales of stock by control persons: it states when and how much stock a control person may sell without becoming an "issuer" and making those that sell the stock "underwriters."

c) **The small issue exemption—regulation D.** In addition to the other security and security transaction exemptions set forth in the Act, section 3(b) of the 1933 Act permits the S.E.C. to exempt security offerings from registration when the protection of the Act is not required and less than $5 million in securities is involved in the offering. Pursuant to this section, the S.E.C. formulated regulation D in 1982. Although formulated under section 3 of the 1933 Act for ***security*** exemptions, this small business exemption is really a ***transaction*** exemption.

(1) Introduction. The S.E.C. adopted regulation D, which contains Rules 501 through 506, in a major initiative aimed at facilitating the capital formation needs of small business. Rules 501 through 503 set forth definitions, terms, and conditions that apply generally throughout the regulation. Rules 504 and 505, respectively, replace prior Rules 240 and 242 and provide exemptions from registration under section 3(b) of the 1933 Act. Rule 506 replaces prior Rule 146 and relates to transactions that are deemed to be exempt from registration under section 4(2) of the 1933 Act. [*See* S.E.C. Release No. 33-6389 (1982)] These provisions apply only to the issuer; control persons may not use them. Regulation D is designed to: (i) simplify and clarify existing exemptions; (ii) expand the availability of existing exemptions; and (iii) achieve uniformity between federal and state exemptions.

(2) **Definitions and terms used in regulation D.** Rule 501 sets forth definitions that apply to the entire regulation D. One of these key definitions is that of "accredited investor," which includes eight categories:

(i) Institutional investors [*see* SA §2(15)(i)];

(ii) Private business development companies [*see* SA Rule 501(a)(2)];

(iii) Tax-exempt organizations [*see* SA Rule 501(a)(3)];

(iv) Directors, executive officers, and general partners of the issuer of the securities [*see* SA Rule 501(a)(4)];

(v) $150,000 purchasers (*see* SA Rule 501(a)(5)];

(vi) Natural persons with $1 million net worth [*see* SA Rule 501(a)(6)];

(vii) Natural persons with $200,000 income [*see* SA Rule 501(a)(7)]; and

(viii)Entities made up of certain accredited investors, such as an entity owned entirely by such investors [*see* SA Rule 501(a)(8)].

(3) **General conditions to be met.** There are several general conditions that apply to all offers and sales effected pursuant to Rules 504 through 506 [*see* SA Rule 502]:

(a) **Integration.** All sales that are part of the same regulation D offering must be integrated. [*See* SA Rule 502(a)] The rule provides a safe harbor for all offers and sales that take place at least six months before the start of, or six months after the termination of, the regulation D offering, so long as there are no offers and sales (excluding those to employee benefit plans) of the same securities within either of these six-month periods.

(b) **Information requirements.** The type of disclosure that must be furnished in regulation D offerings is specified. [*See* SA Rule 502 (b)] If an issuer sells securities under Rule 504 or only to accredited investors, regulation D does not mandate any specific type of disclosure. But if securities are sold under Rule 505 or 506 to any investors that are not accredited, delivery of the information specified in Rule 502(b)(2) to ***all*** purchasers is required. The type of information to be furnished varies depending on the size of the offering and the nature of the issuer (*i.e.,* whether the issuer is a reporting or nonreporting company under the 1934 Act). Reporting companies in essence can use the information they are already filing with the S.E.C. (*i.e.,* annual report, proxy statement, and Form 10K). The issuer, in a Rule 505 or 506 offering, must also give investors the opportunity to ask questions and to obtain any additional information that the issuer can acquire without unreasonable effort.

(c) **Manner of the offering.** The use of general solicitation or general advertising in connection with regulation D offerings is prohibited, except in certain cases under Rule 504. [*See* SA Rule 502(c)]

(d) **Limitations on resale.** Securities acquired in a regulation D offering, with the exception of certain offerings under Rule 504, have the status of securities acquired in a transaction under section 4(2) of the 1933 Act. [*See* SA Rule 502(d)] Issuers are required to exercise reasonable care to ensure that purchasers of these securities are not underwriters and to make reasonable inquiry as to an investor's investment purpose. Also, a legend restricting transfer must be placed on the share certificates.

(4) **Filing notice of sales.** There is a uniform notice of sales form for use in offerings under both regulation D and section 4(6) of the 1933 Act. It is called "Form D." Issuers furnish information on Form D mainly by checking appropriate boxes. [*See* SA Rule 503] The notice is due 15 days after the first sale of securities in an offering under regulation D. Subsequent notices are due every six months after the first sale and 30 days after the last sale.

(5) **Exemption for offers and sales not exceeding $1 million.** An exemption under section 3(b) of the 1933 Act is provided for certain offers and sales not exceeding an aggregate offering price of $1 million during any 12-month period. [*See* SA Rule 504] This exemption is not available to investment companies or to 1934 Securities and Exchange Act reporting companies. Commissions or similar remuneration ***may*** be paid to those selling the offering in a Rule 504 offering.

   (a) Rule 504 does not mandate specific disclosure requirements. However, an issuer proceeding pursuant to the rule is subject to the antifraud and civil liability provisions of the federal securities laws ***and must comply with any applicable state requirements.***

   (b) If the entire offering is made exclusively in states that require the registration and the delivery of a disclosure document, and if the offering is in compliance with these requirements, then the general limitations of Rule 502(c) (on the manner of the offering) and (d) (restrictions on transfer) do not apply.

(6) **Exemption for offers and sales not exceeding $5 million.** An exemption under section 3(b) of the 1933 Act is also provided for offers and sales to an unlimited number of accredited investors, and to no more than 35 non-accredited investors, where the aggregate offering price in any 12-month period does not exceed $5 million. [*See* SA Rule 505] Rule 505 is available to any issuer that is not an investment company.

(7) **Exemption for offers and sales without regard to dollar amount.** Rule 506, which modifies and replaces old Rule 146, relates to transactions that are deemed to be exempt under section 4(2) of the 1933 Act. Like Rule 146, Rule 506 exempts offers and sales to no more than 35 purchasers (accredited investors are not included in counting the 35 investors). Rule 506 modifies the offeree qualification principles of Rule 146 in two ways:

   (i) Rule 506 requires that ***only purchasers*** have to meet the sophistication standard; offerees are not required to. If the purchaser himself cannot meet the sophistication standard (knowledge and experience in financial and business matters), then, similarly to

Rule 146, the investor can employ a sophisticated person to represent him. [*See* SA Rule 506(b)(ii)]

(ii) Rule 506 eliminates the economic risk test for qualifying offerees under Rule 146.

(8) Difference between Rules 505 and 506. Note that the difference between Rules 505 and 506 is that a Rule 505 offering must be limited in amount (to $5 million or less) and that all investors in a Rule 506 offering must be either sophisticated (or be represented by a sophisticated person) or accredited, while in a Rule 505 offering the 35 nonaccredited investors need not be sophisticated or represented by a sophisticated person.

4) Transaction exemption for intrastate offerings.

a) Introduction. Securities that are offered and sold only to persons residing within a single state, when the issuer of the securities is a resident of and doing business in that same state, are exempt from registration under section 5 of the Act. This is known as the "intrastate offering" exemption. The purpose of the exemption is to facilitate the raising of local capital for local businesses. [*See* SA §3(a)(11)] Over the years, a great deal of uncertainty arose in the meaning of some of the terms of the intrastate exemption. For this reason, the S.E.C. adopted Rule 147, which sets forth a specific, objective set of criteria, which, if followed by an issuer, will ensure that the intrastate offering exemption will apply. However, if the issuer cannot qualify an issue under Rule 147, the issuer may still qualify it under the general terms of section 3(a)(11).

b) General requirements of the intrastate offering exemption—section 3(a)(11).

(1) The issue concept. The entire issue of securities must be offered and sold to residents of one state. [*See* SA Release No. 4434 (1961)] Thus, a single offer to a nonresident will destroy the exemption.

(a) Restricting transfers—the good faith test. It is the responsibility of the issuer to make sure that the offering is made only to residents and that no resales (which would destroy the exemption) are made to nonresidents. Those participating in the offering must act in good faith, according to a standard of due care, to see that only appropriate offers and sales are made.

(b) **Resales—the coming-to-rest test.** Resales to nonresidents are possible without destroying the exemption, but only after the original distribution to residents is complete (*i.e.,* only after the offering has come to rest in the hands of residents).

1] **Intent of the purchasers.** The question of whether the issue of securities has come to rest depends on the intent of the original purchasers. If they purchased the securities with the intention of keeping them for investment, then the issue is complete and resales to nonresidents may begin. However, if the purchasers took with the intent to make a further distribution or resale, then the issue has not "come to rest" and resales to nonresidents will destroy the exemption.

2] **Objective standard.** Whether the issue has come to rest (so that resale to nonresidents is then possible) is a fact question, to be determined according to objective factors, such as the length of time the securities are held before resale.

(2) **Residence within the state of issuer, offerees, and purchasers.** The exemption also requires that the entire issue be confined to a single state where the issuer, the offerees, and the purchasers are residents.

(a) **Offerees and purchasers.** With respect to offerees and purchasers, the test for residence is something like "domicile" (*i.e.,* the purchaser must reside in the state with the intent to remain in the state).

(b) **Control persons.** Control persons may use the exemption (if the issuer could), even though such control persons are not residents in the state where the offering is made.

(c) **Issuer.** There are two requirements that the issuer must meet in order to establish residence:

1] **Residence in the state.** The issuer must be a resident in the state where the offering is made. For a corporation, the state of residence is the state of incorporation.

2] **Doing business test.** Since the purpose of the rule is to finance local business, the issuer must also be "doing business" in the state. The tests used to establish "doing business" in the state are (i) whether the issuer is doing a majority of its business in the state, and (ii) whether the proceeds of the offering are used in the state.

c) **Rule 147—objective test for intrastate offering exemption.**

(1) **Background.** The S.E.C. has little control over intrastate offerings, since the initiation and the progress of such an offering is never reported to the Commission. Hence, in the past, many violations of the exemption requirements occurred, and much uncertainty arose over the meaning of some of the terms and conditions involved in the section 3(a)(11) exemption. This resulted in the adoption by the S.E.C. of Rule 147, which is a specific, objective set of criteria for qualifying an issue for the 3(a)(11) exemption.

(2) **Residence.** The issuer, offerees, and purchasers must be residents of the same state. Rule 147 gives specific definitions to the term "residence."

(a) **Residence of issuer in a state.** Residence is defined in Rule 147 as follows: (i) for ***corporations,*** the state of incorporation; (ii) for ***individuals,*** the state of principal residence.

(b) **Doing business.** An issuer is deemed to be "doing business" in a state if: (i) 80% of the consolidated gross revenues are derived there; (ii) 80% of the consolidated assets are held there; (iii) 80% of the proceeds from covered transactions are to be used in the issuer's operations there; and (iv) the issuer's principal office is located there. [*See* SA Rule 147(c)(2)]

(c) **Offerees and purchasers.** Definitions are also given for determination of the state of residence of the offerees and purchasers. Individuals are deemed residents of the state where their principal residence is located. [SA Rule 147(d)(2)]

(3) **Resale of intrastate securities.** No sales can be made to persons not resident in the state of issue during the

time the securities are being offered and sold by the issuer and for an additional period of nine months following the last sale by the issuer of the offering. [*See* SA Rule 147(e)]

(4) **Transfer restrictions.**

(a) **Legend and stop transfer instructions.** To insure that securities issued under this rule do not enter the interstate securities markets prior to the time allowed (*i.e.,* nine months), the S.E.C. requires the issuer to have a restrictive legend placed on each certificate and to see that stop transfer instructions are lodged with the transfer agent for the issued securities. [*See* SA Rule 147(f)(1)(i) and (ii)]

(b) **Transfer letters.** To insure that only resident offerees and purchasers are involved in covered transactions, Rule 147 requires the issuer to obtain a written representation from each purchaser regarding his place of residence. [*See* SA Rule 147(e)(1)(iii)]

9. Liabilities Under the 1933 Act.

a. **Proving fraud at common law.** At common law, a defrauded purchaser of securities had to prove the same things to recover as any other purchaser of goods.

b. **Liability for false or misleading statements or omissions in the prospectus.** Section 11 of the 1933 Act imposes liability on designated persons for material misstatements or omissions in an effective prospectus, unless the defendants can show that they had (after having made a reasonable investigation of the facts) reasonable grounds to believe, and they actually did believe, that the statements made were accurate.

c. **Liability for offers or sales in violation of section 5.** Section 12(1) provides that any person who offers or sells a security in violation of any of the provisions of section 5 of the 1933 Act shall be liable to the purchaser for (i) the consideration paid (with interest), less the amount of any income received on the securities, or (ii) for damages if the purchaser no longer owns the security.

d. **General civil liability under the Act.** The Act also prohibits fraud generally in the offer or sale of securities. It provides that any person who offers or sells a security (whether or not the sale is exempted from registration by the provisions of the Act) by the use or any means of interstate commerce and makes an untrue statement of material fact (or omits to state a material fact) in connection therewith (the purchaser not knowing of such untruth or omission), and who cannot sustain the burden of proof that he did not know and in the exercise of reasonable care could not have known of such untruth, is liable to the purchaser of such security. [*See* SA §12(2)]

10. **Regulation by the States of the Distribution of Securities.** Most states also have securities laws that regulate the original distribution of securities within their borders. When an issuer makes a distribution within a state, both the Securities Act of 1933 and the state law must therefore be complied with. These state laws are generally called "blue sky" laws.

11. **Determining Whether Property Interest Constitutes Security: Application of *Howey* Test--**

Smith v. Gross, 604 F.2d 639 (9th Cir. 1979).

Facts. Gross and others (Ds) represented to Gerald and Mary Smith (Ps) that earthworms were easy to raise and would multiply 64 times per year and that Ds would buy back earthworms produced by Ps at $2.25 per pound. In fact, the earthworms multiplied only about eight times per year and Ds could afford to pay $2.25 per pound only for purpose of resale to other investors at an inflated price. Ps appeal from the district court's judgment dismissing their action against Ds.

Issue. Did the transactions between the parties involve an investment contract type of security?

Held. Yes. Consequently, Ds were in violation of federal securities laws. Judgment reversed.

- The Supreme Court in *Securities and Exchange Commission v. W.J. Howey Co.* (*supra*) set out the conditions for an investment contract. The test is whether the scheme involves "(i) an investment of money (ii) in a common enterprise (iii) with profits to come solely from the efforts of others."

- Ps did invest money in a common enterprise, *i.e.,* one in which the fortune of Ps was interwoven with and dependent upon the efforts and success of Ds.

- With regard to the third element of the Supreme Court test, Ps alleged that they were promised that the effort necessary to raise worms was minimal and alleged that they could not receive the promised income unless Ds purchased their harvest. Thus, the Smiths alleged facts that, if true, were sufficient to establish an investment contract.

G. ISSUANCE OF SHARES BY A GOING CONCERN: PREEMPTIVE RIGHTS, DILUTION, AND RECAPITALIZATIONS

1. Preemptive Rights.

a. **Definition.** A preemptive right is the right of a shareholder to subscribe to a pro rata or proportionate share of any new issuance of shares that might operate to decrease her percentage ownership in the corporation. Thus, if there are 10 common shareholders, each owning 100 shares, and XYZ Corporation plans to issue 1,000 additional shares, then if each shareholder had preemptive rights, each would be entitled to subscribe to an additional 100 shares of the 1,000 new shares to be offered.

b. **At common law.** At common law the shareholders were deemed to have an inherent right to preempt new stock offerings.

1) Generally, however, such rights were recognized only when shares were to be issued for cash (*i.e.,* the corporation could issue additional shares for property or services without preemptive rights attaching).

2) Such rights generally attached only to common stock, although some states held that such rights also attached to preferred stock.

3) Also, the majority view was that preemptive rights attached only to issues of newly authorized stock.

a) Thus, if XYZ Corporation was formed and issued 10,000 of its 100,000 shares of authorized common stock, and later issued another 10,000 shares, preemptive rights did not attach to the second issue (some courts were contra on this). The rationale was that the originally authorized shares constituted the corporation's original plan of financing and could be issued whenever and to whomever the corporation wished.

b) But if XYZ first issued all of its 100,000 authorized shares, later authorized another 10,000 and issued these shares, preemptive rights would apply to the 10,000 shares issued.

c. **Regulation by statute.** Today preemptive rights are generally governed by statute.

1) Some states provide that there are no preemptive rights unless such rights are provided for in the articles.

2) Some states indicate that there are preemptive rights unless they are expressly denied in the articles.

d. **Problem with preemptive rights.** The problem with preemptive rights (as far as the well-being of the corporation is concerned) is that such rights limit the financing opportunities of the corporation (*i.e.*, the corporation is limited to first offering new shares to existing shareholders). Thus, preemptive rights usually appear only in the close corporation situation (where existing shareholders are interested in maintaining management control).

e. **Remedies.** There are several alternative remedies available to protect a shareholder's preemptive rights.

1) **Damages.** Damages are calculated on the basis of the difference between the offering price of the new shares and the cost of acquiring the shares in the market (*i.e.,* the market value).

2) **Equitable remedies.** If the shares are not available in the market, the shareholder with preemptive rights may sue for specific performance (to compel the corporation to issue the additional shares necessary for the shareholder to retain her proportionate interest). When the shares have not yet been issued (but are about to be), the shareholder may get an injunction against issuance of the shares in violation of her preemptive rights.

f. **Damages--**

Stokes v. Continental Trust Co. of City of New York, 78 N.E. 1090 (N.Y. 1906).

Facts. Stokes (P) is a shareholder in the Continental Trust Co. (D), which had 5,000 shares of $100 par value stock authorized and outstanding, P owning 221 shares. A brokerage firm offered to buy an additional 5,000 shares at $450 per share. D sought to increase the authorized shares by 5,000 (which P voted for) and then to issue these shares to the brokerage firm (which P voted against). Prior to the authorization to sell the shares, P protested and offered to buy his proportionate interest (221 shares) in the new offering at $100 par value. His offer was declined and the shares were sold to the brokerage firm. P sues D to compel it to issue new shares to him or for damages.

Issue. Does a shareholder have an inherent right to subscribe to his proportionate interest in newly authorized and issued shares?

Held. Yes. Judgment for P.

- The existing shareholders have an inherent right to a proportionate share of new stock issued for cash.

- Such a right can be waived, but it was not waived here. P protested and offered to buy his proportionate interest prior to the sale to the brokerage firm.

- The price to exercise preemptive rights is not par value but the price fixed for issuing the shares by the board. Here, it was $450 per share. Thus, the damages should be measured by the difference between the market price of the shares at the date of the sale and the price P would have had to pay for the shares at that time ($450).

Comment. The court emphasizes the fact that preemptive rights allow the existing shareholders to maintain their voting interest in the corporation. However, today many commentators emphasize the idea that preemptive rights allow the shareholders to maintain their right to invest their capital in the corporation (and when a corporation is highly successful, this is a valuable right, since it represents an investment opportunity that might not be available to shareholders outside the corporation).

---

g. **Shareholder votes to eliminate preemptive rights.** Note that an issue sometimes arises as to whether the corporation (through a vote of the shareholders) may eliminate preexisting preemptive rights. The trend is toward permitting a majority of the shareholders to eliminate such preexisting rights by amendment.

2. **Equitable Limitations on the Issuance of Shares.**

a. **Fiduciary's objective of gaining control.** As a general rule, it is improper for directors or majority shareholders to issue shares to themselves for the purpose of perpetuating their control.

b. **Duty to issue shares for adequate consideration.**

1) **Introduction.** There are equitable considerations other than whether shares have been issued for property or services equal in value to the par value of the shares (*see* the discussion *supra* on stock watering). The fiduciaries of the corporation (such as directors) have the duty to issue the stock for an adequate price. However, the factual situations must be closely examined to see whether there is any injury involved when shares are issued for at least their par value but for less than their going value.

2) **Initial issuance.** Initially, the shares must be issued for at least their par value. Beyond this creditors cannot complain, and the shareholders do not care about the price per share (as long as they each pay the same amount).

3) **Later issues.** For later issues, it makes no difference to creditors if shares are issued for less than they might be worth (since their interests are not affected), but if stock is reasonably worth $10 per

share and is issued for $5, then the percentage interest of existing shareholders is diluted. But when all existing shareholders buy their pro rata interest in the new shares, it makes no difference (since their interests are not diluted). However, when new shares are to be issued to new shareholders (or to only some of the existing shareholders), all existing shareholders have an interest in seeing that the new shares are issued for an adequate price.

c. **Inadequate consideration--**

Katzowitz v. Sidler, 249 N.E.2d 359 (N.Y. 1969).

Facts. Katzowitz, Sidler, and Lasker were involved in several close corporations as directors, officers, and equal shareholders. They had personal disagreements, and Katzowitz (P) agreed to withdraw from active management of Sulburn Corporation, with the understanding that he would receive the same benefits and compensation as Sidler and Lasker (Ds) and remain an equal shareholder. Sulburn owed each of the three $2,500 in commissions; Ds wanted to issue additional shares to each of the three for the commission amounts, and then loan the $7,500 to another corporation. P objected. Ds called a special meeting of the board of directors; P did not attend. A resolution offering 25 shares to each of the three at one-eighteenth of the book value ($100 per share) was passed. P was sent a commission check for $2,500 and notice that pursuant to preemptive rights he was offered 25 additional shares at $100 per share. He did not purchase the shares. Ds did purchase theirs. Later the corporation was dissolved; Ds received approximately $18,900 each. P then sued to set aside the distributions, to refund to Ds the amount they paid for their additional shares, and to distribute the assets of the corporation equally among the three shareholders. The lower court found for Ds, reasoning that P had waived his rights. P appeals.

Issue. Can a shareholder in a close corporation who refuses to exercise his preemptive rights set aside the issuance of shares to other shareholders as fraudulent when the shares are issued at an inadequate price?

Held. Yes. Judgment reversed.

- ♦ By offering shares according to preemptive rights to a shareholder, the other shareholders in a close corporation cannot force that shareholder to buy the shares at the risk of having his interest in the corporation unfairly diluted.
- ♦ Ds can purchase the shares offered, but the price must be a fair price so as not to dilute P's interest. Here, the stock was sold for $100 per share when the book value per share was $1,800. Therefore, the issuance of the additional stock to Ds was fraudulent.

---

d. **Recapitalization to gain corporate control--**

Lacos Land Company v. Arden Group, Inc., 517 A.2d 271 (Del. Ch. 1986).

Facts. Shareholders of Arden Group, Inc. voted to authorize a recapitalization plan in which a new Class B common stock would be created. The Class B common stock would possess 10 votes per share and be entitled to elect 75% of the members of Arden's board of directors. Class B stock also contained restrictions on transfer, and different dividend provisions. While the stock would be available to all holders of Class A common stock, Arden's board of directors (Ds) admitted that the Class B stock was fashioned mainly to be attractive to Briskin, Arden's principal shareholder and chief executive officer. In actuality, the recapitalization was proposed not to raise capital, but to transfer stockholder control to Briskin. Briskin became CEO 10 years prior, at a time when the company was struggling financially. Under his leadership, the company's stock rose in price from $2 per share to $25 per share. Briskin proposed the recapitalization plan because he wanted to protect his power to control Arden's business future and was worried about possible hostile takeover attempts. Briskin had initially presented his idea to the board of directors. The board established a three-member panel to consider the issue and prepare a report. The report was presented to the board, and it approved the plan and prepared a proxy statement describing the plan for shareholders. The shareholders voted to approve the plan. P, a 4.5% shareholder, brought this action to enjoin issuance of the Class B stock. P claimed that the board and the shareholders only approved the plan because Briskin had threatened to use his power to block any corporate transaction that could dilute his ownership interest if the plan was not approved.

Issue. Can a corporate officer attempt to effectuate a recapitalization plan that would provide him with stockholder control by threatening to use his power to block certain corporate transactions that may be beneficial to the company?

Held. No. Injunction granted.

- Briskin's stated desire to protect his power to control Arden's business future, while it may be a suspect motivation since it may simply be a desire to retain his office, is not wrongful in itself. However, the facts in this case indicate that the board felt pressured to approve the plan and recommend it to shareholders because of an explicit threat by Briskin that unless the plan was approved, he would use his power to block transactions that may be in the best interest of the company if those transactions would dilute his ownership interest. The proxy solicitation materials clearly communicated this threat to the shareholders.
- As a director and officer, Briskin has a duty to act with complete loyalty to the interests of the corporation. He must use his power unselfishly to advance the interests of the corporation and all of its shareholders. His statement that he would not support a beneficial corporate transaction unless steps were taken to protect his personal power indicates a disregard of that duty. As a corporate fiduciary, Briskin has no right to take the position he has, even if he is benevolently motivated in doing so.

H. DISTRIBUTIONS BY A CLOSELY HELD CORPORATION

1. Dividends.

a. **Definition.** A dividend is any distribution of cash, property, or additional shares (a stock dividend) paid to present shareholders as a result of their stock ownership.

b. **Discretion of the directors.** Normally the payment of dividends is within the discretion of the board of directors, even when lawful sources of paying a dividend are available to the corporation. For example, the directors may make a good faith determination that it is better for the corporation if available funds are kept within the corporation and used for expanding the business rather than paying a dividend to the shareholders.

c. **Limitations on paying cash dividends.** The discretion of the directors is limited in several ways:

1) **Contractual restrictions.** The corporation may have previously entered into contractual relationships that limit its ability to pay dividends (such as preferred stock issues, contracts relating to debt securities, or other lending arrangements; *see supra*).

2) **Ceiling on dividends.** State corporate law normally limits the amount of dividends that can be paid since the sources from which dividends can be paid are designated (*i.e.*, dividends may only be paid from earned surplus, etc.).

3) **Abuse of discretion.** There is some judicial control on the discretion of directors in their dividend determinations. That is, the directors must determine the corporation's dividend policy in good faith.

a) For example, minority shareholders might claim that there has been an abuse of this discretion if majority shareholder-directors have refused to pay a dividend in order to squeeze out the minority shareholders.

b) Or the minority shareholders might claim that too much is being paid (*i.e.*, the majority shareholders are taking all of the available cash out of the corporation so that it is crippling the corporation's ability to expand and grow).

d. **Lawful sources of cash or property dividends.** Statutes regulate the sources of funds that can be used for payment of dividends by the corporation. There are several basic tests that have been formulated to determine whether it is proper to pay a dividend:

1) **Balance sheet test.** Under the balance sheet test, dividends may be paid only when (after the payment of the dividend) the assets exceed both the liabilities and the capital stock accounts (*i.e.*, stated capital). For example:

Balance Sheet

Assets	**Liabilities**	
$100,000	$60,000	
	Capital	
	Stated Capital (the aggregate par value and/or stated value of the issued and outstanding shares)	$20,000
	Paid-in Surplus	$10,000
	Earned Surplus	$10,000

a) Dividends that impair stated capital are not permitted. In the above example, dividends over $20,000 would not be permitted.

b) As the source of the dividends, some states would allow use of the paid-in surplus as well as the earned surplus and thus permit a dividend up to $20,000; but most states would limit this to the extent that there were liquidation preferences on the outstanding shares in excess of the par or stated value (for example, there could be preferred shares with liquidation rights such that there would have to be $30,000 in stated capital and surplus in order to cover the par value plus the liquidation preferences. In this case, the dividend would be limited to $10,000 and paid-in surplus could not be used in this instance). Other states allow paid-in surplus to be used only for dividends to preferred shares.

c) In some states the dividend would be limited to earned surplus, $10,000 in this case.

2) **Earned surplus test.** The earned surplus test indicates that dividends can only be paid out of the earned surplus (including current profits) of the corporation. In the above example, $10,000 would be available for dividends.

3) **Solvency test.** Generally speaking, the corporation cannot pay a dividend if it is insolvent or the dividend would make it insolvent.

[*See* the Uniform Fraudulent Conveyance Act, the Federal Bankruptcy Act, and some state corporation laws] Definitions of insolvency include:

a) Liabilities exceed assets.

b) The company cannot meet its debts as they fall due (regardless of whether the value of the assets exceeds the liabilities).

4) **Accounting concepts.** Note the critical importance of accounting concepts to questions concerning dividends. For example, if the real property of the corporation is carried on the books at its historical value of $50,000 when in reality it has a current market value of $100,000, does it affect what is available for dividends?

5) **Questions.** Innumerable questions may arise concerning these tests. For example, what if the corporation has a deficit earned-surplus account (*i.e.,* over its entire history it has not made a profit on a cumulative basis), but it has a profit for the current year (*i.e.,* earned surplus for the current year)—may it pay dividends?

6) **Objectives of dividend law.** Limiting the sources of dividends tends to safeguard the creditors (by providing a cushion of equity dollars above the debt owed by the corporation), to ensure the solvency and future operation of the business, and to provide management with sufficient capital to run and expand the business.

7) **Repurchase of stock.** Note that the same issues (as to appropriate sources) arise in connection with a corporation's repurchase of its own stock.

e. **Stock dividends.**

1) **Definition.** A stock dividend is the issuance by the corporation of additional common shares to its common shareholders without consideration (*i.e.,* there is no distribution of cash or property). This excludes the situation where a dividend of shares in another corporation is distributed, or where shares of another class are distributed.

2) **Effect.** The effect is to give the shareholders more shares, but since the dividend is pro rata, the proportionate interest of each shareholder in the accumulated earnings is not changed.

3) **Accounting for stock dividends.**

a) **In general.** In general, stock dividends may be paid from current profits, earned surplus, paid-in surplus, or reduction surplus. For example, if the company had 1,000 shares of $1 par value outstanding and it issued a stock dividend of an additional 1,000 shares (one new share for each share owned), $1,000 would be transferred from earned surplus to stated capital.

b) **Fair market value.** However, there are situations where the dividend is relatively small and the issuance of the additional shares does not change the market price of the shares issued. In these situations the stock dividend may appear to be a genuine distribution of corporate earnings. Therefore, the New York Stock Exchange and the Accounting Principles Board require that the amount transferred from earned surplus be the fair market value of the securities issued in the stock dividend.

4) **Stock splits.** A stock split is simply splitting existing outstanding shares into more shares. For example, if there are 1,000 shares of $2 par value common stock outstanding and the stock were split two for one, the 1,000 shares would be split into 2,000 shares of $1 par value.

f. Declared and informal dividends.

1) **Declared dividends.**

a) **Revocability.** Once a cash dividend is declared, it becomes a debt of the corporation and may not be revoked. Thus, shareholders may sue for the distribution of the dividend. Stock dividends are revocable (since they do not change the interests of the shareholders).

b) **Record date.** Normally, dividends are declared payable to shareholders "of record" on a certain date. Thus those who own shares and sell them prior to the record date lose their right to the dividend.

c) **Payment date.** Normally, state law provides that dividends must actually be paid within a stated period after the record date.

2) **Informal dividends.** In close corporations, distributions are often made to shareholders without the formal action by directors normally required of dividends. The courts get into many situations where they must pass on whether such distributions amount to dividends, and they tend to find that many of these distributions are dividends despite the informal way they have been distributed.

g. **Compelling dividends.**

1) **Introduction.** As stated above, the directors generally have the discretion to declare or withhold dividends, subject to the limitation that they may not act in an arbitrary or fraudulent manner or in bad faith.

2) **Public companies.** The issue of the directors' discretion does not usually arise in connection with public companies.

3) **Close corporations.** There have been a number of situations where directors have acted in bad faith in the close corporation context. This issue may arise more often than in the public corporation context, since in the close corporation the directors are also often the majority shareholders.

a) **Bad faith--**

Gottfried v. Gottfried, 73 N.Y.S.2d 692 (1947).

Facts. All shareholders of the Gottfried Baking Corporation are the children (and their spouses) of the founders of the business; no dividends had been paid for 14 years. Minority shareholders not employed by the corporation (Ps) sued the directors (Ds, majority shareholders who are employed by the corporation) to compel the payment of dividends. Ps claim that dividends have not been paid due to the animosity of Ds, their desire to coerce a sale of Ps' stock, their avoidance of high personal income taxes, and because Ds have large salaries and bonuses and have received corporate loans.

Issue. If there is adequate surplus to pay a dividend, may the directors refuse to pay one?

Held. Yes. Judgment for Ds.

- Although the corporation has adequate surplus to pay a dividend, there must be a showing of bad faith (a question of fact) by the directors in not paying a dividend for the court to force payment.
- Bad faith is found where the motivation of the directors is their personal benefit, not the general benefit of the corporation.
- All of the matters mentioned by Ps are admissible to show bad faith. But there were also reasons that showed that Ds were acting for the benefit of the corporation (*i.e.,* planned capital expenditures equaled the available cash position of the company).

b) **Accumulation of surplus--**

Dodge v. Ford Motor Co., 170 N.W. 668 (Mich. 1919).

Facts. Shareholders of Ford (Ps) brought an action to prevent the expansion of a new plant and to compel the directors to pay additional special dividends. The company has capital stock of $2 million and $112 million in surplus. Profits for the year were expected to be $60 million. Testimony of the majority shareholder (D) and his counsel showed that D wanted to build a new plant, increase production and employment, and cut the price of cars to the public in order to pass on part of the benefit of the company's earning power to the public. The company had paid large dividends in the years prior to this change in policy by D. D's policy is now to pay only a regular dividend (60% on stated capital) and reserve the remainder of the earnings for expansion and price reductions. Ps charge that D's new purposes are charitable in nature and unlawful.

Issue. When the directors' purpose in not paying a dividend (when there is adequate surplus to do so) is to benefit the interests of persons other than the shareholders, will the court intervene to force payment?

Held. Yes. Judgment affirmed.

- Corporations are organized primarily for the profit of the shareholders. The directors are to use their powers primarily for that end. They have reasonable discretion, to be exercised in good faith, to act for this end. Here, their discretion to expand the business and cut car prices will be upheld—it is part of a long-range business plan; past experience shows Ford management has been capable and acted for the benefit of the shareholders, and it does not appear that the interests of the shareholders are menaced.
- Directors also have the responsibility to declare dividends and their amounts. Their discretion will not be interfered with unless they are guilty of fraud, misappropriation, or (when there are sufficient funds to do so without detriment to the business) bad faith.
- Here, the expansion plans of D may be carried out and there will still be a large amount of surplus available for dividends. Thus, the trial court's order that $19 million be paid in additional dividends is upheld.

---

h. **Accumulated earnings tax.** Since dividends are subject to taxation and thus raise revenue for the Internal Revenue Service, the Internal Revenue Code includes provisions against accumulating earnings without reason. Otherwise, those forming corporations could allow earnings to accumulate in the corporation and then at some point dissolve the corporation and pay a capital gains tax on the liquidating distribution rather than ordinary income rates on the dividends.

2. **Other Distributions by a Close Corporation.** There are many other types

of distributions made by a close corporation, such as for expenses, which may be questioned by regulatory bodies or by others in the corporation as to their appropriateness.

a. **Unauthorized salaries to officers--**

Wilderman v. Wilderman, 315 A.2d 610 (Del. 1974).

Facts. Eleanor Wilderman ("P") and Joseph Wilderman ("D"), owners of Marble Craft Co., were formerly married. P was designated vice president, treasurer, and secretary but primarily was the bookkeeper, and D was president. Both were directors. Although D was authorized by the board to draw a flat salary of $20,800 per year, during the period between 1971 and 1973 he authorized various pay increases and bonuses of substantial amounts. P had received a salary of only $7,800 a year. P sued D and the corporation, as an individual and derivatively on behalf of the corporation, for a ruling that D had made excessive and unauthorized payments to himself, for an order that the excessive salaries and bonuses be repaid to the corporation, for an injunction against future unauthorized payments, for an order that the company's management be subject to a custodian, for an order that the company be compelled to pay dividends, and for an order that contributions made to D's pension plan be reduced to account for the unauthorized salary payments.

Issue. May the president of the corporation sua sponte pay himself more than his authorized salary?

Held. No. D is ordered to repay that which the court finds to be excess compensation.

- The authority to compensate corporate officers is normally vested in the board of directors and is usually a matter of contract. In the absence of a board authorization setting salary, an officer may receive only the amount of compensation reasonably commensurate with his duties.

- There was no authorization given D and no basis for the payments based on duties performed by D. The I.R.S., for example, allowed the corporation to deduct as salary expense only $52,000 of the $92,000 D received in 1971. An expert witness found that a salary of $35,000 was all that was reasonable.

- D should return anything received in the years in question over $45,000.

- The company's board of directors may declare dividends, when appropriate, and if there is a deadlock, the dividends may be declared by the custodian.

- Appropriate adjustments should be made to pension plan contributions on behalf of D to take into account the reduction in salary amounts found to be reasonable.

---

3. Purchase and Redemption by a Corporation of Its Own Shares.

a. Definitions.

1) **Redemption.** The corporation acquires some or all of a class of its outstanding shares by paying its shareholders for the shares being redeemed. The redeemed shares are canceled (so that the stated capital amount is reduced).

2) **Purchase.** The corporation buys some of its shares, but the shares are not canceled (they remain as "treasury shares," authorized but unissued). Hence, stated capital is not affected, but surplus is.

b. **Purposes.** There are many reasons why a corporation may want to redeem or purchase its own shares:

1) The corporation may wish to maintain or acquire control. Often close corporations provide that the shareholder's stock is subject to purchase by the corporation if the shareholder attempts to sell to an outside party, or if the shareholder is an employee, the stock is subject to purchase if the employee leaves the employ of the corporation, etc.

2) The corporation may ***support the market price*** of the stock by buying shares and lessening the supply on the market.

3) The corporation may ***increase earnings per share*** by reducing the number of outstanding shares.

4) The corporation may redeem a preferred or debt issue due to the interest rate involved, or to change the debt-equity ratio, etc.

c. **Issues.** There are several important issues with respect to redemption or purchase.

1) The existence of the power to buy or redeem.

2) Lawful sources to buy or redeem.

3) The duty of directors and majority shareholders to treat all shareholders fairly (such as by paying the fair value for shares purchased, or not overpaying).

4) Protection of creditors.

d. **Change in proportionate interest.** When equity shares are redeemed or purchased, the interest held by the remaining shareholders is proportionately different after the transaction.

e. **Power to purchase or redeem shares.**

1) **Redemption.** The power to redeem equity shares exists only if it is expressly provided for in the articles; with respect to debt securities the power is given in the contract that forms a part of the issuance of the securities (such as a trust indenture). Of course, in some instances the corporation has no choice (*i.e.,* redemption is mandatory, as in the case where the corporation must provide for a "sinking fund" to redeem an issue of its securities).

2) **Purchase.** Most states, by statute, provide that a corporation may purchase its own shares. If there is no statute, the courts generally permit it, as long as the purchase is in good faith.

f. **Lawful sources.**

1) **Redemption.** Most states permit the corporation to redeem its shares out of profits, any type of surplus, or its stated capital. There are, however, certain limitations (discussed below). The rationale for this liberal posture is that at the issuance of the shares a contract was made concerning later possible or mandatory redemption. All interested parties are on notice of these redemption provisions.

2) **Purchase.** Most states allow a purchase of shares only out of earned surplus. Some states permit the use of reduction or paid-in surplus as well. A few permit the use of stated capital for specific and limited purposes, such as to pay dissenting shareholders in a merger the fair value of their shares.

3) **Limitations.**

a) **Offer to all shareholders--**

Donahue v. Rodd Electrotype Co., 328 N.E.2d 505 (Mass. 1975).

Facts. Harry Rodd joined a company and later gained control of it, giving it his name. Gradually he transferred controlling shares to his children, until 1970, when he retired. The board of directors (which then consisted of two of Harry's children and the company attorney) authorized the company to buy some of Harry's remaining shares. When the transaction was complete, the Rodd children owned 75% of the company and a former employee's widow (P) owned 25%. P sued the board and Rodd (Ds) to rescind the corporate purchase, charging breach of fiduciary duty to the minority shareholder, who was not given an equal opportunity to sell her shares at the same price. The lower court held for Ds. P appeals.

Issue. Did this particular purchase of shares by the corporation, authorized by an insider board of directors, violate fiduciary duties to the minority shareholder?

Held. Yes. Judgment reversed.

- Freeze-outs by majority shareholders controlling close corporations (majority withholds dividends or other corporate benefits from minority shareholder, forcing her to sell at an inadequate price) are illegal.
- In a close corporation, shareholders owe each other the same strict fiduciary duty that partners do. This is a higher standard than shareholders and directors in regular corporations owe to the corporation in discharge of their duties.
- To fulfill this duty, when the controlling majority of a close corporation causes the corporation to purchase some of its shares from the controlling majority, it must offer this same opportunity to the minority to sell a pro rata portion of its shares at an identical price.
- This is only fair, since in a close corporation there is no other market for the shares but the controlling majority and purchase of shares represents use of the corporation's assets.

Concurrence. The decision applies only to the close corporation's purchase of its shares, not to other actions or policies of the corporation. The analogy to a partnership is not universally a valid one.

---

b) **Insolvency.**

(1) **General rule.** No repurchase or redemption is permitted if the corporation is insolvent or would be rendered insolvent by the purchase distribution.

(2) **Definition of insolvency.** The definition of insolvency in the various jurisdictions differs.

(3) **Subsequent insolvency.** There are instances when the corporation enters into a contract (at a time when it is solvent) to purchase shares, and at the time that the contract is to be executed, the corporation is insolvent. For example, the corporation may agree to buy a shareholder's stock on an installment basis, and when one of the installments falls due, not have a lawful source for the purchase.

IX. MANAGEMENT AND CONTROL OF THE CORPORATION

A. INTRODUCTION TO MANAGEMENT

The following introductory material applies, to a certain extent, to both closely held and publicly held corporations (discussed in chapter X).

1. The Management Function.

a. **Businessperson's concept.** Businesspersons think of management in terms of a general manager responsible for the direction of the corporation. The management function involves:

1) ***Planning***: deciding what to do (setting objectives, deciding on strategies).

2) ***Organizing***: staffing, dividing responsibility, training, coordinating, communicating, etc.

3) ***Directing***: motivating, supervising, etc.

4) ***Controlling***: reviewing performance, evaluation, correcting direction.

b. **Legal concept.** Most state corporation laws place the ultimate responsibility for the management of the corporation in the board of directors. It is not entirely clear what this means. There are certain boundaries to this responsibility, since on one hand the shareholders are the ultimate owners and have specific management responsibilities. On the other hand, directors normally do not have the time (and often the expertise) to be involved in the routine, detailed, day-to-day management functions (these are officer functions).

1) The shareholders elect the directors and the directors appoint the officers. The directors are responsible for management in the sense that they are really a kind of overall supervisory body to pass on or review major decisions, to designate and remove the chief executive officer, to watch out for signs of dishonesty in the top executives, and to correct incompetence or error on the part of the full-time management.

2) In reality, directors normally perform functions that are less substantive (except in a close corporation) than those they are supposed by law to perform. They often merely serve as a sounding board to the president, they act as a discipline in requiring management to

explain company performance, and they make decisions in times of crisis (change company officers, etc.).

2. **Rights of Shareholders in Management.** As indicated above, the role of directors in management is circumscribed by certain rights given to the shareholders.

   a. **Indirect power.** Shareholders have no direct power over the management of the corporation. Resolutions by shareholders on matters within the discretion of the board are void (even if the shareholders and the directors are the same people) unless ratified by the board.

      1) Of course, shareholders have indirect control, since their ownership allows them to remove directors and replace them with others.

      2) Note also that some decisions have held that transactions entered into by all of the shareholders are valid even without direct approval.

   b. **Close corporations.** In the situation where the directors and the shareholders are really the same people (close corporations), many states have passed statutes that treat the few shareholders as partners. Hence, agreements made by shareholders are often binding on the corporation, and other acts done by shareholders are as effective as if the board had so acted. Some statutes even do away with the board entirely, leaving management of the corporation to the shareholders (normally in situations where there are 10 or fewer shareholders).

   c. **Shareholder approval of major changes.**

      1) **Issues concerning shareholders.** The major issues with respect to shareholders are:

         a) When must shareholder approval of corporate transactions be secured?

         b) When might the directors ask for such approval as a matter of policy (even though it is not required by statute)?

         c) When may shareholders initiate corporate action?

      2) **Major changes.** State corporation law always provides that certain major corporate transactions require shareholder approval. Reasoning from this, courts have held that transactions and decisions that are "not in the ordinary course of business" require shareholder approval (even though not specifically mentioned in the statute). Normally the transactions listed in the statute that require shareholder approval are:

a) **Election and removal of directors.** Shareholders elect directors and can remove them for cause (some states allow them to be removed without cause). Normally, vacancies on the board are filled by the other members of the board.

b) **Bylaws.** The bylaws typically are adopted by the directors in the organizational meeting. They may be changed by the directors, although shareholders normally have the ultimate authority to amend the bylaws.

c) **Organic changes.** The power to make organic changes in the corporation—merging the corporation into or consolidating it with another corporation, selling the entire corporation's assets or dissolving it, reducing the capital, or amending the certificate of incorporation—resides with the shareholders.

d) **Amendments to the charter.** Shareholders must approve amendments to the corporate charter. But this area has had a long history as to whether and to what extent such amending power can be exercised.

e) **Other matters.** State law differs in granting to shareholders the approval power of many diverse subjects.

f) **Initiation.** State law also differs in naming the matters where, and the procedures by which, shareholders may initiate corporate action (such as calling shareholder meetings).

3. Action by Directors.

a. Appointment of directors.

1) **First board.** The first board of directors is the incorporators. They hold office until the first meeting of shareholders or until they resign and new directors are elected.

2) **Number of directors.** The articles and bylaws indicate how many directors there shall be. Some state laws require a minimum number. Delaware law permits a board of only one. If the articles permit it, the number may be changed by amendment of the bylaws.

3) **Acceptance.** Directors must accept and consent to act as directors.

4) **Qualification.** Some states require that directors own stock in the corporation. The election of unqualified persons is voidable, but their acts while directors are effective.

5) **Vacancies.** Normally the remaining board members may fill vacancies on the board.

b. **Term as directors.**

1) **Period of appointment.** Most state laws indicate that directors are elected for a one-year term or until their successors are elected. However, articles or bylaws may specify a different period. Some states provide for longer periods.

2) **Resignation.** Directors may resign at any time.

3) **Removal.** Most state corporation laws indicate that directors may be removed at any time by the vote of the shareholders. In addition, for certain causes (such as insanity), board members may usually be removed by the board.

c. **Formal aspects of board action.** In order to be valid, the board must act as a board by resolution or vote at properly called meetings at which there is a quorum present. Statutes indicate how meetings are to be called, the notice requirements, the number necessary for a quorum and for resolutions to pass, etc.

4. **Action by Officers.** It is assumed by corporation law that the directors will delegate certain responsibilities to executive employees (officers), retaining for themselves the overall supervisory role. However, the modern trend in public corporations is for more and more responsibility and authority to gravitate toward the executive officers, since as business becomes more and more complex, the information and expertise necessary to make decisions rests with executive management.

a. **Management levels.** Corporation law usually indicates by statute the top-level officers of the corporation (president, vice president, secretary, treasurer, etc.). Something is also said about the duties of these officers. Below this level of executive officers there may be other levels of managers (where normally the law of agency is applicable), down to the blue-collar worker (where labor law governs).

b. **Tenure of officers.** As agents of the corporation, officers are bound by a duty of loyalty and obedience to the corporation (*i.e.,* to the directives of the board of directors). In theory, this renders officers liable to the corporation in damages for breach of this duty. Normally, however, infractions of this duty are handled by reprimand, transfer, demotion, or dismissal. In essence then, officers hold their positions at the discretion of the board.

c. **Executives and their external representation of the corporation.**

1) **Types of authority.** The authority of an officer comes from the board of directors or the bylaws. Thus, officers act in an agency role.

   a) **Authority.** The Restatement (Second) of Agency states, "Authority is the power of the agent to affect the legal relations of the principal by acts done in accordance with the principal's manifestations of consent to him."

   b) **Actual authority.** Certain authority and powers are given officers in the articles, the bylaws, the corporation laws of the state, and resolutions of the board. Authority that is necessarily and reasonably implied from express authority can arise from a course of acquiescence in the conduct or acts of officers.

   c) **Apparent authority.** Authority created by some action of the corporation can create the impression in the mind of the third party that the agent has authority when he does not. If an agent acts outside his actual authority, the third party dealing with the agent may be able to hold the corporation on the basis of apparent authority, but the corporation may have an action against the agent.

   d) **Inherent authority.** By virtue of their positions of responsibility, officers may be said to have certain inherent powers of authority. For example, the president is often deemed to have the authority necessary to make decisions and run the corporation on a day-to-day basis. Of course, major decisions (such as whether to sell a major portion of the company's assets) must have the approval of the board.

   e) **Unauthorized acts—ratification.** Courts often hold that acts by corporate officers that would otherwise be unauthorized (outside the scope of their authority) are valid by ratification or adoption by the board or the shareholders or by estoppel.

2) **Liability for torts or crimes.** The corporation is responsible for the torts and crimes committed by corporate officers in the course of and within the scope of their employment.

B. THE CLOSE CORPORATION

Close corporations are those with very few shareholders. In effect, a close corporation is an incorporated partnership, since most often the few shareholders involved also assume roles as officers of the corporation. The chief problems associated with close corporations are discussed below.

1. **Control Problems.**

   a. The formal roles assigned by law to managers of the corporation may not be relevant—*i.e.,* the distinctions between the role of shareholders, the board, officers, etc.

   b. Formalities of notices, meetings, quorums, etc., may not be as relevant as in other situations, since there is little possibility of injury to outsiders—shareholders and creditors or the public—from internal deviations from formal corporate requirements.

   c. Minority shareholders usually want more control in a close corporation, so voting requirements are usually set at higher percentages (often a unanimous vote is required). Alternatively, there may often be various types of voting agreements to give those in management positions (but without stock interests) a greater voice and more control (such as by putting shares in a voting trust).

   d. There are often agreements between the corporation and one or more founding members (directors and shareholders) who are not in day-to-day management, for services or supplies, etc., from the founder and his other businesses. These create conflict situations, but they are often the very reason for the formation of the corporation.

2. **Provisions for Transfer.** Public companies try to make their stock marketable. Close corporations try to control the transfer of stock, so that the nature of the partnership is preserved. Therefore, there are restrictions on transfers such as buyout arrangements in case of death or other contingencies, etc.

3. **Provisions for Resolution of Disputes.** Since there are often provisions for higher percentages (sometimes unanimous) for voting and buy-out arrangements for stock, disputes and disagreements can arise and paralyze decisionmaking. Provisions for resolving such disputes must be developed, such as arbitration proceedings.

4. **Other Problems.** Most of the other problems already discussed apply in equal measure to close corporations (*i.e.,* piercing the corporate veil, promoters, stock issuance, etc.).

C. SHAREHOLDER AGREEMENTS AFFECTING ACTION BY DIRECTORS

1. **Traditional Rule.** The traditional view has been that shareholders cannot make agreements with each other as to how they will vote as directors. Directors must be free to act independently in their roles as directors in order to faithfully execute their fiduciary duty to the corporation (part of which is to protect the interests of ***all*** shareholders, including minority shareholders). Of course, shareholders can agree on how they will vote as shareholders to

elect directors, and then the directors may act as they choose. Note how this traditional notion conflicts with what is practical in the close corporation context. For the same reason, most courts hold that directors may not agree with other board members in advance of a vote as to how they will vote individually.

a. **Shareholder agreements where there are minority shareholders--**

McQuade v. Stoneham, 189 N.E. 234 (N.Y. 1934).

Facts. A corporation had 2,500 shares outstanding: Stoneham had 1,306, McQuade (P) 70, and McGraw 70. They agreed to use their best efforts to elect themselves directors and officers, to take salaries, and to perpetuate themselves in office (and not to amend the articles, bylaws, etc., as long as any of the three owned stock). Stoneham appointed the other four directors. Three years later, at a directors' meeting, Stoneham and McGraw (Ds) refused to vote, allowing the other four directors to outvote P in removing him as an officer; at a later shareholders' meeting P was removed as a director. P sued for specific performance of the shareholder agreement. The trial court found for P, and Ds appeal.

Issue. May shareholders agree among themselves as to how they will act as directors in managing the affairs of the corporation?

Held. No. Judgment reversed.

♦ Shareholders may not agree to control the directors in the exercise of their independent judgment. They may combine to elect directors, but they must let the directors manage the business, which includes the election of officers.

---

2. **Special Recognition of the Closely Held Corporation.** The trend toward recognizing the close corporation as a separate situation continues in the judicial opinions in this area. Also, more and more states are passing statutes that define the close corporation and set forth special rules to govern it.

a. **Principal case--**

Galler v. Galler, 203 N.E.2d 577 (Ill. 1964).

Facts. Emma Galler's (P's) deceased husband and his brother (D) owned 95% of the corporation's stock. An employee owned the remaining stock, which was repurchased by D after this suit began. P, her husband, D, and his wife all signed a shareholders' agreement that provided that the four of them would vote for themselves as the corporation's four directors, that an annual dividend of $50,000 would be paid as long as the corporation's accumulated earned surplus was $500,000 or more, and that upon the death of either brother, the corporation would give the widow a salary continuation contract for a five-year period. P demanded performance, and D refused. P sues for an accounting and specific performance.

Issue. When substantially all of the shareholders of a close corporation enter a shareholders' agreement that provides for actions to be taken by the corporation, will the court sustain such an agreement although it deviates from state corporation law practice?

Held. Yes. Judgment for P.

- Courts have allowed close corporations to deviate from corporate norms in order to give business effect to the intentions of the parties.
- Here, substantially all of the shareholders of the corporation entered the agreement. The agreement did not injure creditors, other shareholders, or the public. The duration of the agreement is until the death of P. This period is not too long. The purpose of the agreement (maintenance of the widow) is proper. The provision for a dividend is valid since a base surplus is required to be maintained.
- The terms of the agreement are upheld, to P's benefit.

See MBCA 7.32 (RB at + 8.01

---

b. Agreement of all shareholders--

Zion v. Kurtz, 405 N.E.2d 681 (N.Y. 1980). Policy case

Facts. Zion (P) put up some collateral to permit Kurtz (D) to buy control of a corporation. P ended up owning all of the Class A (nonvoting) stock and D owned all Class B (voting) stock. As part of the deal, P and D agreed that no business would be transacted without the agreement of P. D, the controlling shareholder, had the corporation enter into two transactions without P's approval. P brought suit to cancel the two transactions. D won in the trial court; P appeals.

Issue. Under Delaware law, may all shareholders of a general corporation agree that no action will be taken without the consent of the minority shareholder?

Held. Yes. Judgment reversed.

- Delaware law, which the parties agreed would apply to this situation, provides that a corporation is to be governed by its board of directors, except when all shareholders agree and a provision is put in the articles of incorporation that the shareholders may govern the corporation.
- Here, the corporation was not formed as a close corporation and no provision was put in the articles. However, the parties did agree in writing, no third parties are

adversely affected by the agreement, and there is a provision that D would take the necessary steps to implement the agreement, which D failed to do (*i.e.,* get a provision put in the articles).

Dissent. The general rule is that no agreements that deprive the board of the power to run the corporation are valid. The exception is where the parties have complied with a set of procedures as set forth by state law. However, here the parties did not comply with the provisions of the state law—no statement was put in the articles of incorporation. This requirement should be ***strictly*** construed; it was put there to protect third parties that might deal with the corporation by putting them on notice that they are dealing with a different situation. It makes no difference that in this situation no third party was actually injured by the agreement of the parties and their failure to put notice in the articles.

---

3. The Inherent Power of the Shareholders--

Auer v. Dressel, 118 N.E.2d 590 (N.Y. 1954). Proper role of shareholders

Facts. Shareholders sued to compel the president to call a special meeting of shareholders of Class A stock. The bylaws provide that the president must call a meeting when requested by a majority of the voting shareholders. Holders of 55% of the Class A stock (the voting stock) asked for the meeting. Members of this class were entitled to elect nine of the 11 directors; but four had changed sides and had helped to vote the old president (Auer) out of office. The purpose of the meeting was (i) to pass a resolution asking that the fired president be rehired; (ii) to amend the articles and bylaws so that vacancies on the board would be filled by the shareholders of the class that the removed directors represented; (iii) to hear charges against the four disloyal directors in order to remove them; and (iv) to amend the bylaws so that a quorum requires 50% of all directors.

Issue. May the president refuse to call a shareholders' meeting that has the purposes as stated above?

Held. No. Order for the meeting is granted.

- The purposes of the meeting were proper and the president must call it. This is state law; corporate officers have no discretion.
- There is nothing invalid about shareholders expressing themselves in a resolution that the president should be rehired. However, without a special provision in the charter, the shareholders cannot reinstate the removed officer directly (this is the responsibility of the directors).
- Shareholders who elect directors have the inherent right to remove them for cause (after notice and hearing). Thus, it is not inappropriate for these shareholders to amend the articles and bylaws so that they can elect successor directors who have

been removed. (Note that existing provisions in the articles and bylaws gave this right to the directors.)

Dissent.

- There is no basis for calling a meeting, since none of the proposals made by the Class A shareholders can be acted on by the shareholders at the proposed meeting.
- It would be an idle gesture for the shareholders to indicate their support of the ousted president, since management is vested in the directors, and they are the only ones with the right to hire and fire officers.
- The present articles provide that directors are to be removed by the directors. Class A shareholders elect nine directors; common shareholders the other two. But once they are elected, vacancies (whether from removal or resignation) are to be filled by all directors. To allow the Class A shareholders to amend the articles to permit Class A shareholders (rather than the directors) to fill Class A director vacancies would be to alter the voting rights of the common shareholders (*i.e.,* they would have less power than they currently do under the articles and bylaws). State law requires that whenever the voting rights of a class of stock are adversely affected, they must be allowed to vote on the matter. Hence, a meeting of Class A shareholders to vote on this matter is illegal.
- Shareholders can remove directors for cause, but not before the expiration of their terms simply to change corporate policy.
- Also, the means for trying the four directors seems to be improper. For example, it is impossible to have all of the shareholders act as the tribunal, and it appears that those against the firing of Auer have solicited proxies already to remove the four. It is questionable whether solicitation of proxies is an appropriate method to convict directors of fraud.

Comment. Nothing is said in the case about what state law provided concerning removal of directors (*i.e.,* where this power was vested).

D. SHAREHOLDER POWERS—MEETINGS AND VOTING

1. **Introduction.** The law regards shareholders as the owners of the corporation, the object of management's fiduciary duty, and the ultimate source of corporate power. Shareholders have two ways to exercise this power—the vote and the derivative suit (discussed *infra*).

2. **Right to Vote.** Shareholders vote annually to elect directors and on important corporate issues. In effect, the shareholders have indirect control over management. If the corporation is small and the number of shareholders relatively small, this control is meaningful. However, with the larger corporations this control may be illusory, since management really controls what happens and manipulates far-removed and disinterested shareholders to its wishes.

a. **Who may vote.**

1) The right to vote is held by the shareholders of record who hold shares with voting rights. Normally, the right to vote follows legal title.

2) There must always be one class of shares with voting rights. If there is more than one class of shares, one or more of these classes may have restrictions on the right to vote. However, some states do not allow nonvoting common stock to be issued.

3) Only shareholders of record may vote. That is, management sets a date when all those holding shares with voting rights on that date will be able to vote at a future date.

b. **Allocations of voting power.** The right to vote may be allocated to others not owning the shares:

1) **Proxies.** A shareholder may give a proxy to another to vote the shares. Normally, proxies are revocable.

2) **Voting trusts.** A voting trust is another device to assure control of the corporation to some interested party. This device is often used because proxies are normally revocable.

a) Shareholders transfer legal title to their shares to a trustee and receive a "voting trust certificate." The trustee then has the right to vote the shares for the life of the trust.

b) Normally, trusts are irrevocable by the shareholders, regardless of whether there was consideration given the shareholder. But most states limit the permissible duration of such trusts.

c) An action for specific performance is available to compel the trust to perform according to its terms.

d) Shareholders receive all of the other usual benefits of being a shareholder (such as dividends).

3) **Pooling agreements.** Shareholders may exchange promises to vote their shares in some specific way, or as some part of the group shall direct. In the absence of fraud or illegal motives, such pooling agreements are specifically enforceable.

4) **Fiduciaries.** Shares of stock may be held by a trustee, custodian, guardian, or other fiduciary.

5) **Joint ownership.** Shares may be held by two or more persons—joint tenants, partners, etc.

6) **Pledges.** Shares may be pledged as security for a debt (and voting rights transferred).

7) **Brokers.** Brokers may hold stock in their names as agents for clients.

c. **Other limitations on the voting power of shareholders.**

1) **Introduction.** Shareholders cannot make agreements relative to their voting power that will interfere unduly with the interests of minority shareholders or disrupt the normal operations of the corporate system.

2) **Majority approval.** Matters requiring shareholder approval usually need only a majority of the shareholders. However, often those controlling the corporation at its formation attempt to provide in the articles and/or bylaws that a greater percentage is required. This assists those with a smaller percentage of the voting power to prevent change in the company.

a) Most courts have held that shareholder agreements that require unanimous shareholder approval for change are invalid. But many that require less than unanimous approval but more than a majority have been approved (such as a provision that 75% of the voting power must agree to a sale of the corporate assets).

3) **Shareholder agreements for action as directors.** Most courts hold that shareholders cannot make agreements as to how they will vote as directors (*see* the discussion *supra*).

d. **Shareholders' meeting.** Shareholders can only act at a meeting (although some states permit action based on unanimous written consent, or the consent of some specified percentage of shareholders), duly called, with notice, where a quorum (normally a majority) is present, and by resolution passed by the required percentage. The bylaws normally require an annual meeting and permit special meetings to be called by officers or shareholders holding a specified percentage of the voting shares.

e. **Proxy dispute--**

Salgo v. Matthews, 497 S.W.2d 620 (Tex. 1973).

Facts. Matthews (P) represented a faction that was trying to take control of General Electrodynamics Corporation from Salgo (D). Meer, the election inspector appointed by Salgo to act at the shareholders' meeting, refused to recognize certain disputed proxies solicited by P, without which P was unable to carry a majority vote. The disputed shares were in the name of Pioneer Casualty Company, which was in bankruptcy, and the beneficial title had been transferred to Shepherd, also in bankruptcy. A court order had authorized Pioneer's receiver to give Shepherd a proxy to vote Pioneer's shares. Meer took the position that Shepherd could not execute a proxy in favor of P (*i.e.,* that only Shepherd's bankruptcy trustee, as the beneficial owner of the General Electrodynamics stock, could do so). P petitioned the court to require the president, D, to reconvene the shareholders' meeting and declare P (and his slate) directors of the corporation. The trial court granted injunctive relief. D appeals.

Issue. May a corporation require that its shares be voted only by their beneficial owner?

Held. No. But the trial court is reversed.

- ♦ In the first place, the trial court erred in granting P injunctive relief absent a showing that P could not have obtained adequate relief by statutory remedy of quo warranto after the election.
- ♦ Under a bylaw providing that stock is transferable only on the corporation's books, eligibility to vote at corporate elections is determined by the corporate records rather than by the ultimate judicial decision of beneficial title. Shares may be voted only by the legal owner as shown on the corporation's records or by his authorized agent. Here, Pioneer had legal title, and it could only act through its trustee, who appointed Shepherd, who appointed P.

---

3. Types of Voting.

a. **Straight voting.** On most matters shareholders having shares with voting power get one vote for each share held. Thus, a majority of those voting have the power to pass resolutions requiring shareholder approval.

b. **Cumulative voting.** For ***directors,*** voting may be on a cumulative basis. The purpose of cumulative voting is to assure minority shareholders of representation on the board.

1) **Introduction.** Each voting share is given one vote for each director to be elected. If there are eight directors to be elected, and the shareholder has 100 shares, she has 100 votes for each director, or a total of 800 votes. The shareholder may then cumulate her votes and cast them all for one director, or vote as many votes for each director as she chooses. The effect in many cases is to allow minority shareholders to cumulate enough votes to elect a director when they would not be able to under the "majority rule" normally in effect. For example, if there are eight directors to be elected, a shareholder with 12.5% of the voting stock could elect one director.

2) **The formula.**

$$X = \frac{Y \times N}{1 + N} + 1$$

X (number of shares needed to elect a given number of directors) = [Y (number of shares voting at meeting) × N (number of directors desired to elect)] / [1 + N (total number of directors to be elected)] + 1

Example: If a minority shareholder wishes to assure election of one director on a board of eight and there are 1,500 shares, with 900 expected to vote at the meeting:

$$X = \frac{900 \times 1}{1 + 8} + 1 = 101 \text{ shares required.}$$

3) **Right to cumulative voting.** In many states cumulative voting is mandatory. In other states it is permissive. In some states the right is given in the state constitution, and in others it is merely statutory.

4) **Ways to avoid cumulative voting.**

a) **Classification of directors.**

(1) The fewer the directors being elected, the larger the percentage of the outstanding shares required to elect one director. Hence, one way to avoid the effect of cumulative voting is to stagger the election of directors (*e.g.*, nine directors, with three elected each year).

(2) Some states have prohibited classification of directors. In other states, state law specifically permits the classification of directors.

b) **Effectiveness not guaranteed--**

Humphrys v. Winous Co., 133 N.E.2d 780 (Ohio 1956).

Facts. Winous Co. (D) had a board of directors of three members. The members were classified such that no two were elected at the same time (*i.e.*, one was elected each year). Humphrys (a shareholder) sued the company, claiming that the classification was invalid because it nullified the state code section that guaranteed the right to vote cumulatively. The state code also expressly allowed classification of directors. The trial court held for D, and the court of appeals reversed. D appeals.

Issue. Does a statute that provides for cumulative voting in corporate elections guarantee the effectiveness of the exercise of that right (*i.e.,* that the minority will gain representation on the board of directors)?

Held. No. Court of appeals reversed.

- Ohio has been concerned with the rights of minority shareholders since 1893 and has maximized their voting strength by guaranteeing the right to vote cumulatively for directors.

- But the right to cumulate votes cannot be said to nullify the right to classify directors, which is also provided by state law.

- Therefore, the code guarantees to minority shareholders only the right to vote cumulatively but does not necessarily guarantee the effectiveness of that right to elect minority representation on the board.

- However, the same scheme used by D would not be valid any longer (*i.e.*, as to new corporations) since state law has been amended to require that classes of directors cannot be smaller than three directors.

Dissent. Since the legislature provided for classification of directors and cumulative voting in the same act, it could not have intended the one provision to completely nullify the other, as in this case.

---

c) **Reduce the size of the board.** If the minimum number of board members required by state law is three, reducing the board to that size maximizes the number of shares that a minority shareholder must own to elect one director in cumulative voting.

4. **Restrictions on Voting at the Shareholder Level and Proxies Coupled with an Interest.**

a. **Voting agreements.** In a voting agreement, shareholders exchange promises to vote their shares in some specific way, or as some part of the group shall direct. In the absence of fraud or illegal motive, such agreements are generally held to be specifically enforceable.

1) **Compared with voting trusts--**

Ringling Brothers-Barnum & Bailey Combined Shows v. Ringling, 53 A.2d 441 (Del. 1947).

Facts. Ringling (P) owned 315 shares of a corporation, Haley (D) 315, and North 370. P and D entered an agreement for 10 years that they would act jointly in exercising their voting rights and if they could not agree, that the decision would be made by an arbitrator. At a shareholder meeting they could not agree, and D voted his shares rather than following the direction of the arbitrator. P sued D for specific performance of the contract. The trial court upheld the agreement to arbitrate. D appeals.

Issue. When two of three shareholders of a corporation agree that they will vote together and that if they do not vote together, an arbitrator will decide how they should vote, does the agreement empower the arbitrator to enforce his decision?

Held. No. Judgment reversed.

- ♦ The agreement did not provide that on violation either party could vote the shares of the other, or that the arbitrator could vote them. It simply provided that in case of disagreement the arbitrator would make a decision as to how the votes should be made. If one party refuses to vote in accord with the arbitrator, it simply means that these votes should not be counted. Thus, the six persons elected directors by the votes of the other two shareholders should hold office, and the remaining director should be elected at the next shareholder meeting.

---

2) **Issues associated with pooling agreements.** The two major issues are whether pooling agreements are void as against public policy, and, if they are valid, how and against whom will they be enforced. For example, it has been held valid for shareholders to get together and create a majority shareholder interest in voting to elect a certain slate of directors. This has been upheld even where cumulative voting has existed. But note that whenever anything smacks of fraud, such agreements may be overturned. For example, if A agrees to vote with B if B releases A from a personal debt, this may be enough to cancel the agreement. The time period of the agreements is also an important factor, since voting trust statutes normally limit the duration.

   a) Courts have split in the situation represented by the *Ringling Brothers* case. Some have indicated that a vote cannot be split from its shares (in an arbitration) and have refused to uphold such agreements. What was the result in the *Ringling Brothers* case itself—did the court really effectuate the intent of the parties? Other courts have specifically enforced such agreements.

b) The statutes of Delaware now allow voting agreements for a period of no longer than 10 years. Irrevocable proxies are recognized as valid, if there was the requisite interest (an interest in the stock or any interest in the corporation is sufficient). Thus, it appears that Delaware, by statute, avoided the difficult line-drawing problems created by the *Ringling Brothers* case.

3) **Liberal voting agreements.** Some states have liberal rules concerning the validity of voting agreements. Some allow the management of the corporation to be transferred from the directors to the shareholders, when all of the shareholders agree in a voting agreement to provisions restricting the power of directors by requiring a shareholder vote.

4) **Proxies coupled with an interest.** A proxy that is expressly made irrevocable is irrevocable. "Coupled with an interest" means that there is some consideration received by the shareholder where the shareholder borrows money, pledges stock, and grants the lender a proxy to vote the shares.

b. Voting trusts.

1) **Introduction.** The voting trust was developed to meet the limitations and problems associated with proxies and shareholder pooling agreements. The purpose of the trust is to assure control of the corporation to some interested party. It is often employed with public companies as well as with close corporations.

a) Shareholders transfer legal title to shares to a trustee and receive a "voting trust certificate." The trustee has the right to vote the shares for the life of the trust.

b) Trusts are irrevocable by the shareholder regardless of whether there was consideration given the shareholder. But most states limit the permissible duration of such trusts. Some states provide for revocation by a vote of a specified percentage of the shares subject to the trust.

2) **Duty of trustees--**

Brown v. McLanahan, 148 F.2d 703 (4th Cir. 1945).

Facts. The directors and trustees (Ds) of a 10-year voting trust of all the voting shares (preferred and common stock) passed an amendment to the articles of incorporation of the company near the end of the trust's term. The amendment allowed the debenture holders (which included Ds) to vote; previously, only preferred and common stockholders had enjoyed that right. When the company went bankrupt, was reorganized, and the 10-year voting trust was created, the debentures and the preferred stock were issued to the holders of the corporation's first lien bonds; hence, the debenture holders and the preferred stockholders were the same individuals. Much of the preferred stock had been traded during the term of the trust, so that Ds, who held a substantial amount of debentures, were seeking to preserve their voting control over the corporation and to dilute the power of the preferred stockholders by allowing debenture holders to vote. Brown (P), who held trust certificates representing 500 preferred shares, sued in a class action, alleging that passing the amendment allowing debenture holders to vote was a violation of Ds' duties as trustees. The district court granted Ds' motion to dismiss, and P appeals.

Issue. Was the passage of the amendment that diluted the voting power of the preferred stock held in a voting trust for which Ds served as trustees a violation of Ds' duties as trustees?

Held. Yes. Judgment reversed.

- ♦ A trustee may not exercise his powers in a way that is detrimental to the "cestuis que trustent" (in this case, the actual owners of the preferred shares held in trust). Since the amendment granting the debenture holders the right to vote diluted the value of the preferred stockholders' rights to vote, it was a violation of Ds' duties as trustees.

---

3) **Nonvoting stock as a trust--**

Lehrman v. Cohen, 222 A.2d 800 (Del. 1966).

Facts. The Cohen family (D) and Lehrman (P) owned equal voting power in the Giant Food Corporation (each owning different classes of common stock). Each elected two directors to a four-person board. At the time P acquired all of the AL class of stock, D (who owned the AC class of stock) insisted that a new class of stock be created (one share of AD voting stock, with no dividends or redemption rights but with the power to elect a fifth director) in order to break the voting deadlock. The AD stock was issued to Danzansky, the company lawyer, who elected himself the fifth director. Cohen then resigned as president, and Danzansky was elected president at a shareholders' meeting (AC and AD stock voting in favor) with a large salary and stock options and an employment contract. Danzansky then resigned as a director and elected another person in his place; the board then ratified his election as president and the employment contract (the AL directors voting against it). P (owner of the AL stock) then sued on the basis that (i) the AD stock arrangement was an illegal voting trust since in effect it gave a portion of the AL and AC stock voting power (10% from each) to AD (like a trustee), and the AD stock had no other rights except voting, and (ii) stock having only voting rights but no other rights is illegal under state law. Summary judgment was granted in favor of D; P appeals.

Issue. Does creation of a new class of voting stock (without any other rights) create an unlawful voting trust?

Held. No. Judgment affirmed.

- The first test for a voting trust is whether the voting right is separated from the other incidents of ownership. AC and AL owners retained all of their rights.
- The rationale of the voting trust statute is to avoid secret uncontrolled combinations of shareholders from acquiring voting control of the corporation. This is prevented by requiring that voting trusts be disclosed to the corporation. The rationale of P is not supported by this purpose, since creation of a new class of voting stock is fully disclosed.
- State law does not require that each class of stock created have voting and all the other rights of each other class. Specifically, state law allows creation of stock having no voting rights.

Comment. Note that one limitation on the formation of voting trusts is that the trust be formed for a proper purpose. In this case this was to break a voting deadlock problem. The burden is normally on the attacking party to show that the purpose is improper.

---

5. **Restrictions on the Transfer of Shares.** Normally, the shareholders of a close corporation wish to keep it that way; thus, they desire to prevent the transfer of shares without approval of the transferee. Restriction on the transfer of shares is accomplished in one of three ways:

   (i) By provision in the articles,

   (ii) Through bylaws, or

   (iii) By private agreement among the shareholders.

   Such a restriction may or may not be stated on the share certificates themselves.

   a. **General rules.**

      1) **Restraints on alienation.** Restraints on alienation of shares are permissible if (i) the person taking the stock is aware (has notice) of the restraint and (ii) the restraint is not "unreasonable" (*i.e.,* the restraint is not total; the shareholder may still sell her stock at somewhere near its true value).

      2) **Forms of restraints.**

a) **Absolute prohibition.** One form is for absolute prohibition of sale without the approval of the shareholders, the board, etc.

b) **Right of first refusal.** Another is to give the other shareholders a right to buy the stock before it can be sold to an outside party.

c) **Option.** Another form is that of an option given to specified parties to buy the stock on certain specified events.

3) **Notice.** In order to sustain a restriction, it is safest if the restraint is stated on the share certificate, ensuring that the transferee has notice of the restriction.

4) **Price.** The price of transfer may be set in a number of ways:

(i) By mutual agreement.

(ii) By appraisal of market value, etc.

(iii) By reference to book value.

b. **Reasonable restrictions valid--**

Ling and Co. v. Trinity Savings and Loan Association, 482 S.W.2d 841 (Tex. 1972).

Facts. Bowman (D) borrowed money from Trinity (P) and pledged 1,500 shares of Ling and Company common stock as security for the loan. When D defaulted, P sued to foreclose the security interest and to sell the stock at a public sale. Ling objected to a public sale, arguing that its articles of incorporation imposed a limitation on the transfer of the stock, requiring that it first be offered to the corporation's other shareholders of the same class and that written approval be obtained from the New York Stock Exchange before any sale. The limitation requiring an offering to other shareholders of the same class appeared on the stock certificate but was not in bold type or otherwise conspicuous. The lower court entered summary judgment for P, and the state circuit court of appeals affirmed.

Issue. Were the restrictions on the transfer of the stock valid?

Held. Yes. Judgment reversed.

♦ Although the state law of the forum generally requires restrictions to be conspicuously noted on the certificate, if P is aware of the restrictions, conspicuous notice on the certificate is not required. Summary judgment for P should not be granted without conclusive proof that P lacked notice of the restrictions on transfer.

♦ Both restrictions are reasonable since allowing shareholders of the same class to purchase before a public sale has not been shown to be unduly burdensome, and the approval of the New York Stock Exchange was required by the exchange while Ling was a member.

---

c. **Rule of construction.** The rule of construction relating to restraints is that they are construed narrowly so as to give maximum scope to the ability of the shareholder to transfer the shares.

E. DISSENSION AND DEADLOCK

Often disputes arise in close corporations between the ownership factions. Various methods are resorted to in order to resolve them:

(i) Negotiation;

(ii) Legal action (enforcing shareholder agreements, corporate procedures, suits, etc.);

(iii) Arbitration; and

(iv) Dissolving the corporation.

In each of these methods, the court must consider all of the parties affected: shareholders, employees, creditors, customers, and the public.

1. Deadlock on the Board of a Close Corporation--

Gearing v. Kelly, 182 N.E.2d 391 (N.Y. 1962).

Facts. The bylaws of Radium Chemical Co. provided for a board of four members, a majority constituting a quorum. Gearing (P) and her mother owned 50% of the stock, but only P was on the board. The two defendants (Ds) owned 50% of the stock and were on the board. A board meeting was called, P refused to attend, the fourth director resigned at the meeting, and Ds elected a new fourth director. P had refused to attend since she knew that she would be outvoted in electing a new director and that control of the corporation would pass to Ds. P sued to set aside the election.

Issue. When a director-shareholder intentionally refuses to attend a board meeting to prevent a quorum, may the court deny the director's equitable suit to nullify a director's election where the requisite quorum was not present at the meeting?

Held. Yes. New election denied.

- ♦ Justice does not require that there be a new election in these circumstances. Control had already passed from P and her mother when they earlier had allowed a fourth director supporting Ds to be elected.
- ♦ If there were to be a new election, Ds would outnumber P and the result would be the same as it is now.

Dissent. The election is void since there was not a quorum. In disputes for control of a close corporation, where both sides own equal amounts of stock, the court should not assist either side. It is proper for P not to attend the meeting where she is outnumbered and to seek a solution of the deadlock through other means (*i.e.,* negotiation with Ds).

---

2. **Dissolution.** Every state corporation law provides for dissolution procedures.

   a. **Judicial discretion--**

In re Radom & Neidorff, Inc., 119 N.E.2d 563 (N.Y. 1954).

Facts. Radom and Neidorff each owned 50% of the corporate stock of a business; Neidorff died and his wife inherited the stock. Radom and Mrs. Neidorff (brother and sister) did not get along, and although the corporation was very successful, Radom petitioned under section 103 of the General Corporation Law for dissolution. The petition cited that the directors were deadlocked, the shareholders' meeting was unable to elect new directors, and Mrs. Neidorff would not sign Radom's salary checks although he was running the business. Mrs. Neidorff had also sued Radom in a derivative action over misappropriation of corporate funds. Profits had averaged $71,000 per year, and there was $300,000 cash on hand. Radom had offered three years ago to buy Mrs. Neidorff out for $75,000. Mrs. Neidorff claimed that she did not interfere in running the business, that she would allow a third director to be appointed by an independent body, and that the refusal to sign salary checks was a result of the pending derivative suit. The lower court dismissed without a hearing.

Issue. If the court has discretion, should it allow dissolution when the two sole shareholders are feuding but the corporation is successful?

Held. No. Decision affirmed.

- ♦ The statute grants the court discretion to dismiss when the petition is brought by 50% of the ownership, the directors are evenly divided and deadlocked, and new directors cannot be elected.
- ♦ The court usually grants dissolution when the corporate purposes cannot be obtained, efficient management is impossible, and the dissolution will be beneficial to the shareholders and not harm creditors or the public. But here, the

business is successful and able to operate; Mrs. Neidorff will allow an additional director to be appointed.

Dissent. The state law provides that when certain conditions exist, a petition for dissolution may be made to the court. The court cannot dismiss without holding a hearing. The lower court did not do this. And, in this situation, dissolution should be ordered. The shareholders are feuding, there is no likelihood that this will change, the board and shareholders are deadlocked, and there is no other alternative remedy.

Comment. Probably what the court is doing is preventing Radom, who is able to control the business because of his expertise, from taking over the business for much less than it is worth. In effect, what the court is saying is, buy out Mrs. Neidorff for a fair price.

---

b. **Involuntary and voluntary dissolution.** Usually the statutes of the state provide for two bases of dissolution.

   1) **Involuntary dissolution.** On petition of a shareholder and on certain conditions, the court may order the corporation to dissolve. Several bases are named on which the court will consider dissolution: the directors are deadlocked, the assets of the corporation are being wasted, etc.

   2) **Voluntary dissolution.** In most instances, state law provides that if a certain percentage of the shareholders agree (normally a high percentage, such as two-thirds), the court must order dissolution.

3. **Oppression of the Minority Shareholder--**

Davis v. Sheerin, 754 S.W.2d 375 (Tex. Ct. App. 1988).

Facts. Davis (D) and Sheerin (P) formed a corporation in 1955, with D owning 55% and P owning 45%. D was an employee (and president), responsible for managing the corporation. In 1985, D refused P's request to inspect the books of the corporation, claiming that P no longer owned any stock (supposedly having gifted the stock to D in the late 1960s). P sued; after a jury trial, the jury found that P owned 45% and a "buyout" of the 45% interest by D was ordered for $550,000. D challenges the buyout requirement.

Issue. Is a court-enforced buyout an appropriate remedy in these circumstances?

Held. Yes. Lower court opinion affirmed.

♦ Texas law does not explicitly provide for a buyout remedy for aggrieved minority shareholders of a corporation.

- Texas law does provide, however, that in certain circumstances (including one in which those in control of a corporation engage in illegal, oppressive, or fraudulent conduct) a receiver may be appointed to liquidate the corporation.

- Texas courts have not held that a buyout is an appropriate remedy, but the courts of other states have, since it is a less extreme remedy than a liquidation.

- Even though Texas statutory law does not provide for such a remedy, we feel that the remedy is an appropriate one.

- The issue here is whether it is appropriate in this case. In general, it is appropriate where the majority is attempting to squeeze out the minority (who do not have a ready market for their shares but are at the mercy of the majority). Oppressive conduct may include many different kinds of acts: broadly speaking, it means conduct that reasonably can be said to frustrate the legitimate expectations of the minority, particularly when the expectations being frustrated are those that were the basic reason the minority invested in the corporation in the first place.

- Oppression does not have to mean fraud, illegality, or deadlock. It is just burdensome, harsh, unfair conduct in dealing with the affairs of the corporation.

- Here, conspiring to deprive P of his ownership of stock in the corporation, especially when the corporate records clearly indicate such ownership, qualifies as oppression.

- Furthermore, there are no other lesser remedies that could adequately remedy the situation. Damages and certain injunctions could remedy the breaches of fiduciary duties (paying excessive legal fees, etc.) that have been occurring, but not the problem of trying to deprive P of his ownership interest.

---

4. Appointment of a Provisional Director--

Abreu v. Unica Industrial Sales, Inc., 586 N.E.2d 661 (Ill. App. Ct. 1991).

Facts. Abreu's (P's) husband, Manny, co-founded Ebro Foods, Inc. and owned 50%; the other 50% was owned by LaPreferida, Inc. (co-owned by Ralph and William Steinbarth (Ds); LaPreferida was the distributor of Ebro's products). Manny died; P inherited his interest in Ebro and became its president and a director. Ralph Steinbarth formed Unica (D) to compete with Ebro; it took away Ebro's business with Kraft Foods; Ds also tried to obtain Ebro's formulas so they could manufacture Ebro's products themselves. P sued Ds and Unica in a derivative suit under Illinois Business Corporation Act section 12.55(b), which provides for alternative remedies to dissolution in cases where there is a close corporation and hostile factions exist and create oppression of one of the ownership interests. This section provides for a court-appointed provisional director. The trial court found there was fraudulent self-dealing by Ds, removed Ralph as an Ebro director (leaving P and one of Ds' nominees in a deadlock), and, to resolve the deadlock, appointed the general manager of Ebro, Silvio Vega, P's son-in-law, as the third director, indicating he could vote only if there was a deadlock between the other directors. Ds appeal on the basis that Vega is not impartial, thus, his appointment is a violation of the court's discretion in appointment of a provisional director, and that Vega has improperly exercised the duties of such a director.

Issues.

(i) Must a provisional director be strictly impartial under the state statute?

(ii) Did the provisional director improperly exercise his authority?

Held. (i) No. (ii) Yes. Judgment affirmed in part and reversed in part.

- The state statute does not require strict impartiality in appointment of a provisional director. The trial court must consider the best interests of the corporation; if based on the particular situation, there is no strictly impartial third party to appoint who has the skills necessary in the urgent time frame to meet the crisis involved, the court may use its discretion to appoint the best person it can find. Here, Vega was appointed in the best interests of the corporation, although he was not strictly impartial. He knew the business, was a CPA, and was the best person for the job under the time constraints involved.

- Vega acts under the supervision of the court; he is to vote only if there is a deadlock. There are two instances where he has acted beyond his authority—appointment of a new auditor without a vote of the board (a board function), and to reimburse P for expenses of this appeal. This was taken to the board, Ds' board member asked for time to study the proposal, and Vega voted with P to pay P's expenses. This action is reversed; it was a reasonable request for time to study the matter, so there is not yet a deadlock here.

16.01
16.02, 16.04, 16.05

F. ACTION BY DIRECTORS AND OFFICERS

1. **Formal Aspects of Board Action.** As noted above, the general rule is that the board must act as a board, by resolution or vote at properly called meetings, at which there is a quorum, or in some way approved by state law as an alternative (*i.e.,* by unanimous written consent), for an action by the board to be valid.

2. **Required Action by Shareholders.** The same problem of required action (and acquiescence) by directors of corporate agents' actions occurs when corporate law requires formal action by shareholders and the directors do not get this shareholder approval.

3. **Officers.** *See* the general discussion *supra* concerning officers and their authority.

a. **Reliance on representations of the officers--**

In the Matter of **Drive-In Development Corp.,** 371 F.2d 215 (7th Cir. 1966).

Facts. The parent company of Drive-In (D) wanted to borrow money from the National Boulevard Bank (P). P required that D guarantee the loan, which guarantee was signed by Maranz as "Chairman" and attested to by Dick as "secretary." P asked for a resolution of D's board showing the authority of Maranz to sign the guarantee. P received a certified copy (by Dick as secretary) of D's board minutes, showing the authorization of Maranz to sign the guarantee. Later D went into Chapter XI proceedings under the Bankruptcy Act, and P filed its claim for the amount of the unpaid loan. The referee disallowed P's claim on the basis that D's corporate minutes did not show the authorization to make the loan guarantee. Testimony of D's directors was unclear as to whether Maranz had ever been authorized to enter the guarantee on behalf of D. From a judgment affirming the referee's decision, P appeals.

Issue. May a plaintiff who enters into a guarantee transaction with a corporation on the representations of its officers that they had authority to enter the transaction rely upon these representations?

Held. Yes. Judgment reversed.

- ♦ Here, the officers of D appeared to be acting within the scope of their apparent authority.

- ♦ D's officers had no actual, express authority. But it is the secretary's duty in the corporation to keep the corporate records, and once P received a copy of the certification of board resolutions, it was reasonable for P to assume that D's officers had the authority to enter into the guarantee agreement. P had no duty to investigate further.

---

b. **Apparent authority--**

Lee v. Jenkins Brothers, 268 F.2d 357 (2d Cir. 1959).

Facts. The president of Jenkins Brothers (D) hired Lee (P) as an employee of the corporation and in the presence of another vice president orally offered P a pension of $1,500 per year beginning in 30 years. The board of directors never approved the pension. P was later fired and was never paid the pension. P sued both the corporation and the president.

Issue. Did the president have the authority to bind the corporation to a long-term contract without board approval?

Held. Yes.

- The president has the authority to bind his company by acts arising in the usual and regular course of business but not for contracts of an "extraordinary" nature. It is not extraordinary to hire employees for a specific number of years; however, lifetime employment contracts are extraordinary since they are of long duration, and they are restrictive of shareholder rights to manage the corporation.
- Here, the agreement on the pension was not unreasonable; it benefited the corporation and was not unduly restrictive of the shareholders' management rights.
- Thus, there is a question of fact—whether the president had apparent authority to enter the contract. This factual question is decided by looking at all of the circumstances: the reasonableness of the contract, the officer negotiating the contract, the number of shareholders, who the contracting third party is, etc.

G. TRANSACTIONS IN CONTROLLING SHARES

1. **Introduction.** The most complex problem involving the sale of corporate stock is the situation in which a shareholder owning a majority interest (or a controlling minority interest) of the shares sells that control in a transaction from which the other shareholders are excluded (the controlling shareholder receiving a premium price per share on the stock over book or market value), or when all sell, but the owner of the control shares receives more per share than the other shareholders. Since a person purchasing "control" can dictate the affairs of the corporation, "control" is something of value.

2. **General Rule.** The general rule is that a shareholder may sell his stock to whomever he wants to at the best price he can get. Most courts would say that a majority shareholder has the same right. Thus, it is not illegal per se for the majority shareholder to agree to have a majority of the board of directors resign and the purchaser's appointees elected (where this would naturally occur anyway).

3. **Types of Purchase Transactions.** Purchase of control may occur in several ways:

a. **Purchase of stock.** The purchaser may approach the shareholders directly to purchase their shares. The purchaser may buy all or only a controlling portion of the outstanding stock. When all is purchased, one price may be offered to controlling shareholders and a lower price to the minority shareholders.

b. **Purchase of assets.** The purchaser offers to buy X Corporation's assets; the corporation itself holds a vote of its shareholders on the offer (normally a majority vote is required to sell). If the necessary majority vote is secured, the purchaser deposits the purchase price with X, and this price is distributed pro rata to all X shareholders.

4. **Exceptions to the General Rule.** There are many exceptions to the general rule that a shareholder may sell to whomever he wishes for whatever price. In fact, it may be that despite the general rule, in fact sale of control is not possible unless all minority shareholders are given exactly the same terms as the majority shareholders. In other words, the courts often apply the theory that one share owned by a minority shareholder ought to be worth the same as one share owned by a majority shareholder.

a. **Theory of "corporate action."** In situations in which the purchaser has first approached a majority shareholder and bought his stock (in X Corporation) and then either merged X or bought its assets (giving the remaining minority shareholders of X in this transaction less than what the majority shareholders of X had previously been paid), some courts hold that the entire acquisition was really a "corporate action" and that the premium received by the majority should be placed in a pool and distributed pro rata to all shareholders.

b. **Theory of misrepresentation.** Sometimes the majority will be involved in misrepresentation to the minority shareholder. For example, the majority shareholder may know that the purchaser is willing to pay $10 per share. It may buy the minority stock for $8 per share and then sell it and their own stock for $10 per share to the purchaser.

c. **Looting theory.** In a situation in which the purchaser buys only the controlling stock, the controlling shareholders may be liable to the minority when the purchaser later "loots" the corporation (if the majority shareholders knew or had reason to know that the purchaser intended to loot the corporation). Paying a "premium" is one indication or notice of possibly intended "looting."

1) **Looting--**

DeBaun v. First Western Bank and Trust Co., 120 Cal. Rptr. 354 (1975).

Facts. DeBaun and Stephens (Ps) held 30 of the 100 shares of stock in a photo finishing business where they worked. They were also directors. After the death of the founder, who held the balance of the stock in 1964, the 70 shares passed to a testamentary trust administered by First Western (D). Ps and another managed the business very successfully until 1968. In 1966, D decided to sell the 70 shares (on the basis that it was not an appropriate trust investment) without informing Ps. After an appraisal and aid from a broker, D located a tentative buyer, Mattison. About the same time, DeBaun learned of the proposed sale and submitted an offer, which was refused. D, after receiving a sketchy balance sheet of the trust through which Mattison was seeking to purchase the shares, ordered a Dunn and Bradstreet report on Mattison (which report noted pending litigation, past bankruptcies, and existing tax liens against corporate entities in which Mattison had been a principal).

Also, one of the officers of D had knowledge that there was an unsatisfied judgment that had been rendered against Mattison in favor of D's predecessor. Mattison explained these problems on the basis that he usually acquired failing companies and tried to turn them around. The public records of Los Angeles County, which were not checked by D, revealed $330,886 in unsatisfied judgments against Mattison and his entities and 54 pending actions totaling $373,588, as well as 22 recorded abstracts of judgments against him for $285,700 and 18 tax liens aggregating $20,327. Notwithstanding the information available to D, on the basis of the fact that one of D's officers knew Mattison and that Mattison was warmly received at an exclusive club, D accepted Mattison's offer of $50,000 in securities with the balance of the purchase price to be paid out of the revenues of the corporation (even though D knew that Mattison would be forced to make some of these payments out of the capital assets of the corporation). D sold Mattison the shares in July, and in less than one year the corporation's net worth of $220,000 was reduced to a net deficit of over $200,000 by Mattison's diversion of corporate assets to himself through various schemes. Ps sued D to recover for its breach of duty to minority shareholders in selling to Mattison. The trial court found for Ps and awarded damages of $438,000 ($220,000, or the net asset value at the time of sale by Mattison, plus $218,000 as the discounted value of the anticipated corporate profits for the next 10 years). D appeals.

Issue. Does a controlling shareholder owe the other shareholders a duty not to sell its controlling interest to an individual who was likely to loot the corporation?

Held. Yes. Judgment affirmed.

- D knew of Mattison's numerous financial failures and that Mattison could not meet his obligations to pay for the corporation without using its assets.
- A majority shareholder owes a duty to the minority shareholders to investigate an individual and not to sell to him if they reasonably should know he will loot the corporation. D breached its duty to P by selling to Mattison.

---

d. **Sale of a corporate asset.** When the purchaser buys only the majority stock, the majority may be liable for any premium received if the corporation has some particular "corporate asset" that creates this premium, since this asset belongs to all shareholders equally. But what constitutes a "corporate asset"? Isn't this involved in every corporate sale, so that whenever a purchaser offers to buy control he must give this same offer to minority shareholders?

1) **Fiduciary relationship--**

Perlman v. Feldmann, 219 F.2d 173 (2d Cir. 1955).

Facts. Perlman and other minority shareholders (Ps) brought a derivative shareholder action against Feldmann (D), president, chairman of the board, and 37% owner, for selling his shares at $20 per share to customers of the corporation (who thus gained control of the corporation's steel supplies in a shortage war market). After the sale the directors resigned, and the purchasers appointed a new board. The existing market price at the time of sale was $12 per share.

Issue. May the controlling shareholder be held for any "premium" price he receives for a sale of corporate control, when the motivation for the acquisition is the purchase of a particular "corporate asset" for which the premium is paid?

Held. Yes. Case remanded to determine stock's value.

- The director and majority shareholder is in a fiduciary position to the corporation and to the minority shareholders.

- In some instances such a fiduciary can sell control, even to the corporation's customers. But here the sale included an element of corporate goodwill (the ability to charge high prices in wartime and require advance funding on orders from the corporation's customers) and thus unusual profit to D that really belonged to all of the shareholders (*i.e.,* to the corporation). D has the burden to prove otherwise.

- Although this type of action is normally a derivative one, with recovery going to the corporation, here Ps can recover individually since, if the corporation recovered, those buying the corporation (who participated in the wrong) would share in the recovery.

- The case is remanded to the trial court on the issue of what the stock was worth without control. The premium belongs pro rata to all shareholders.

Dissent. What fiduciary duty is owed as a director? What as a majority shareholder? There is none here.

e. **Sale of a corporate office.** Normally, in a purchase transaction, the majority also agrees to assist the purchaser in the accomplishment of some corporate action requiring the exercise of their corporate office. For example, the majority (having representation on the board of directors) may agree that in connection with the sale of their shares they will have the board resign and be replaced with the purchaser's nominees. Some courts have held that any premium paid to majority shareholders must be distributed pro rata to all shareholders when a premium price has been paid based on the majority's exercise of its "corporate office" (on the basis that this belongs to the corporation as a whole, not to the majority shareholder exclusively).

X. CONTROL AND MANAGEMENT IN THE PUBLICLY HELD CORPORATION

A. CORPORATE "SOCIAL RESPONSIBILITY"

1. **To Whom Do Fiduciary Duties Run?** A number of academics have cheered the prospect that management of large businesses might have discretion to pursue goals other than profit maximization. These academics argue that management should use whatever discretion it might have to meet what they call the corporation's "social responsibility." Insofar as this argument seeks to justify expenditures that would otherwise not be made, it has elicited a number of objections: (i) diverting funds in this way is functionally equivalent to levying a tax and then deciding how the proceeds should be spent, a distinctly political process without the checks established by the political process; (ii) management lacks information about the real consequences of diverting funds; (iii) management cannot know how much diversion is justified; and (iv) management could readily use "social responsibility" as an excuse for inferior business results caused in fact by managerial shirking or pursuit of self-interest.

2. **The Rise of Corporate Constituency Statutes.** Beginning in the early 1980s, over half of the states have enacted statutes that authorize—and in some instances appear to command—directors to consider the interests of nonshareholder constituencies like employees, creditors, customers, and local communities. Many of these statutes apply only to corporate control transactions. (The threat of hostile takeovers prompted the lobbying that resulted in the enactment of these statutes.) Only a few of these statutes contain command language, and they may command precious little because they practically bar enforcement.

3. **Objections to Constituency Statutes.** Requiring or permitting directors to serve both shareholders and nonshareholders may diminish the incentive to engage in economically efficient risk-taking. It may also expose directors to increased risk of litigation and liability—because the interests of these constituencies conflict—while rendering them effectively responsible to none. Constituency statutes put directors to the task of ascertaining the public interest, a task to which they may not be well-suited by virtue of personal characteristics or incentives. Moreover, nonshareholders can negotiate contractual protection much more readily than shareholders seeking protection for their contingent interest in the residual.

4. **The ABA Position.** The ABA Committee on Corporate Laws urges that courts interpret these constituency statutes as permitting directors to "take

into account the interests of other constituencies but only as and to the extent that the directors are acting in the best interests, long as well as short term, of the shareholders and the corporation."

B. DIVORCE OF CONTROL FROM OWNERSHIP—SHAREHOLDERS AND DIRECTORS

In the large corporation with many shareholders, control of the corporation can be maintained with ownership of a minority percentage of the voting stock. This is done through installing management in the corporation and from this position soliciting voting proxies from the other shareholders. Because shareholders tend to vote with current management and proxy contests are expensive, control is normally easily maintained.

1. **Control by Management.** The first trend away from shareholder control of the large corporation took place with a minority interest controlling the board of directors. During this period, the board was separate from management (the officers). The latest trend is for public corporations to be controlled by management, who determine who will be directors and who controls the proxy machinery.

2. **Institutional Ownership and Takeover Bids.** Control is also changing due to these factors:

    a. **Institutions.** Increasingly, the stock market and thus ownership of the major corporations is being concentrated in the hands of institutions (bank trust departments, insurance companies, mutual funds).

    b. **Takeover bids.** Also, there is a strong trend for the merging of companies to occur through the method of the takeover bid (*i.e.,* Company A makes an offer directly to the shareholders of Company B to buy controlling stock of Company B).

3. **Composition of the Board of Directors.** Corporate responsibility issues raise the issue of the proper composition of the board of directors. There have been several suggestions:

    a. **Government intervention.** The government should have a "public interest" representation on the board of the largest corporations.

    b. **Shareholder representation.** Various shareholder groups should be specifically represented.

    c. **Employee representatives.** The employees should have their representatives on the board.

    d. **Career directors.** There should be paid career directors who represent various interests and serve as directors on many corporations.

4. Shareholder Voting.

a. **Introduction.** The law regards shareholders as the owners of the corporation, the object of management's fiduciary duty, and the ultimate source of corporate power. Shareholders have two ways to exercise this power—the vote and the derivative suit.

b. **Allocations of voting power.** The right to vote may be allocated to others not owning the shares.

1) **Proxies.** A shareholder may give a proxy to another to vote the shares.

2) **Other means.** There are other means of allocating voting power, such as voting trusts (discussed *supra*).

C. CORPORATE GOVERNANCE TODAY

Recent business failures and scandals, such as the collapse of the Dot-coms, Enron, Arthur Andersen, WorldCom, etc. led to increased political pressure to enact new corporate governance legislation. The Sarbanes-Oxley Act was adopted in 2002 in the wake of these scandals. (*See infra*, E.2., for a summary of Sarbanes-Oxley provisions.) The Act has since been met with much criticism by corporate governance experts, who claim that the act is ineffective and costly.

D. PROXY REGULATION

1. Regulation Under State Law.

a. **Power of attorney.** A proxy is a power of attorney to vote shares owned by someone else. At common law such proxies were illegal, but statutes permit proxies.

b. **Power to revoke.**

1) **In general.** A proxy establishes an agency relationship. This relationship is generally revocable at any time (such as by the grant of a subsequent proxy, or by the shareholder personally attending the shareholder meeting and voting).

2) **Irrevocable proxies.** A proxy that is expressly made irrevocable and is coupled with an interest is irrevocable.

a) "Coupled with an interest" means that some consideration was received by the shareholder for the grant of the proxy. An example would be the situation in which the shareholder borrows money, pledges his stock, and grants the lender a proxy to vote the shares.

b) Statutes often limit the duration of an irrevocable proxy.

2. Regulation Under the Securities Exchange Act of 1934.

a. Introduction to the Securities Exchange Act of 1934. The Securities Exchange Act of 1934 ("1934 Act") is a federal act that regulates a wide variety of transactions involving the securities markets. Two specific requirements of the 1934 Act are mentioned here (others are discussed throughout the remainder of the outline).

1) Registration and reporting requirements. Section 12 of the 1934 Act requires a company to register its securities with the Securities and Exchange Commission ("S.E.C.") and thereafter to file periodic reports on the company's financial condition, if the company's securities are (i) traded on a regulated securities exchange or (ii) traded over the counter and the company has assets of at least $10 million ***and*** 500 or more shareholders of a class of equity securities (such as common stock). Companies that have so registered with the S.E.C. are called "registered companies."

2) Proxy solicitation. Section 14 of the 1934 Act also regulates the solicitation of voting proxies from shareholders of companies registered under section 12.

b. Proxy solicitation rules.

1) Basic provision of the 1934 Act. Section 14(a) of the 1934 Act provides:

> It shall be unlawful for any persons, by the use of the mails or by any means or instrumentality of interstate commerce or of any facility of a national securities exchange or otherwise, in contravention of such rules and regulations as the Commission may prescribe as necessary or appropriate in the public interest or for the protection of investors, to solicit or to permit the use of his name to solicit any proxy or consent or authorization in respect of any security (other than an exempted security) registered pursuant to section 12.

2) Rules adopted by the S.E.C. Under the authority given by section 14 of the 1934 Act, the S.E.C. has adopted several rules for the regulation of proxy solicitation of registered securities. These rules are designed to accomplish three objectives.

a) Full disclosure. Those soliciting proxies or attempting to prevent others from soliciting them must give full disclosure of all material information to the shareholders being solicited. [Rule 14a-3 to a-6]

b) **Fraud.** Resort to the use of fraud in the solicitation is made unlawful. [Rule 14a-9]

c) **Shareholder solicitation.** Shareholders may solicit proxies from other shareholders, and management must include in its proxy statement proposals made by shareholders. [Rule 14a-8]

3) **Remedies for violation.**

a) **Appropriate remedies.** If the proxy rules are violated, courts will fashion an appropriate remedy. The "fairness" of the transaction involved is taken into consideration in the type of remedy granted.

b) **Actions by the S.E.C.** The S.E.C. may bring actions seeking administrative remedies, such as an injunction preventing solicitation of proxies, preventing the voting of shares obtained through improper proxy solicitation, or requiring resolicitation (and these actions may be enforced in the federal district courts).

c) **Private actions.** The courts have held that a private cause of action is implied under section 14.

d) **Materiality.** It need not be shown that the violation (such as a misstatement or omission) caused the outcome of the voting on the matter. All that need be shown is that such statements were material and could have had a propensity to affect the voting.

e) **Relief granted.** As stated above, the court will fashion whatever relief is appropriate to remedy the violation, whether damages or rescission of the transaction, etc.

4) **Solicitation.** Rule 14a-1 defines a "solicitation" as a "communication to security holders under circumstances reasonably calculated to result in the procurement, withholding, or revocation of a proxy."

a) **Example.** When Company A has agreed to merge with B, C makes a counter-proposal, and a federal agency must first pass on any merger proposal, A places newspaper ads directed to B's shareholders and employees suggesting that they would be better off with the merger into A. It was held that where this occurred three months prior to the formal proxy solicitation, no solicitation was involved. [Brown v. Chicago, Rock Island & Pacific Railroad Co., 328 F.2d 122 (7th Cir. 1964)]

b) **Use of shareholder lists--**

Studebaker Corp. v. Gittlin, 360 F.2d 692 (2d Cir. 1966).

Facts. New York law required that a corporation permit a shareholder to inspect the list of shareholders if the shareholder owned or represented 5% of any class of outstanding stock and he did not intend to use the list for a purpose other than one related to the business of the corporation. Gittlin (D) owned 5,000 shares himself and solicited authorizations from others owning 145,000 shares of Studebaker (P) stock (combined totaling more than the required 5%). In soliciting the authorizations D did not comply with several of the federal proxy rules (such as Rule 14a-3, which requires disclosure of information concerning the purpose of soliciting a proxy). After getting the authorizations, D began an action in New York state court to force management to give the list (which it refused to do). P's management then began an action, on behalf of the corporation, in federal court for an injunction against the state court proceeding, alleging that the purpose of getting the list was for a corporate takeover, and therefore that the solicitation was the first step in a proxy solicitation, which was done without complying with federal law. The court found for P and D appeals.

Issue. When a shareholder intends to use the shareholder list to make a corporate takeover attempt, and a proxy solicitation is necessary as part of this attempt, is a request for authorization by shareholders to use their rights as shareholders to get a shareholder list a proxy solicitation?

Held. Yes. Judgment affirmed.

- ♦ The corporation has standing to bring an action for an injunction against a shareholder for violation of the proxy solicitation rules.
- ♦ When a communication to shareholders seeks support as part of a plan that will end in solicitation of the shareholders' proxies, such a communication is a solicitation of a proxy and must comply with the federal rules. This rationale applies since misinformation can be communicated that may render the later proxy solicitation ineffective.

---

3. **Proxy Forms, Statements, Annual Reports.** The proxy rules regulate the type of forms used, and the content of proxy statements, and annual reports of reporting companies, where a proxy solicitation is to be made.

   a. **Failure to disclose material information in S.E.C. reports--**

In the Matter of **Caterpillar, Inc.,** S.E.C. Rel. No. 34-30532 (1992).

Facts. In 1989, Caterpillar, Inc's. (D's) Brazilian subsidiary had 5% of D's sales, but 23% of its net profits, due to some unusual occurrences, such as currency exchange rates. D's management knew that the situation in Brazil was highly unusual; at a board meeting in January 1990, it informed the board members that the Brazil subsidiary had had an unusual effect on 1989 earnings and that the situation was volatile and could significantly impact 1990 earnings. However, D failed to mention Brazil in its 10K report. Then, at its April 1990 board meeting, D's management told the board that a new president had been elected in Brazil whose inflation fighting program would likely adversely impact D's earnings. Again, nothing was mentioned of this fact in D's first quarter 10Q report to the S.E.C. On June 25, 1990, D issued a press release that the projected results for 1990 would be much lower than anticipated. The S.E.C. charged D with violation of Item 303 of Regulation SK in its year-end 10K report for 1989 and its first quarter 10Q report for 1990. This regulation requires a registrant to disclose material information that will likely affect the company's operations.

Issue. Does a company meet the S.E.C. filing requirements if it fails to disclose in its 10K and 10Q reports possible material consequences from operations in a foreign subsidiary?

Held. No.

- D failed to disclose material information in its 10K report that was necessary for an investor to understand, through management's eyes, the results of its 1989 operations. Item 303(a) of Regulation SK requires registrants filing 10K reports to provide such information as necessary to understand the results of operations, including discussion of any unusual items and any known trends or uncertainties that have had or will have a material impact on sales or earnings.

- In its 10Q report, D failed to report known uncertainties from operations in Brazil that could have a material effect on D's future operations. Item 303(b) requires registrants filing 10Q interim reports to discuss material changes from the end of the preceding year. Regulation SK has also been interpreted to require registrants to provide interpretative comments representative of future performance and disclosure of the likelihood of certain prospective developments.

4. **False or Misleading Statements.** Rule 14a-9 prohibits materially false or misleading statements or omissions in connection with the solicitation of proxies.

   a. **Rescission of a merger--**

J.I. Case Co. v. Borak, 377 U.S. 426 (1964).

Facts. A shareholder sued for damages and rescission of a merger that was effected through circulation of a false and misleading proxy statement. The shareholder claimed damages under section 27 of the 1934 Act.

Issues. When there are false and misleading statements in the proxy statement in violation of section 14(a) of the 1934 Act, and when the transaction (merger) is now complete and the proxies solicited were necessary to the shareholder vote approving the transaction:

(i) Do the shareholders have a derivative cause of action under section 14(a) of the 1934 Act?

(ii) If so, will the court grant the remedy of unwinding the merger?

Held. (i) Yes. (ii) Yes. Case remanded for trial on the merits.

- ♦ A private right of action in the form of a derivative action by shareholders is implied under the 1934 Act for alleged violations of the proxy rules.
- ♦ The court may provide such remedies as required to make effective the purpose of the 1934 Act, including unwinding a merger. Remedies are not limited to prospective relief.

---

b. **Causation.** When it is shown that a proxy solicitation contained a material defect, such as ***materially*** misleading statements of fact, a plaintiff does ***not*** also have to show that the misleading statement was the cause of the shareholders voting as they did. It must only be shown that the proxy solicitation was necessary to the transaction that resulted in the detriment to the plaintiff. [*See* Mills v. Electric Auto-Lite Co., 396 U.S. 375 (1970)]

c. **Materiality--**

TSC Industries, Inc. v. Northway, Inc., 426 U.S. 438 (1976).

Facts. National Industries, Inc. bought 34% of the common stock of TSC Industries, Inc. and put five persons on the TSC board (one becoming chairman of the board, another chairman of the executive committee). Then a proposal was made by National to buy TSC in a stock-for-stock exchange. The board of TSC approved (the five National directors abstaining). A shareholder of TSC brings this action, claiming that there were false and misleading statements in the proxy statement issued by National to solicit approval of the merger. The following were claimed as violations:

> The president of National was the chairman of the board of TSC, and the vice president was the chairman of the executive committee. Also, because it owned 34% of the common stock of TSC, National may have been in "control" of TSC.

The opinion issued by a brokerage firm that the terms of the transaction were fair was modified by a later statement indicating that the price on part of the stock issued by National would decline. Also, about 9% of the stock purchases of National were by a mutual fund with connections to National or by National itself (which may have manipulated the stock price of National).

Issue. Were the statements or omissions "material"?

Held. No. Summary judgment is denied.

- ♦ A statement is "material" if there is a substantial likelihood that a reasonable shareholder would consider it important in deciding how to vote.
- ♦ Summary judgment issues only when the statements are such that reasonable minds cannot differ on the question of materiality. This is not the case here.
- ♦ The proxy statement did reveal that National controlled TSC (*i.e.,* the stock ownership was revealed; the fact that National had five people on the board was revealed, etc.).
- ♦ The brokerage firm indicated that a premium over market price was being paid for the TSC shares; even with the second letter revealing that this firm thought that the price of the National shares would decline, the fact that a premium is being paid is not disputed. Also, there is nothing to prove that the stock purchases by National and the mutual fund were for the purpose of manipulating the market price of National; nor is there anything to prove that such purchases were coordinated with the merger of TSC.

d. Qualitative terms and proxy solicitation of unneeded minority votes--

Virginia Bankshares, Inc. v. Sandberg, 501 U.S. 1083 (1991).

Facts. In 1986, First American Bankshares, Inc. ("FABI"), a bank holding company, began a freeze-out merger under Virginia state law in which First American Bank of Virginia (85% owned by FABI and 15% owned by 2,000 minority shareholders) was merged into Virginia Bankshares, Inc., a wholly owned subsidiary of FABI. FABI got an investment banker to give a report that $42 per share was a fair price. Virginia law required that the merger be submitted to vote at a shareholders' meeting, preceded by a statement of information given to shareholders. FABI instead solicited proxies for voting at the annual shareholders' meeting. In the proxy solicitation materials, FABI urged approval of the merger because (i) it was an opportunity for minority shareholders to achieve a "high" value, and (ii) the price offered was "fair." Most minority shareholders approved, but P did not; she sued for damages in district court, on the basis that section 14(a) and Rule 14a-9 were violated by material misrepresentations in the proxy materials. She also sued under state law for breach of fiduciary duties by the directors of FABI. P alleged that the directors had not believed the price was fair or high. The jury found for P and awarded her an additional $18 per share. The circuit court affirmed. The Supreme Court granted certiorari.

Issues.

(i) Were the qualitative statements in proxy statements about a "high" price, etc., material and misleading?

(ii) Is there a federal claim under the proxy rules when the plaintiff is a minority shareholder whose vote is not required to approve the transaction and by solicitation of proxies no state law remedies otherwise available to the plaintiff have been lost?

Held. (i) Yes. (ii) No. Judgment reversed.

- If a director makes a statement in proxy material of his reasons for doing something (or of his beliefs or opinions) and it is shown that the director did not really have these reasons or hold these beliefs, these statements can be material. These matters can usually be documented from corporate records. And here, the word "high" is not too vague; it has a basis in provable facts from established criteria in valuing companies. For example, P showed that the book value used to calculate $42 per share was not based on the appreciated value of the bank's real estate; that market value as used was not reliable since the market for the stock was thin; and that undisclosed valuations by the bank showed a value of $60 per share.

- But in addition to showing an opinion or belief that was not in fact held, P ***must also show*** that the statement also said or implied something false or misleading about the subject matter. Here, not only did the directors give an opinion that the value was high (and this was a reason for the merger), but also there is an implied misstatement of actual fact that this was the reason and that the price was in fact high, which P showed proof of otherwise.

- Here, one director of Virginia Bankshares was also a director of FABI, which was not disclosed. Virginia state law provided that such a freeze-out merger could be attacked afterward by minority shareholders if they could show conflicts of interest that may have injured them. This provision could be avoided if: (i) minority shareholders approved the transaction after disclosure of the material facts concerning the transaction; (ii) the directors ratified the transaction after disclosure; or (iii) the transaction could be proved to be fair. P argues that because the proxy solicitation allowed Ds to avoid these state law provisions (otherwise available to the minority shareholders) because the minority approved the transaction in the proxies, then there is causation (the proxy solicitation provided an essential link in the chain of approving the transaction, and a section 14(a) cause of action should exist).

- However, in this case there is no such causal sequence. This procedure is too hypothetical. It allows actions when the shareholders' vote is not necessary to the transaction.

- Implied private rights of action under federal securities laws are based on congressional intent. They should not be expanded beyond that intent. Congress was not clear in how far an implied private right should go in the case of section 14(a). However, when it did want private rights, it specified them in specific sections of the securities laws. So policy concerns must be looked at to determine the scope of the private right in this case.

  It is too speculative to allow a dissatisfied minority shareholder to allege that without the proxy solicitation a timid management would not have been able to pass the corporate action, which approval was secured by misrepresentation.

  And, on the other hand, directors in the future would simply make a few statements about plans to proceed without minority endorsement (if they did not get it in the proxy solicitation).

- There have been cases in which proxy solicitation has been a link in the process of preventing a class of shareholders from resorting to a state remedy otherwise available; *e.g.*, a minority shareholder induced by a misleading proxy statement to forfeit a state-law right to an appraisal remedy. [Swanson v. American Consumers Industries, Inc., 475 F.2d 516 (7th Cir. 1973)] But this case does not require the court to decide whether section 14(a) provides a cause of action for lost state remedies since there is ***no*** indication that will occur here. Virginia law indicates that minority shareholder ratification of a merger overcomes any problem of a conflict of interest. But state courts would not accept the giving of proxies based on a material misrepresentation as a minority shareholder approval.

Concurrence (Scalia, J.). There is a standard misrepresentation of fact here; *i.e.,* that of the directors' opinion ***and*** of the accuracy of facts on which the opinion was assertedly based. No new rule is needed to decide the case.

Concurrence and dissent (Stevens, Marshall, JJ.). Shareholders may bring an action for damages under section 14(a) whenever materially false or misleading statements are made in proxy statements. The fact that solicitation of proxies is not required by law or by the bylaws of the corporation does not authorize corporate officers to avoid the constraints of the Securities Exchange Act.

Dissent (Kennedy, Marshall, Blackmun, Stevens, JJ.). The majority has misrepresented the status of non-voting causation in proxy cases. Courts have applied this theory to cases for 25 years. The Court simply wanted to restrict a well-established implied right of action.

5. **Shareholder Proposals.** Management must include in its solicitation proposals made by shareholders, when such proposals are "proper subjects." The statement may be up to 200 words. Several bases for rejecting shareholder proposals are set forth in Rule 14a-8.

   a. **Shareholder proposal properly rejected--**

Rauchman v. Mobil Corp., 739 F.2d 205 (6th Cir. 1984).

Facts. Olayan, a Saudi Arabian, was up for reelection to Mobil's (D's) board of directors at its annual shareholders' meeting. Rauchman (P), a shareholder, submitted a shareholder proposal for inclusion in D's proxy statement that the bylaws be amended so that no citizen of an OPEC country could be elected to D's board. D refused to include the proposal on the grounds that the proxy rules (section 14a-8(c)(8)) allowed a company to exclude proposals that relate to an election to the office of the board of directors. The S.E.C., agreeing with D's position, granted D a no-action letter. P sued in federal district court under section 14(a) and Rule 14a-8. The district court granted D summary judgment. P appeals.

Issues.

(i) Does P have a private right of action under section 14(a) and Rule 14a-8?

(ii) Was P's proposal properly excluded by D?

Held. (i) Yes. (ii) Yes. Judgment affirmed.

♦ We assume a private cause of action exists for a violation of Rule 14a-8.

♦ On the merits, D properly excluded the proposal. A shareholder could not both vote for P's proposal and still vote to elect Olayan to the board, so the proposal improperly relates to a matter concerning election to the board.

---

6. **Civil Liability.** The courts will fashion whatever relief is appropriate to remedy a violation of the proxy rules. In some instances damages may be awarded. For example, damages might be awarded to an individual shareholder suing for loss in the value of his shares due to violations (insurgents gain control in a contest through misleading statements violating the proxy rules; market price of the stock drops).

E. CORPORATE DISCLOSURE REQUIREMENTS

Various corporate disclosure requirements have been enacted in an attempt to "level the playing field" and keep all investors and potential investors fully informed.

1. **S.E.C. Rules.** S.E.C. Regulation FD provides that a company disclosing material nonpublic information to securities market professionals must promptly thereafter publicly disclose that information. Another S.E.C. rule addresses concerns over the independence of outside auditors, requiring disclosures in the proxy statement regarding the non-audit functions being performed by the outside auditor and other matters possibly affecting the independence of the auditor.

2. **Sarbanes-Oxley Act.** Calls for reform following corporate accounting irregularities lead to the enactment of the Sarbanes-Oxley Act of 2002. Following are some important provisions of the Act.

   a. Section 201 prohibits accounting firms from providing an audit client with a wide variety of non-audit services, including: bookkeeping, appraisal or valuation services, internal auditing services, investment banking services, and legal and expert services that are unrelated to the audit.

   b. Section 301 requires all listed companies to have audit committees consisting entirely of independent board members. The audit committee must "be directly responsible for the appointment, compensation, and oversight of the work" of the independent auditor, and the audit firm must report directly to the audit committee.

   c. Section 302 mandates that, in connection with each filing of a company's periodic reports, its CEO and CFO each certify that he reviewed the report, that to his knowledge it contains no material misstatement or omission, and that the financial statements and other financial information in the report fairly present the firm's financial condition and results of operations.

   d. Section 402(a) prohibits companies from making or arranging for a personal loan to any director or executive officer or extending credit to a director or executive officer.

   e. Section 404 requires that annual reports filed with the S.E.C. be accompanied by an acknowledgement by management of its obligation to establish and maintain adequate internal controls. Management must also give its assessment of the effectiveness of these controls. In addition, the independent auditor's report must attest to management's assessment of the company's internal controls.

XI. DUTY OF CARE AND THE BUSINESS JUDGMENT RULE

A. INTRODUCTION

By law, directors have the duty of management of the corporation. This duty is normally delegated to the officers; thus, the directors must supervise the officers. The legal duties of the directors and officers are owed to the corporation; performance of these duties is enforceable by an action on behalf of the corporation brought by an individual shareholder (called a "derivative suit," discussed *infra*).

B. FIDUCIARY RELATIONSHIP OF DIRECTORS TO THE CORPORATION

Directors and officers are said to occupy a "fiduciary" position in relationship to the corporation and the management of its affairs (since they manage on behalf of the shareholders). This relationship has resulted in several legal standards.

1. **Duty of Loyalty or Good Faith.** Directors and officers are bound by rules of fairness, loyalty, honesty, and good faith in their relationship to, dealings with, and management of the corporation.

2. **Duty of Reasonable Care.** In addition, directors and officers must exercise reasonable care, prudence, and diligence in the management of the corporation.

3. **Business Judgment.** Finally, a third standard is imposed on officers and directors—that of the "business judgment" rule.

    a. There is some confusion in the courts over the negligence standard to be applied to officers and directors. For example, are directors really responsible for management? Or is there a more limited role for directors? If so, then negligence is failure to perform with the care expected of directors (but not necessarily failure to perform with the prudence that a director would give to his own personal business dealings; thus, a different standard of care would apply to directors and to officers).

    b. Because of the reluctance of the courts to hold directors truly responsible for the management of the corporation, courts have adopted the "business judgment" rule, which says that when a matter of business judgment is involved, the directors meet their responsibility of reasonable care and diligence if they exercise an honest, good-faith, unbiased judgment. When this standard is applied, a director would only be liable (if his actions were in good faith) if he were guilty of gross negligence or worse.

C. DAMAGES

1. **Cause of Action.** To form a cause of action, it must be shown that the director or officer failed to exercise reasonable care and that as a direct and proximate result the corporation has suffered damages.

2. **Joint and Several Liability.** Either one director may be held liable for his own acts, or all directors may be held liable (all those participating in the negligent act). When more than one director is held responsible, liability is joint and several.

D. CASES AND APPLICATIONS

1. **Duty of Care Owed by Bank Directors--**

Litwin v. Allen, 25 N.Y.S.2d 667 (1940).

Facts. A shareholder (P) brought a derivative action against the directors of Guaranty Trust and its wholly owned subsidiary (the Guaranty Company). The Trust Company purchased some bonds from Alleghany Corporation and gave an option to Alleghany to repurchase them in six months for the same price. If Alleghany did not repurchase, the subsidiary (Guaranty Company) was obligated to purchase the bonds at the same price from the Trust Company. Alleghany could not get a loan, and so the subsidiary bought the bonds at $105 (market value was then in the $80s). The bonds subsequently dropped drastically in price, and the Guaranty Company lost substantial amounts of money.

Issue. Has there been a violation of the director's duty of due care in entering the transaction with Alleghany Corporation?

Held. Yes. Judgment for P.

- ♦ The duty of due care is higher for bank directors than for other companies since banks are affected with the public interest. Thus, bank directors must exercise the care of "reasonably prudent bankers."
- ♦ The purchase by Guaranty subject to the option to buy in Alleghany at the same price is an ultra vires act of the corporation (*i.e.,* against public policy for the bank to give such an option).
- ♦ Furthermore, all of the directors of both companies that voted for or ratified the purchase have violated their duty of due care. They have not shown sufficient diligence in allowing the bank to purchase bonds with an option to sell at the same price (all of the risk is on the bank for a drop in price; if the price rises, they get no gain).

- The directors are responsible for the losses from holding the bonds up to the expiration date of the option.

Comment. This case indicates that the standard of care may vary according to the kind of business involved and the precise circumstances in which the directors acted.

2. Business Judgment Rule--

Shlensky v. Wrigley, 237 N.E.2d 776 (Ill. App. Ct. 1968).

Facts. Shlensky (P), a minority shareholder in the corporation (D) that owns Wrigley Field and the Chicago Cubs, brought a shareholder's derivative suit against the directors of the corporation for their refusal to install lights at Wrigley Field and schedule night games for the Cubs as other teams in the league had done (to increase revenues). The directors' motivation was allegedly the result of the views of Mr. Wrigley (also a defendant), the majority shareholder, president, and a director of the corporation, who wanted to preserve the neighborhood surrounding Wrigley Field and who believed that baseball was a daytime sport. The lower court dismissed P's action.

Issue. May a shareholder bring a derivative action when there are no allegations of fraud, illegality, or conflict of interest?

Held. No. Judgment affirmed.

- The court will not disturb the "business judgment" of a majority of the directors—absent fraud, illegality, or a conflict of interest. There is no conclusive evidence that the installation of lights and the scheduling of night games will accrue a net benefit in revenues to D, and there appear to be other valid reasons for refusing to install lights—*e.g.,* the detrimental effect on the surrounding neighborhood.

- Corporations are not obliged to follow the direction taken by other similar corporations. Directors are elected for their own business capabilities and not for their ability to follow others.

3. Informed Judgment in Merger Proposals--

Smith v. Van Gorkom, 488 A.2d 858 (Del. 1985).

Facts. Shareholders (Ps) of Trans Union sued Trans Union seeking rescission of a merger into New T Company (a wholly owned subsidiary of defendant Marmon Group, controlled by Pritzker), or alternatively, damages against members of Trans Union's board (Ds).

Trans Union was a profitable, multi-million dollar leasing corporation that was not able to use all of the tax credits it was generating. Several solutions were explored. Van Gorkom (chairman) asked for a study by Romans (financial officer) regarding a leveraged buy-out by management. Romans reported that the company would generate enough cash to pay $50 per share for the company's stock, but not $60 per share. Van Gorkom rejected the idea of this type of buy-out (conflict of interest) but indicated he would take $55 per share for his own stock (he was 65 and about to retire). On his own, Van Gorkom approached Pritzker, a takeover specialist, and began negotiating a sale of Trans Union. He suggested $55 per share and a five-year payout method without consulting the board or management. The price was above the $39 per share market value, but no study was done by anyone to determine the intrinsic value of Trans Union's shares. In the final deal, Trans Union got three days to consider the offer, which included selling a million shares to Pritzker at market, so that even if Trans Union found someone else who would pay a better price, Pritzker would profit: For 90 days Trans Union could receive but not solicit competing offers.

Van Gorkom hired outside legal counsel to review the deal, ignoring his company lawyer and a lawyer on the board. He called a board meeting for two days later. At the meeting, Trans Union's investment banker was not invited, no copies of the proposed merger were given, senior management was against it, and Romans said the price was too low. Van Gorkom presented the deal in 20 minutes, saying that the price might not be the highest that could be received, but it was fair. The outside lawyer told the board that they might be sued if they did not accept the offer and that they did not need to get an outside "fairness" opinion as a matter of law. Romans said he had not done a fairness study but that he thought $55 per share was on the low end. Discussion lasted two hours, and the merger offer was accepted.

Within 10 days, management of Trans Union was in an uproar. Pritzker and Van Gorkom agreed to some amendments, which the board approved. Trans Union retained Salomon Bros. to solicit other offers. Kohlberg, Kravis, Roberts & Co. made an offer at $60 per share. Van Gorkom discouraged the offer and spoke with management people who were participating in it. Hours before a board meeting to consider it, it was canceled, and was never presented to the board. General Electric Credit Corp. made a proposal at $60 per share, but wanted more time, which Pritzker refused to give, so it too was withdrawn.

On December 19, some shareholders began this suit. On February 10, 70% of the shareholders approved the deal. The trial court held that the board's actions from its first meeting on September 20 until January 26 were informed. Ps appeal.

Issue. Did the directors act in accordance with the requirements of the business judgment rule?

Held. No. Judgment reversed and case remanded.

- The business judgment rule presumes that directors act on an informed basis, in good faith, and in an honest belief that their actions are for the good of the company. Plaintiffs must rebut this presumption. There is no fraud here, or bad faith. The issue is whether the directors informed themselves properly. All reasonably material information available must be looked at prior to a decision. This is a duty of care. And the directors are liable if they were grossly negligent in failing to inform themselves.

- The directors were grossly negligent in the way they acted in the first board meeting that approved the merger: They did not know about Van Gorkom's role, and they did not gather information on the intrinsic value of the company. Receiving a premium price over market is not enough evidence of intrinsic value.

- An outside opinion is not always necessary, but here there was not even an opinion given by inside management. The Van Gorkom opinion of value could be relied on had it been based on sound factors; it was not and the board members did not check it. The post-September market test of value was insufficient to confirm the reasonableness of the board's decision.

- Although the 10 board members knew the company well and had outstanding business experience, this was not enough to base a finding that they reached an informed decision.

- There is no real evidence of what the outside lawyer said, and as he refused to testify, Ds cannot rely on the fact that they based their acts on his opinion.

- The actions taken by the board to review the proposal on October 9, 1980, and on January 26, 1981, did not cure the defects in the September 20 meeting.

- All directors take a unified position, so all are being treated the same way.

- The shareholder vote accepting the offer does not clear Ds because it was not based on full information.

Dissent. There were 10 directors; the five outside ones were chief executives of successful companies. The five inside directors had years of experience with Trans Union. All knew about the company in detail. No "fast shuffle" took place over these men. Based on this experience, the directors made an informed judgment.

---

4. Liability for Illegal Acts of Employees--

In re **Caremark International, Inc. Derivative Litigation,** 698 A.2d 959 (Del. Ch. 1996).

Facts (by casebook editor). This case involved a proposed settlement of five derivative suits filed on behalf of Caremark International, Inc. against individual defendants who constitute the company's board of directors (Ds). The suit alleges that members of the board breached their fiduciary duty of care to the corporation in connection with alleged violations by employees of federal and state laws regulating health care providers. The allegations followed a four-year federal government investigation of Caremark. As a result of those investigations, Caremark was indicted with multiple felonies and pleaded guilty to a single felony of mail fraud. Caremark was required to pay fines and reimburse various parties in the amount of $250 million. This suit was filed on behalf of the corporation seeking to recover this money from the individual members of the board of directors. The parties have entered into settlement negotiations and now petition the court to approve their settlement agreement. The agreement provides, among other things, that the board establish a compliance and ethics committee to monitor compliance with applicable laws, and that corporate officers serve as compliance officers who report to this committee. The balance of the agreement requires the board to discuss changes in health care regulations semi-annually, and basically, not to violate these laws.

Issue. Can a settlement agreement be considered fair even if the benefits it provides are very modest?

Held. Yes. Proposed settlement approved.

- ♦ The ultimate issue for this court is whether the proposed settlement appears to be fair to the corporation and its absent shareholders, all of whom will be bound by the settlement. The complaint here charges the directors with allowing a situation to develop and continue which exposed the company to enormous liability. In so doing, the complaint alleges, the directors violated a duty to be active monitors of corporate performance. In this case, subordinate employees of the company committed the actions subjecting Caremark to liability, not members of the board of directors. The question then is what is the scope of the duty of the board to prevent this type of activity by subordinate employees.

- ♦ To show that the directors breached their duty of care by failing to adequately control employees, plaintiffs would have to show either "(1) that the directors knew or (2) should have known that violations of the law were occurring and, in either event, (3) that the directors took no steps in a good faith effort to prevent or remedy that situation, and (4) that such failure proximately resulted in the losses complained of . . ."

- ♦ After a careful review of relevant case law, I am of the opinion that a director's obligation includes a duty to attempt in good faith to assure that a corporate information and reporting system exists, and that failure to do so under some circumstances may render a director liable for losses caused by noncompliance of employees with applicable legal standards. However, only a sustained or systematic failure of the board to exercise reasonable oversight will establish the lack of good faith that is necessary to liability. In this case, the corporation had in place a committee charged with overseeing corporate compliance with applicable laws, which in my opinion, represents a good faith attempt to be informed of relevant facts. In light of this, I find the claims against the directors to be very weak. There is no evidence in this record that the directors lacked good faith in their monitoring responsibilities, or that they conscientiously permitted a known violation of the law to occur.

- The proposed settlement agreement provides very modest benefits indeed. However, in light of the weakness of the plaintiffs' case, I find the settlement to be fair.

---

5. Fiduciary Duties in the Absence of a Request for Shareholder Action--

Malone v. Brincat, 722 A.2d 5 (Del. 1998).

Facts. The plaintiffs (Ps) are individuals who held shares of Mercury Finance Company ("Mercury") from 1993 to 1998. Mercury is a publicly traded company. Ps filed suit against the directors of Mercury for breach of their fiduciary duty of disclosure. Ps' complaint also named KPMG Peat Marwick L.L.P. ("KPMG") as a defendant, and alleged that KPMG aided and abetted Mercury's directors in breaching their duties. Ps alleged that between 1993 and 1998, the directors disseminated to shareholders information containing overstatements of Mercury's earnings, financial performance, and shareholder equity in violation of their fiduciary duty of disclosure. Ps alleged that this same financial misinformation was included in all of Mercury's S.E.C. filings, and every communication from the directors to the shareholders. Ps contend that as a direct result of these false disclosures, the company has lost all or virtually all of its value, and they seek class action status to pursue damages against Mercury's board of directors and KPMG (Ds). Ds filed motions to dismiss the action for failure to state a claim upon which relief may be granted. The Court of Chancery dismissed Ps' complaint with prejudice, holding that under Delaware law, directors have no fiduciary duty of disclosure in the absence of a request for shareholder action.

Issue. Do the fiduciary duties of care, loyalty, and good faith apply when directors disseminate information to shareholders even when no shareholder action is sought?

Held. Yes. Judgment to dismiss the complaint affirmed. Judgment to dismiss the complaint with prejudice reversed.

- In the absence of a shareholder request for action, Delaware law does not require directors to provide shareholders with information concerning the finances or affairs of the corporation. However, whenever directors communicate publicly or directly with shareholders about the corporation's affairs, directors have a fiduciary duty to the shareholders to exercise due care, good faith, and loyalty. This is true with or without a request for shareholder action. Dissemination of false information could violate one or more of these duties.

- The issue here is not whether the directors breached their duty of disclosure. It is whether they breached their more general duty of good faith and loyalty by knowingly communicating false information about the company's financial condition. We find that when directors deliberately misinform shareholders about the business of the corporation, either directly or by a public statement, there is a violation of fiduciary duty. We therefore disagree with the Court of Chancery that a claim cannot be articulated on these facts.

- However, we find that the dismissal of the complaint ***was*** proper, but should have been without prejudice. It appears that Ps are claiming an injury to the corporation in that the misleading statements caused it to lose nearly all of its value. However, Ps never expressly asserted a derivative claim on behalf of the corporation. Nor did they comply with chancery court rules that require a pre-suit demand or particularized allegations why demand is excused. In short, if Ps intended to file a derivative suit, they have not followed proper procedures, and their complaint must be dismissed. However, the dismissal is without prejudice to allow Ps to replead to assert a derivative claim and any damages or equitable remedies sought on behalf of the corporation.

---

6. Special Committees of the Board Reviewing Board Actions--

Gall v. Exxon Corp., 418 F. Supp. 508 (S.D.N.Y. 1976).

Facts. Gall (P) brought a shareholder's derivative action alleging that directors of Exxon (D) had given $38 million improperly as campaign contributions to secure political favors in Italy. P claimed violations of the 1934 Act for filing false reports with the S.E.C. and soliciting proxies from shareholders without revealing the illegal contributions, and for a breach of fiduciary duties, and waste and spoliation. D formed a special committee of the board of directors to investigate the charges, and the committee determined that the corporation would not be aided by bringing suit against any of the directors since most of the directors involved had little actual knowledge of the nature or legality of the payments and since all such payments had ceased in 1972. D moved for summary judgment, arguing that the decision of the committee was within the sound business judgment rule and should not be disturbed by the court.

Issue. Is this decision (made by a special committee of the board of directors) not to bring a cause of action held by the corporation within the sound business judgment of the corporate management?

Held. Yes, but summary judgment denied.

- The directors are empowered to determine by the exercise of their business judgment whether bringing the cause of action would benefit the corporation, and absent prejudice in the decision, the court should allow the decision to stand.

- However, P will be given time for discovery to determine whether there was prejudice in the decision before summary judgment will be granted.

Comment. The special committee consisted of directors who had had no knowledge of the illegal contributions at the time they were made.

---

7. Termination of a Shareholder's Derivative Suit--

Zapata Corp. v. Maldonado, 430 A.2d 779 (Del. 1981).

Facts. Maldonado (P), a shareholder in Zapata Corp. (D), instituted a derivative action on D's behalf. The suit alleged breaches of fiduciary duty by 10 of D's officers and directors. P brought this suit without first demanding that the board bring it, on the ground that the demand would be futile since all directors were named as defendants. Several years later, the board appointed an independent investigating committee. By this time, four of the defendants were off the board, and the remaining directors appointed two new outside directors. These new directors comprised the investigating committee. After its investigation, it recommended that the action be dismissed. Its determination was binding on D, which moved for dismissal or summary judgment. The trial court denied the motions, holding that the business judgment rule is not a grant of authority to dismiss derivative suits, and that a shareholder sometimes has an individual right to maintain such actions. D filed an interlocutory appeal.

Issue. Did the committee have the power to cause this action to be dismissed?

Held. Yes. Trial court interlocutory order reversed; case remanded for proceedings consistent with this opinion.

- A shareholder does not have an individual right, once demand is made and refused, to continue a derivative suit. Unless it was wrongful, the board's decision that the suit would harm the company will be respected as a matter of business judgment. A shareholder has the right to initiate the action himself when demand may be properly excused as futile. However, excusing demand does not strip the board of its corporate power. There may be circumstances where the suit, although properly initiated, would not be in the corporation's best interests. This is the context here.

- The court must find a balancing point when bona fide shareholder power to bring corporation causes of action cannot be unfairly trampled on by the board, but when the corporation can rid itself of detrimental litigation. A two-step process is involved. First, the court must recognize that the board, even if tainted by self-interest, can legally delegate its authority to a committee of disinterested directors. However, the court may inquire on its own into the independence and good faith of the committee and the bases supporting its conclusions. If the court is satisfied on both counts, the second step is to apply its own business judgment as to whether the motion to dismiss should be granted. Thus, suits will be heard when corporate actions meet the criteria of the first step, but when the result would terminate a grievance worthy of consideration.

---

8. Demand on the Board in Derivative Suits--

Aronson v. Lewis, 473 A.2d 805 (Del. 1984).

Facts. Lewis (P) was a shareholder of Meyers Parking Systems; he brought a shareholder's derivative suit challenging transactions between Meyers and one of its directors, Fink, who owns 47% of its stock. Meyers's board approved an employment contract for Fink, 75 years old, for $150,000 a year plus an override on profits; on termination Fink was to receive at least $100,000 a year for life; Fink was to devote substantially all of his time to the business. Also, Meyers made $225,000 in interest- free loans to Fink. P alleged there was no business purpose and a waste of corporate assets in these transactions. P did not make a demand on the board before bringing the derivative suit because: (i) all directors were named as defendants and they participated in the wrongs; (ii) Fink picked and controlled all directors; and (iii) to bring this action, the defendant directors would have to have the corporation sue themselves. P sought cancellation of the employment contract. The defendant directors bring an interlocutory appeal of a trial court finding for P that no request for action need be made on the board of directors.

Issue. When state law requires that demand on the directors be made prior to bringing a shareholder's derivative suit, will such a demand be excused?

Held. Yes. While the trial court finding for P is reversed, P is given leave to amend his complaint.

- The demand requirement is to ensure that shareholders first pursue intracorporate remedies and to avoid strike suits.

- The issue of the futility of a demand is bound up with the business judgment rule; directors apply it in addressing a demand notice. The business judgment rule can only be claimed by disinterested directors whose conduct meets the rule's standards. The business judgment rule applies in a board's determination of whether to pursue a derivative suit ***and*** whether to terminate one already brought by a shareholder (where demand on the board was excused).

- This case involves the question of when demand is futile and thus excused. The trial court test was whether the allegations in the complaint, when taken to be true, show that there is a reasonable inference that the business judgment rule is not applicable for purposes of a presuit demand. This test means that when director action itself is challenged, demand futility is almost automatic. There must be a better test.

- The test is: Based on the ***particularized*** facts alleged, is there a reasonable doubt that (i) the directors were disinterested and independent, ***and*** (ii) the challenged transaction was the product of a valid exercise of business judgment?

- A ***general claim*** that Fink controls the board and owns 47% of the stock does not support a claim that the directors lack independence. P must allege particularized facts showing the control and showing that entering the contract was a breach of good faith or shows control.

- A bare claim that the defendants would have to sue themselves is also not enough. Particular facts again must be alleged showing lack of director independence or failure to adhere to standards of the business judgment rule.

---

9. Terminating Derivative Suits--

Cuker v. Mikalauskas, 692 A.2d 1042 (Pa. 1997).

Facts. PECO, a publicly traded utility, sold electricity and gas to residential and commercial customers. A 1991 management audit criticized PECO's methods of credit and collection, especially its method of collecting on overdue accounts. Following the audit, a group of PECO's minority shareholders filed a demand on PECO alleging that the officers had damaged the corporation by mismanaging the credit and collection functions. The shareholders demanded that PECO authorize litigation against the officers to recover for the monetary damages sustained by PECO. Less than one month later, a second set of minority shareholders filed suit against PECO's officers and directors alleging the same issues. The nondefendant members of PECO's board created a special litigation committee to investigate the allegations. The special committee consisted of three outside directors who had never been employed by PECO and were not named in either the demand or the lawsuit. After an extensive investigation over many months, the committee prepared a 300-page report in which it concluded that there was no evidence of bad faith, self-dealing, concealment, or other breaches of duty of loyalty by any of the defendant officers. PECO's board reviewed the report, and the 12 nondefendant members voted unanimously to reject the demand, and terminate the lawsuit. However, the Pennsylvania court of common pleas rejected PECO's motion for summary judgment, stating that a corporation lacks power to terminate pending derivative litigation under the business judgment rule. The question was certified to the Pennsylvania Supreme Court.

Issue. Does the business judgment rule permit a board of directors to terminate derivative lawsuits brought by minority shareholders?

Held. Yes. Judgment reversed and case remanded.

- Although this court has not adopted the "business judgment rule," nor used the term in a corporate context, we find that it is the law of Pennsylvania. Under the business judgment rule, an independent board of directors may terminate shareholder derivative actions brought by minority shareholders. What is needed then is a procedural mechanism for implementing this rule, and judicial review of the board's decision.

- A court must examine the circumstances surrounding a board's decision to terminate litigation in order to determine if the conditions warrant application of the business judgment rule. Factors to be considered include whether the board or its special committee was disinterested, whether it was assisted by counsel, whether it prepared a written report, whether it was independent, whether it conducted an adequate investigation, and whether it rationally believed its decision was in the best interests of the corporation. If all of these criteria are satisfied, the business judgment rule applies and the court should dismiss the action.

- We believe that the lower courts need specific guidance on how to manage these cases. Therefore, we specifically adopt sections 7.02-7.10 and section 7.13 of the American Law Institute's Principles relating to derivative actions. These sections set forth the considerations and procedures we outline in this decision.

XII. DUTY OF LOYALTY AND CONFLICT OF INTEREST

A. SELF-DEALING

1. **Introduction.** The officers and directors owe a duty of loyalty to the corporation. This means that the directors must place the interests of the corporation above their own personal gain. Problems arise because directors have other business involvements, and it is often for this reason that they are placed on the board. Therefore, no rule of law that prevents a corporation from dealing with its own directors is feasible, but it is difficult to develop rules that properly circumscribe these dealings.

2. **Contracts of Interested or Interlocking Directors.**

   a. **Introduction.** Over time, there has been an evolution in the rules applied by the courts.

   b. **Early rule.** The early common law rule was that any contract between a director and his corporation, whether fair or not, was voidable. This rule applied not only to individual contracts with directors, but also to the situation of interlocking directorates (two or more corporations having common directors). It was even applied to the situation where one corporation owned the majority of the stock of another and appointed its directors (parent-subsidiary relationship).

   c. **Disinterested majority rule.** Later the courts began to hold (and many still do) that conflict of interest dealings were voidable only when the director had not made a full and complete disclosure of the transaction (its value, his interest, profit, etc.) to an "independent board" (quorum of noninterested directors), or the transaction was shown to be unfair and unreasonable to the corporation. The burden of proof as to the fairness of the transaction was on the director.

   d. **The liberal rule.** Many courts now hold that it makes no difference whether the board is disinterested or not. The issue is whether the transaction is fair to the corporation. Part of "fairness" is that the director's interest be fully disclosed, however. When the board is not disinterested, the contract will be given very close scrutiny.

   e. **State statutes.** Many states have adopted statutes that combine elements from all of the previous judicial positions.

      1) **Intrinsic fairness test--**

Marciano v. Nakash, 535 A.2d 400 (Del. 1987).

Facts. The Marcianos owned 50% of Gasoline, Ltd., and the Nakashs were the officers and owned 50%; the board was evenly divided and deadlocked. The Nakashs, through corporations they owned, loaned the corporation $2.5 million; the loans were not approved by a majority of the directors or shareholders. Finally, the corporation was placed under the court's custody to be liquidated because of the deadlock. The Marcianos claimed that the loans should be invalidated since they were made by interested directors. The lower court approved the loans as valid liquidation claims since the loans were "fair." The Marcianos appeal.

Issue. Is the intrinsic fairness test the appropriate standard for reviewing transactions made by interested directors?

Held. Yes. Judgment affirmed.

- The common law rule was that transactions approved by interested directors were voidable, unless ratified by disinterested shareholders.

- Delaware subsequently passed section 144 of the corporation law, which provides several situations where interested transactions can be validated. None of these situations applies here.

- In addition, Delaware courts have also held that interested director transactions may be approved by the courts if such transactions are "intrinsically fair" (considering the effect of the transaction on the corporation and its shareholders, the motives of the directors, and other factors).

- These loans represent a situation in which the intrinsic fairness test is relevant; due to the shareholders' deadlock, there could be no ratification. Due to the directors' deadlock, approval of any corporate action was destined to be interested. Thus, transactions should be approved based on their intrinsic fairness.

3. **Executive Compensation.** The issue of compensation involves both directors and officers. The most frequently used rationales for attacking executive compensation are (i) that self-dealing is involved; (ii) that retroactive payments without a prior agreement are invalid as being without consideration; and (iii) that compensation is excessive and results in corporate waste.

    a. **Closely held businesses.** The issues are somewhat different with close corporations than with public companies. In a close corporation the shareholders (also directors and officers) normally will try to take all of their compensation as salary for tax reasons (salary is deductible to the corporation and is only taxed once to the shareholders, whereas dividends are taxed twice—once as corporate earnings and the second time in the hands of the shareholder as a dividend).

1) **Tax rules.** The issue for tax purposes is whether the salary is "reasonable." Factors such as the size of the company, the position of the person, and the salaries for comparable companies in the industry are looked at. When compensation is attacked in a shareholder action, these same factors also are looked at.

2) **Authorization.** It is also important whether the executive has had his compensation properly authorized (by an independent board and perhaps by shareholders). Thus, the issues of whether the board is interested, etc., are raised in this area as well.

3) **Typical forms of compensation.**

a) Salary.

b) Bonuses.

c) Stock plans (options, etc.).

d) Deferred compensation (cash payments to be made after the employee retires, etc.).

e) Pension or profit-sharing retirement plans.

f) Fringe benefits.

b. **Publicly held corporations.** Publicly held corporations have problems similar to those of closely held corporations, except that ratification (as by the board of directors) is less likely to be by "interested" groups. Also, a greater variety of compensation plans is used in the public company context.

1) **Must prove waste--**

Heller v. Boylan, 29 N.Y.S.2d 653 (1941).

Facts. In 1912, the shareholders of American Tobacco Company adopted a bylaw providing for an incentive compensation system whereby the president and the vice presidents divided 10% of the company's annual profits over the earnings from comparable company properties held in 1910. This system occasioned salaries and bonuses totaling $15,457,919 for 1929 through 1939 for the six officers. This is a shareholder's derivative suit brought by seven out of the company's 62,000 shareholders (the seven owning 1,000 out of a total of over 5 million shares), protesting these payments as waste and spoliation of corporate property (in that they bore no reasonable relationship to the value of the services for which they were given) by the majority shareholders. The bylaws had been ratified twice, in 1933 and 1940, and had been held valid by the court on a prior occasion.

Issue. Did the huge bonus payments to the president and vice presidents mandated by the shareholder-adopted bylaw amount to waste or spoliation of corporate assets to the detriment of minority shareholders?

Held. No.

- Although the sums are large, the shareholders adopted the bylaw and have ratified it, so the court will not replace the shareholder's judgment with its own.

- If a bonus payment bears no reasonable relationship to the value of services for which it is given, then the majority shareholders cannot give it, since to do so is waste and adversely affects the minority shareholders. But there must be proof of waste (beyond the mere amount of the payments, as here). Since the plaintiff has entered no such proof, the court will not substitute its judgment for that of the shareholders.

2) **Excessive compensation and severance benefits--**

Brehm v. Eisner, 746 A.2d 244 (Del. 2000).

Facts. The Walt Disney Company hired Ovitz as its president in October of 1995. The 1995 board of directors approved a lucrative five-year compensation package consisting of an annual salary of $1 million, along with a bonus and stock options. The contract also contained a generous severance package in the event that Ovitz left Disney's employment before the five-year term and it was not his fault. Shortly after Ovitz began work, problems with his performance arose. The situation deteriorated over the first year, and in December of 1996, Disney's chairman, Eisner, agreed to allow Ovitz to terminate his contract under the non-fault basis provided by the employment agreement. The 1996 board of directors voted to approve the non-fault termination of the agreement. The severance package agreed to by the board was valued at over $140 million. Certain Disney shareholders (Ps) filed this derivative suit alleging that the 1995 board of directors breached its fiduciary duty in approving an excessive and wasteful employment agreement with Ovitz, and that the 1996 board of directors breached its fiduciary duty in approving the nonfault termination of the employment agreement. The lower court dismissed the complaint and Ps appeal.

Issues.

(i) Did the 1995 board of directors breach its fiduciary duty by failing to properly inform itself of the terms of the employment agreement before approving it?

(ii) Did the 1996 board breach its fiduciary duty by approving the non-fault termination of the employment agreement?

Held. (i) No. (ii) No. Judgment affirmed.

- ♦ The record indicates that the board relied on a corporate compensation expert in evaluating the employment contract. The fact that the expert did not quantify the potential severance benefits to Ovitz in the event of non-fault termination does not create a reasonable inference that the board failed to consider the potential cost to Disney in the event of early termination of the contract. The standard for judging the informational component of the board's decision does not require that it be informed of every fact. The board is only required to be ***reasonably*** informed. In this case, although the board did not calculate the exact amount of the payout, it was fully informed about the manner in which such a payout would be calculated. The 1995 board relied on an expert's opinion, and is entitled to the presumption that it exercised proper business judgment in so relying. Ps have produced no evidence to indicate the reliance was not in good faith, or that the expert was not selected with due care.

- ♦ Disney and Ovitz negotiated for the severance payment, and the board considered, using its business judgment, the value of the contract against the value of this particular employee to the company. At the time the contract was negotiated, other companies were interested in hiring Ovitz for high-level executive positions with attractive compensation packages. A board's decision on executive compensation is entitled to great deference. It is the essence of business judgment for a board to determine if a particular individual warrants high compensation, and the court will not apply 20/20 hindsight to second guess the board's opinion except in rare cases when a transaction is so egregious on its face that the board's approval cannot meet the business judgment test. This is not that rare case.

- ♦ Nor can we find that the 1996 board committed waste in approving termination of the employment contract on a non-fault basis. The terms of the agreement limit good cause for termination to gross negligence or malfeasance. While Orvitz may not have put forth his best efforts during his employment at Disney, we cannot find evidence of conduct rising to the level of gross negligence or malfeasance. The complaint fails on its face to meet the waste test because it does not allege with particularity facts tending to show that no reasonable businessperson would have made the decision the 1996 board made in approving the non-fault severance package.

---

4. **Obligation of Majority Shareholders to Minority.** Shareholders are not free in every instance to cast their votes as they want to. They have responsibilities in some cases (just as directors and officers have a duty of loyalty) to the other shareholders. For example, a shareholder cannot sell his vote (*i.e.,* accept a cash bribe for voting his shares in a certain way). And a majority vote is not always effective when it is "unfair" to the minority shareholders.

a. **Duty of loyalty and good faith.** In effect, the majority shareholder(s) have a fiduciary relationship to the corporation and the minority shareholders. This duty is manifest in several circumstances.

1) For example, if a majority shareholder deals with the corporation (such as in a contractual relationship), the transaction will be closely scrutinized to see that minority shareholders are treated fairly. An example would be the situation in which a corporation loans a majority shareholder money.

2) In addition, if the majority has the voting power to effectuate a corporate transaction, the effect on minority shareholders may be reviewed by the courts to see that the majority acted in "good faith" and not to the specific detriment of the minority shareholders.

b. **Subsidiary relationship--**

Sinclair Oil Corp. v. Levien, 280 A.2d 717 (Del. 1971).

Facts. Sinclair Oil (D) owned 97% of the stock of a subsidiary involved in the crude oil business in South America; D appointed all of the subsidiary's board members and officers. Then over six years D drained off dividends from the subsidiary to meet its own needs for cash. The dividends paid met the limitations of state law, but exceeded the current earnings of the same period. Levien (P), a shareholder of the subsidiary, filed a derivative suit, charging that the dividend payments limited the subsidiary's ability to grow; also, that in a contract between D and the subsidiary for the purchase of crude oil, D had failed to pay on time and had not purchased the minimum amounts as required by the contract.

Issue. Is the intrinsic fairness test the appropriate standard to define the fiduciary duty of the parent corporation to its controlled subsidiary?

Held. Yes. Judgment for D on the dividend and expansion questions; judgment for P on the breach of contract issue.

- ♦ When there is self-dealing, the intrinsic fairness test must be applied, which puts the burden on the majority shareholder to show that the transaction with the subsidiary was objectively fair. On the dividend issue there was no self-dealing (since the parent did not receive something from the subsidiary to the exclusion or detriment of the minority shareholders; they shared pro rata in the dividend distributions). On the expansion issue, D did not usurp any opportunities that would normally have gone to the subsidiary. Thus, the business judgment rule applies; the court will not disturb a transaction under this rule unless there is a showing of gross overreaching, which there was not.

- ♦ However, D did make its payments under a crude oil contract with the subsidiary on a late basis and failed to purchase the required minimum amounts of crude oil.

Comment. This case is confusing. The court should have decided on one standard to apply in situations of transactions where the majority controls the corporation. If the standard is the intrinsic unfairness test, then one element is self-dealing. Where it is absent, there is no violation.

---

c. **Burden of showing unfairness--**

Weinberger v. UOP, Inc., 457 A.2d 701 (Del. 1983).

Facts. Weinberger (P) was a former shareholder of UOP (D). He sued to challenge a cash-out of minority shareholders and then a merger between UOP and its majority shareholder, Signal (D), which eliminated UOP's minority shareholders. Several years earlier, Signal had acquired 50.5% of UOP's stock in a friendly transaction. Signal then elected six of UOP's 13 directors. Five of these six were either directors or employees of Signal. When UOP's chief executive officer retired, Signal caused him to be replaced by Crawford, an officer of one of Signal's subsidiaries. Crawford was made a director of both UOP and Signal.

Signal then turned its attention toward acquiring UOP's outstanding shares. Two of Signal's officers and directors, who were also on UOP's board, conducted a feasibility study. The study concluded that acquisition of UOP's stock at a price of up to $24 per share would be a good investment. Signal's executive committee met with Crawford, and the price of $21 per share was discussed. Crawford termed that price "generous," and a consensus that a $20-$21 price would be fair was reached.

The proposal was publicly announced, UOP's outside (non-Signal) directors were informed, and Crawford retained UOP's investment banker to render a fairness opinion as to the price offered. The study was conducted in less than a week, and the fairness opinion letter was typed either immediately prior to or during Signal and UOP's board meeting where it was discussed. The $21 per share price was inserted in the letter's final draft just before it was typed, after being hastily examined by the person in charge of the project.

The two boards met simultaneously and were hooked up to each other by telephone. Signal adopted a resolution authorizing it to propose to UOP a cash merger of $21 per share. The feasibility study, which had suggested a higher price, was not discussed. UOP's outside directors voted to accept Signal's offer.

The merger was then submitted to UOP's shareholders at their annual meeting. Again, the feasibility study was not disclosed, nor was the hurried method by which the fairness opinion was reached. UOP's shareholders overwhelmingly voted to approve the merger. At trial, on the suit brought by P, the court ruled that the terms of the merger were fair and entered judgment in favor of Ds. P appeals.

Issue. Was the minority shareholder vote an informed one, thus requiring P to bear the burden of showing that the transaction was unfair to the minority?

Held. No. Judgment reversed and case remanded for further proceedings.

- Although the majority shareholder bears the ultimate burden of showing that a cash-out merger is fair, P must first show some basis for invoking the fairness doctrine. The burden shifts to P when the action has been approved by an informed vote of the minority. If the vote was not an informed one, the test of fairness has not been met and the burden remains with the majority shareholder.

- All aspects of the fairness issue must be examined as a whole. The concept has two elements: Fair dealing and fair price. In this case, there is reversible error as to both.

- Fair dealing requires candor between the parties to a transaction. This is especially true when one holds dual directorships, as here. Those Signal directors who also served on UOP's board owed a fiduciary duty to UOP's shareholders. They were obliged to disclose the information contained in the feasibility study and the circumstances surrounding the preparation of the fairness opinion. UOP's shareholders were denied critical information; their vote was not an informed one and was meaningless.

- Delaware courts have used the "weighted average" method to determine a fair price for stock. This narrow method is outmoded, and we now adopt a more liberal approach. All relevant factors involving the value of a company are to be considered. Elements of future value that are known or susceptible of proof as of the date of the merger may be taken into account, along with elements of rescission damages. Only the speculative effects of the merger may not be considered. Thus, the trial court is given broad discretion to fashion the financial remedy available to the minority in a cash-out merger.

B. CORPORATE OPPORTUNITIES AND OTHER DUTIES TO THE CORPORATION

1. **Corporate Opportunities.** The duty of loyalty of directors and officers to the corporation prevents them from taking opportunities for themselves that should belong to the corporation.

   a. **Use of corporate property.** For example, clearly a director may not use corporate property or assets to develop his own business or for other personal uses.

   b. **Corporate expectancies.** Furthermore, a director or officer may not assume for himself properties or interests in which the corporation is "interested," or in which the corporation can be said to have a tangible "expectancy," or ones that are important to the corporation's business or purposes.

1) For example, if the corporation has leased a piece of property, a director cannot buy the property for himself. And if it is "reasonably foreseeable" that the corporation would be interested in the property, then there is the necessary expectancy. When opportunities relate very closely to the business of the corporation, there is also the necessary expectancy.

c. **"Line of business" test rejected--**

Northeast Harbor Golf Club, Inc. v. Harris, 661 A.2d 1146 (Me. 1995).

Facts. Harris (D) was the president of Northeast Harbor Golf Club, Inc. (P) for almost 20 years. P also had a board of directors responsible for making and approving policy decisions. P owned real estate on part of which it operated a golf course. P's board occasionally discussed developing the surrounding real estate to raise funds, but never took any steps to do so. In 1985, D purchased some property abutting the golf course, known as the Gilpin property, in her own name. She did not disclose her intention to purchase the property to the board of P prior to the purchase, but informed the board at its annual meeting months later and indicated that she had no plans to develop the property at that time. The board took no action in response to the purchase. Several years later, D purchased another parcel of property abutting the golf course known as the Smallidge property. Again, she formally disclosed the purchase to the board at the annual meeting months afterward, and indicated she had no present plans to develop the property. In 1988, D began obtaining approval for a housing subdivision on the Gilpin property. The board learned of the proposed subdivision and took no action. Two years later, D was asked to resign as president and did so. The board then filed suit against D, alleging that she breached her fiduciary duty to act in the best interests of the corporation by purchasing the lots without providing notice and an opportunity for P to purchase the property, and by subdividing the lots for development. The board simultaneously resolved that the proposed development was contrary to the best interests of the corporation. The trial court held for D, finding that the real estate opportunity was not in P's "line of business." P appeals.

Issue. Is the "line of business" test the best way to analyze corporate opportunity doctrine cases?

Held. No. Judgment vacated.

♦ This case requires us to define the scope of the corporate opportunity doctrine in the state of Maine. The trial court applied a test known as the "line of business" test outlined in *Guth v. Loft, Inc.,* 5 A.2d 503 (Del. 1939). Under that test, a corporate officer or director may not take for himself an opportunity that the corporation is financially able to undertake, and which is "from its nature, in the line of the corporation's business and is of practical advantage to it, is one in which the corporation has an interest or a reasonable expectancy, and, by embracing the opportunity, the self-interest of the officer or director will be brought into direct conflict with that of his corporation." Applying the *Guth* line of business test, the trial court found that real estate acquisition and development was not in P's line of business. In addition, the court found that P lacked the financial ability to purchase either property. The court also emphasized D's good faith as evidenced by her long and dedicated history of service to P.

- While we agree with the court's analysis under this test, we find the line of business test itself flawed in several aspects. First, the question of whether a particular activity is within a corporation's line of business is conceptually difficult to answer. In this case, P had made a policy judgment that development of property surrounding the golf course was detrimental to the best interests of the club. Therefore, purchasing the surrounding land with the intention of insulating the club from future development would have enhanced the ability of the club to implement that policy. Second, considering the financial ability of the corporation to take advantage of the opportunity may unfairly favor an inside director who has control of the facts relating to corporate finances.

- Other courts have combined the "line of business" test with a "fairness" test that requires consideration of the circumstances and ethics of the situation. [*See* Miller v. Miller, 207 N.W.2d 71 (Minn. 1984)] However, we find that this test only complicates the issue.

- The American Law Institute ("ALI") has recently developed a disclosure-oriented rule, which we adopt here. The ALI rule states in part that a director or senior executive "may not take advantage of a corporate opportunity unless: (1) The director or senior executive first offers the corporate opportunity to the corporation and makes disclosure concerning the conflict of interest and the corporate opportunity; (2) The corporate opportunity is rejected by the corporation; and (3) Either: (A) The rejection of the opportunity is fair to the corporation; (B) The opportunity is rejected in advance, following such disclosure, by disinterested directors, or, in the case of a senior executive who is not a director, by a disinterested superior, in a manner that satisfies the business judgment rule; or (C) The rejection is authorized in advance or ratified, following such disclosure, by disinterested shareholders, and the rejection is not equivalent to a waste of corporate assets."

- The central feature of the ALI test is the strict requirement of full disclosure. Under this standard, P has the burden to show that the opportunity is a corporate opportunity, and that D did not offer it to P or that P did not reject it properly. If P did not reject the opportunity properly, then D may defend her actions on the basis that her taking the opportunity was fair to the corporation. But if she failed to offer the opportunity at all, she may not defend on this basis.

- ♦ We find the ALI test to be superior to its predecessors and adopt it here. We therefore vacate the judgment of the trial court and remand the case for consideration of the issues under the ALI test.

Comment. Upon remand, the trial court held that both the Gilpin and Smallidge properties were corporate opportunities, and that D breached her fiduciary obligations by not offering them to the club's board. However, by that time, the six-year statute of limitations had run.

---

2. **Defenses to the Charge of Usurping a Corporate Opportunity.**

   a. **Individual capacity.** Defendants may claim that the opportunity was presented to them in their individual capacities, and not as fiduciaries of the corporation.

   b. **Corporation unable to take advantage of the opportunity.** The law is that an officer or director may take advantage of a corporate opportunity when it is disclosed to the corporation first and the corporation is unable to take advantage of it.

   c. **Corporation refuses the opportunity.** If the corporation, by independent directors or shareholders, turns down an opportunity, fiduciaries may take advantage of the opportunity.

3. **Remedies.** If the fiduciary has usurped a corporate opportunity, the corporation has the following remedies:

   a. **Damages.** When the opportunity has been resold, the profits made by the fiduciary may be recovered by the corporation.

   b. **Constructive trust.** The corporation may force the fiduciary to convey the property to the corporation at the fiduciary's cost.

4. **Competition with the Corporation.** Another area of conflict of interest arises when a director or officer enters into competition with the corporation.

   a. **Use of corporate assets, property, trade secrets, etc.** Clearly a fiduciary may not use corporate assets, property, materials, trade secrets, etc., to form a competing business.

   b. **Formation of a competing business.** However, a fiduciary (without using corporate assets) may leave the corporation and form a competing business. In some instances the conduct of the fiduciary while still with the corporation and preparing to leave to form the new business is questioned.

5. **Duty of Impartiality.** Directors must act in the best interests of the corporation as a whole and without partiality to any particular group of shareholders.

XIII. TRANSACTIONS IN SHARES: RULE 10b-5, INSIDER TRADING, AND SECURITIES FRAUD

A. PURCHASES OF SHARES FROM INDIVIDUAL HOLDERS AND SALES BY "INSIDERS"

1. **The Problem.** The typical problem involves the situation in which someone related to the corporation (such as an officer, a director, or a shareholder owning a large amount of stock) is in a position to have inside information about how the corporation is doing, and hence, what the corporation's stock is or will be worth. This person ("insider") then buys stock (with an advantage over the seller) or sells it (with an advantage over the buyer). The issue concerns what duty the corporate "insider" may owe to the other party.

2. **Common Law Approach.** The majority of jurisdictions held that directors and officers owed no special duty to present or prospective shareholders and could deal with them at arm's length, with no duty of disclosure of inside information required.

   a. **Majority rule.** A majority of courts have held that directors or officers have no duty to disclose information to an outsider when stocks are traded in an anonymous transaction on a stock exchange. [*See* Goodwin v. Agassiz, 186 N.E. 659 (Mass. 1933)] In *Goodwin v. Agassiz,* a director of a mining company purchased stock from a shareholder in an anonymous transaction on the Boston Stock Exchange prior to the release of information about the company that raised the price of the corporation's stock. The director was aware of the information at the time of the transaction, but the court held that he owed no duty to disclose it to the shareholder.

   b. **Minority rule.** The minority of jurisdictions held that directors or officers had a fiduciary duty to disclose facts to an outsider. For example, in *Hotchkiss v. Fischer,* 16 P.2d 531 (Kan. 1932), a widow shareholder asked a director before a board meeting whether the company was going to pay a dividend; he showed her financial statements and told her he did not know. He then bought her stock for $1.25 a share. The board declared $1 a share dividend three days later. The director was held liable.

   c. **Special circumstances rule.** A number of courts took the position that a duty of disclosure is owed only if there are special facts or circumstances making nondisclosure unfair. For example, in *Strong v. Repide,* 213 U.S. 419 (1909), a director, president, and 75% shareholder used a straw figure to purchase a minority interest, knowing that the United States government was going to buy company property. Here, the Court held that the defendant had a duty of disclosure.

3. **Modern Approach Under State Law.** State courts are beginning to follow the federal securities laws and outline an additional duty of loyalty of corporate fiduciaries—that of not using "inside information" available to them as fiduciaries in dealing with "outsiders."

B. DEVELOPMENT OF FEDERAL CORPORATION LAW: RELATING PRIMARILY TO INSIDERS

1. **Introduction.** Two sections of the Securities Exchange Act of 1934 deal with purchases and sales by insiders (section 10(b) and Rule 10b-5, and section 16).

2. **Section 10(b) and Rule 10b-5.** Rule 10b-5 makes it unlawful, in connection with the purchase or sale of any security, for any person, directly or indirectly by the use of any means or instrumentality of interstate commerce, or of the mails, or of any facility of any national securities exchange, to:

   (i) Employ any device, scheme, or artifice to defraud;

   (ii) Make any untrue statement of a material fact or to omit to state a material fact necessary in order to make the statements made, in the light of the circumstances under which they were made, not misleading; or

   (iii) Engage in any act, practice, or course of business conduct that operates or would operate as a fraud or deceit upon any person.

   a. **Transactions covered by Rule 10b-5.**

      1) **Purchases and sales.** Rule 10b-5 applies to both purchases and sales in all contexts.

      2) **Remedies.**

         a) **Private right of action.** The rule does not specifically give a private right of action, but the courts have implied such a cause of action. [*See* Kardon v. National Gypsum Co., 73 F. Supp. 798 (E.D. Pa. 1947)] Thus, a private party may bring an action for an injunction, for damages, or for rescission.

         b) **Actions by the S.E.C.** The S.E.C. may sue to enjoin fraudulent acts, or for other appropriate remedies.

      3) **Securities.** A "security" must be involved. The term is broadly defined. Note that the rule applies to all types of securities transactions (those on an exchange, etc.).

4) **Jurisdiction.** Interstate commerce must be involved (some means of interstate commerce must be used).

5) **Statute of limitations.** There is no specific statute of limitations; courts refer to the statute of a relevant state.

6) **Liable parties.** The rule is extremely broad in its application. It applies to "any person" that is "connected with" a securities transaction. Thus, accountants, lawyers, and others involved in some way with a securities transaction may be held liable.

b. **Elements of a Rule 10b-5 cause of action.**

1) **Misrepresentation, fraud, or deception.** Rule 10b-5 requires that there be some misrepresentation, omission, or other deception in connection with the purchase or sale of securities. An issue has arisen in several contexts as to whether there has actually been such a "deception."

a) **Situations in which no one may have been deceived.** The first context in which the issue has arisen occurs when no one may have been deceived by the "fraud."

(1) **When all corporate directors are involved in the deception.** The cases have held that even when all the directors of a corporation are involved in perpetrating the deception there may still be a "fraud" on the corporation and its shareholders. [*See* Hooper v. Mountain States Securities Corp., 282 F.2d 105 (5th Cir. 1960), *cert. denied*, 365 U.S. 814 (1961)]

(2) **Fraud by all of the promoters, directors, and all present shareholders.** There is also authority for the proposition that even when all of the directors and all of the shareholders of the corporation are involved in the fraud, the corporation may still recover for the fraud. These situations occur when a corporation is initially being formed and all parties relating to the corporation are part of the fraudulent scheme. [*See* Bailes v. Colonial Press, 444 F.2d 1241 (5th Cir. 1971)]

b) **Sufficient connection.** The language of Rule 10b-5 requires that a defendant's fraud, misrepresentation, or omission must be "in connection with" the purchase or sale of a security by the plaintiff. The issue is whether the fraud or deception is so remote from the plaintiff's purchase or sale transaction as to snap the necessary "connection."

(1) **Fraud as part of the securities sales transaction.** The fraud may occur as part of the securities sales transaction itself. For example, A sells to B, having inside material information that he does not disclose to B. It is clear in these cases that a sufficient connection exists.

(2) **Fraud separate from the actual sales transaction.** The more difficult cases are those in which a defendant's fraud is not directly related to the securities transaction itself. Thus, the issue is whether there is a sufficient connection.

c) **Breach of fiduciary duties as "fraud."** Federal courts have split on the question of whether a breach of fiduciary duty under state corporate law (*e.g.,* breach of the directors' duty of loyalty or of due care) is a sufficient "fraud" for Rule 10b-5 purposes. But the trend of opinions is now ***against*** finding a Rule 10b-5 cause of action.

(1) **Cause of action permitted.** Some decisions can be read as permitting a 10b-5 cause of action even though a state cause of action for breach of fiduciary duty is also available. For example, a 10b-5 cause of action has been allowed in situations in which a corporation (and its directors) issued stock for inadequate consideration—a breach of fiduciary duty under state law. [*See* Hooper v. Mountain States Securities Corp., *supra*]

(2) **Cause of action denied.** Other decisions have held that no cause of action is available under Rule 10b-5 when state law provides an adequate remedy. For example, Rule 10b-5 has been held not to cover a cause of action for diversion and misuse of corporate assets by management, traditionally within the province of state law. [Mutual Shares Corp. v. Genesco, Inc., 384 F.2d 540 (2d Cir. 1967)]

2) **Purchase or sale requirement.**

a) **Definition of "purchase" and "sale."** Rule 10b-5 expressly covers only the "purchase" or "sale" of a security. "Purchase" and "sale" are defined to include "any contract" to purchase or sell. This suggests that something beyond a mere offer to purchase must be involved before Rule 10b-5 applies.

b) **Purchase or sale by the defendant.** Clearly the defendant's fraudulent activity must be in connection with the purchase or sale of a security.

(1) **Actual purchase or sale.** Formerly, there was some indication that the defendant had to actually be involved in the purchase or sale of the securities (such as by trading in the market). But *S.E.C. v. Texas Gulf Sulphur Co., infra,* indicated that the defendant could be held liable, without itself purchasing or selling the securities, as long as the defendant's activity was "in connection with" the purchase and sale of a security (here the defendant corporation was held for a misleading press release that might have caused reasonable investors to rely thereon in the purchase or sale of the company's securities).

(2) **Aiders and abettors.** Even when the idea was prominent that a defendant had to actually be the purchaser or seller, liability was held to extend to those found to have aided or abetted the defendant.

c) **Purchase or sale by the plaintiff.** In most situations the courts have required that the plaintiff either be an actual "purchaser" or "seller" in order to have standing to maintain a Rule 10b-5 cause of action. The issue can arise in several contexts. The Supreme Court has held that a plaintiff who is not an actual purchaser or seller does not have standing to sue ***even if fraud prevented the plaintiff from purchasing shares***. [*See* Blue Chip Stamps v. Manor Drug Stores, 421 U.S. 723] In *Blue Chip Stamps*, Blue Chip was subject to an antitrust consent decree requiring it to offer a substantial number of its shares to retailers who have used its stamp service. Two years after the offering, Manor Drug Store, one of the nonpurchasing offerees, sued under Rule 10b-5 on the basis that the prospectus was overly negative, so that Manor did not purchase, allowing Blue Chip to then offer the shares to the public at a higher price. The Court refused to expand Rule 10b-5 to cover such a situation, explaining that it would be too easy for a plaintiff to simply testify "I would have purchased," without any supporting evidence. An actual transaction must take place.

3) **Scienter.** A major issue in actions brought under Rule 10b-5 concerns the standard of care a defendant will be held to in a securities transaction. Historically, various jurisdictions have disagreed about what the standard should be (intentional conduct vs. negligence, etc.). The issue has now been resolved by the Supreme Court, which has held that for liability to exist under Rule 10b-5, it must be shown that the defendant has "scienter" (*i.e.,* actual intent to deceive, manipulate, or defraud). [*See* Ernst & Ernst v. Hochfelder, 425 U.S. 185 (1976)] In *Ernst*, an accounting firm, Ernst & Ernst,

failed to discover that the president of a firm it audited was embezzling client funds. The clients of the firm sued alleging that if Ernst had not been negligent in its audit, it would have discovered the president's fraud, and that through its negligence, Ernst aided and abetted the perpetration of a fraud. The Supreme Court held that Rule 10b-5 does not apply when the defendant has been negligently nonfeasant in performing its duties. A plaintiff must show intentional conduct.

a) **Recklessness sufficient.** Note that some lower courts have found defendants liable under Rule 10b-5 on the basis of reckless conduct.

b) **Rule 10b-5 inapplicable when state law remedy is adequate.** Rule 10b-5 was not meant to regulate all forms of corporate mismanagement—an area traditionally covered by state law. It was meant to control only the securities markets and fraud in the purchase and sale of securities, primarily in situations in which there has been an affirmative misrepresentation or omission of material facts. Courts will normally find Rule 10b-5 inapplicable when there is an adequate state law remedy available. This was the case in *Santa Fe Industries v. Green*, 430 U.S. 462 (1997). Santa Fe Industries owned more than 90% of the stock of a subsidiary corporation. Wishing to eliminate the minority shareholders of the subsidiary, Santa Fe used a Delaware short-form merger statute to merge the subsidiary corporation, paying cash to the minority shareholders. The minority shareholders sued in federal court to enjoin the merger or for damages under Rule 10b-5, which they alleged was violated because there was no business purpose for the merger other than to freeze out minority shareholders, and because a grossly inadequate price was offered for their stock. The Supreme Court noted that the transaction was permitted by state law, there was full disclosure of the facts to the shareholders, and no misrepresentations were made. Moreover, the minority shareholders had an adequate state remedy for the wrong alleged in the complaint in that state law provided for court appraisal of the fair market value of their shares. Therefore, Rule 10b-5 did not apply. Rule 10b-5 may still apply in other situations in which the court considers the available state law remedies inadequate. It also seems clear that based on *Green* (at a minimum in the future), all plaintiffs who wish to state a Rule 10b-5 cause of action will attempt to show that there has been a material misrepresentation or omission of fact, whatever other fraud or deception might be present.

c) Scienter inferred from pattern of conduct--

In re Enron Corporation Securities, Derivative & ERISA Litigation, 235 F. Supp. 2d 549 (S.D. Tex. 2002).

Facts. Following the collapse of Enron Corporation, a class action lawsuit was filed on behalf of purchasers of Enron's publicly traded securities from October 19, 1998 through November 27, 2001. The lawsuit named as defendants several banks and investment companies, several of Enron's top level executives, as well as Vinson & Elkins (Enron's outside counsel), Citigroup (Enron's lead underwriter), and Arthur Andersen (Enron's accountants/auditors) (Ds). Members of the class (Ps) alleged that Ds are liable for making false statements, or failing to disclose adverse facts while selling Enron securities and/or participating in a scheme to defraud or a course of business that operated as a fraud or deceit on purchasers of Enron's securities during the specified time period. The complaint alleged that Ds engaged in an enormous Ponzi scheme using non-arm's length transactions with Enron-controlled entities and accounting tricks that violated Generally Accepted Accounting Principles ("GAAP") in order to inflate Enron's reported revenues and profits, conceal its growing debts, maintain its artificially high stock price and investment grade credit rating, and allow the individual defendants to personally enrich themselves by looting the corporation. Ds also caused Enron to present materially misleading statements in its financial statements, press releases, S.E.C. filings, and prospectuses. Ds moved to dismiss the action, arguing that the complaint contained only undifferentiated, boilerplate allegations repetitively applied to each defendant, and did not adequately state a claim with specificity under section 10(b).

Issue. Does the complaint sufficiently state claims under section 10(b) and Rule 10b-5?

Held. Yes. Motion to dismiss denied.

- We must examine the complaint's allegations against each specific defendant to determine whether it states a claim with specificity under section 10(b) and raises a strong inference of the requisite scienter that would warrant denial of this motion to dismiss. Viewing all of the allegations together, we find that the complaint raises a strong inference of the scienter required to state an action under section 10(b). We find that the scienter pleading requirement is partially satisfied by the allegation of a regular pattern of conduct involving the creation of unlawful, Enron-controlled partnership entities, the sale of unwanted Enron assets to these entities in transactions that were clearly not made at arm's length, in order to shift debt from Enron's balance sheet and shift sham profits onto its books at critical times, such as when quarterly or annual reports were due to the S.E.C. We note that many of these transactions were undone once the reports had been made. Ps' complaint also effectively pleads the common motive of obsession with monetary gain. It alleges that extraordinary fees and interest rates were pocketed by the cooperating Ds, and this only expanded the mirage of corporate success they fraudulently created.

- Viewing the allegations together, we find that Ps have stated a claim against Citigroup and the other banks as violators of section 10(b) and Rule 10b-5 because they knowingly, or at least recklessly, made material misrepresentations that operated as a fraud or deceit upon Enron investors through their disguised loans to Enron in the amount of $2.4 billion. The complaint alleges that Citigroup and the other banks involved advanced funds to the company at key times to allow them to complete bogus transactions just before year- or quarter-end in order to create false profits and conceal billions of dollars of debt. The banks also disguised billions of dollars in loans to Enron as sales transactions. Citigroup allegedly made false and misleading statements in the Registration Statements and Prospectuses for Enron securities sales for which it was an underwriter, and issued numerous analysts' reports that included false and misleading information about Enron's financial condition. These actions served to artificially inflate the price of Enron's stock. Citigroup also allegedly helped Enron structure and finance some of the illicit partnerships it used to inflate its earnings and conceal its debt, and engaged in disguised loans that allowed Enron to falsify its financial condition. Citigroup alone earned $70 million per year for its participation in the scheme.

- Enron's outside general counsel, Vinson & Elkins, argues that it merely represented and kept confidential the interests of its client. But the complaint alleges that the law firm participated in writing, reviewing, and approving Enron's S.E.C. filings, shareholder reports, and financial press releases, and in creating the illicit partnerships whose principal purpose was to engage in transactions with Enron and allowed Enron insiders to operate on both sides of the transactions. The attorneys knew that these partnerships were not independent third parties but were manipulative devices designed to take debt off of Enron's books, and to personally enrich the individual defendants. The disclosures the law firm made in S.E.C. filings gave the impression that the transactions with these entities were fair to the company, and made at arm's length. The firm frequently made statements to the public about Enron's financial situation. It made these allegedly fraudulent misrepresentations to potential investors, credit agencies, and banks. The law firm also agreed to overlook accounting irregularities in documents prepared by Arthur Andersen. The firm engaged in these activities in exchange for very lucrative fees. Under the Rules of Professional Conduct, an attorney may not counsel or assist a client in conduct that the lawyer knows is criminal or fraudulent, and when an attorney takes the affirmative step of making statements about a client's financial condition, the attorney does have a duty to third parties not to knowingly or recklessly issue materially misleading statements on which they intend or have reason to expect those third parties to rely. Thus, we find that Ps' complaint adequately states a claim under section 10(b) and Rule 10b-5 against Vinson & Elkins.

- Ps' complaint alleges numerous violations of GAAP committed by Arthur Andersen. Enron was Arthur Andersen's second largest client, and the complaint alleges Andersen earned extremely lucrative fees from its participation in the Enron scheme. As lead auditor, Andersen was privy to the smallest details of

Enron's alleged fraudulent activities. Andersen documents reveal that Andersen knew and was concerned about, but still covered up or ignored, Enron's fraudulent accounting practices and the enormous number of related party transactions that had taken place. Andersen also knew that Enron used at least 600 offshore tax haven entities to shift income, minimize taxation, circumvent United States laws, and maintain secrecy. Andersen's improper accounting practices allowed Enron to conceal over $50 million in debt. The pleaded facts give rise to a strong inference of scienter, and we find Ps have adequately pled a securities fraud claim against Andersen under section 10(b) and Rule 10b-5.

---

4) **Materiality.** The misrepresented or undisclosed fact must be a "material" one. A number of tests of "materiality" have been suggested by the courts.

   a) **Reasonable person standard.** In *List v. Fashion Park, Inc.*, 340 F.2d 457 (2d Cir. 1965), *cert. denied,* 382 U.S. 811 (1965), the court stated that the "basic test of materiality . . . is whether a reasonable man would attach importance (to the misrepresented fact) in determining his choice of action in the (securities) transaction in question."

      (1) In a situation where the impact of a fact is uncertain, it has also been suggested that in applying this materiality test, the probability that the event will occur must be balanced against the magnitude of the event if it did occur. For example, a high-probability, high-magnitude event is clearly material.

      (2) In *S.E.C. v. Texas Gulf Sulphur Co.*, *infra,* the issue was whether the corporation had met its disclosure responsibility concerning a huge potential ore discovery. It had issued a press release that acknowledged drilling operations but hedged as to the possible results (even though the known information was favorable and the magnitude of the potential effect on the company was huge).

   b) **Value of the corporation's securities.** Another test used for materiality is whether the fact in "reasonable contemplation" would affect the value of the corporation's securities. [*See* Kohler v. Kohler, 319 F.2d 634 (7th Cir. 1963)]

   c) **Consider all of the facts.** Under whatever test is used, it is clear that the courts consider all of the facts to determine whether the undisclosed information might reasonably have influenced the plaintiff's conduct.

d) **Examples of material facts.** Examples of material facts include the intention of company management to pay a dividend, or a significant drop in the profit level of the company.

5) **Privity.**

a) **Early view.** The early view was that the plaintiff had to be in privity with the defendant in order to maintain a Rule 10b-5 action.

(1) **Face-to-face transactions.** The early view was developed in cases in which the plaintiff had dealt in a face-to-face manner with the defendant in a securities transaction.

(2) **Transactions over the securities markets.** However, Rule 10b-5 actions began to be brought in securities transactions consummated on the securities exchanges and in the over-the-counter market. Here there are many varied fact situations, but in each instance the buyer does not know who the seller is. For example, A puts a buy order with her broker for 100 shares of XYZ Corporation. The order is executed over a securities exchange, and A never sees the seller.

b) **Later decisions.** Subsequent decisions moved away from requiring privity.

(1) **Affirmative misrepresentations.** Rule 10b-5 has been applied to situations in which there are affirmative misrepresentations made even though there is no privity of contract. For example, in *Mitchell v. Texas Gulf Sulphur Co.*, 446 F.2d 90 (10th Cir. 1971), where the plaintiffs sold their stock in reliance on the defendant corporation's misleading press release, the defendants were held liable even though the plaintiffs could not show that they had bought their stock from the defendants.

(2) **Total nondisclosure.** There has been some speculation by commentators that when material facts are never disclosed, there may be a requirement of some semblance of privity between the plaintiff and the defendant.

6) **Reliance.** "Reliance" is a showing by the plaintiff that she personally actually relied on the material fact that was misrepresented.

a) **Affirmative representations and open-market transactions.** In cases involving situations in which there are affirmative misrepresentations and the plaintiffs purchase or sell securities on the open market, two types of cases arise:

(1) **Actual reliance.** It is possible that a plaintiff could argue that she actually read and relied on the statements made by the defendant. If there is a reliance requirement, this pleading would fulfill it.

(2) **Effect on the market.** The other alternative is for the plaintiff to allege that the defendant's statements affected the market price at which the plaintiff sold her stock. The plaintiff in this situation need not argue that she actually read or relied on the defendant's statements at all.

(a) Class actions have been allowed when no actual proof has been required from each plaintiff in the class of actual reliance. [*See* Green v. Wolf Corp., 406 F.2d 291 (2d Cir. 1968)]

(b) So while there may be no case that specifically dispenses with the reliance requirement in situations of affirmative misrepresentation, there are cases that seem to indicate that a plaintiff whose loss can be shown to have been caused by market factors affected by a defendant's statements can recover without a showing of specific reliance on these statements.

b) Nondisclosures. Another type of situation sometimes occurs; here the defendant does not disclose material facts. The issue here is whether the plaintiff would have acted differently if she had known of the material facts. This issue is related to the "causation" question (below).

(1) In *Shapiro v. Merrill Lynch, Pierce, Fenner & Smith,* 495 F.2d 228 (2d Cir. 1974), the court indicated that to the extent reliance was necessary the test was simply one of "causation in fact." That is, the proper test is to determine "whether the plaintiff would have been influenced to act differently than he did act if the defendant had disclosed to him the undisclosed facts." The plaintiff will allege this, and the court will decide it based on the probabilities (given the factual setting).

7) Causation and causation-in-fact.

a) **Introduction.** Courts have consistently stated that "causation" is a necessary element in a private action for damages under Rule 10b-5. That is, the defendant's action must have "caused" the plaintiff's injury (for example, the misrepresentation must have caused a drop in the price of the stock).

b) **Relationship to other elements.**

(1) **Reliance.** There is a relationship between causation and reliance. The reason for the reliance requirement is to ensure that the conduct of the defendant caused the plaintiff's injury.

(2) **Materiality.** There is also a relationship between causation and materiality. Causation is, in practice, largely determined by the answer to the threshold question of materiality. Once it is shown that a defendant has misrepresented or omitted to state a material fact, then it is practically a foregone conclusion that the defendant's conduct will be held to have "caused" the plaintiff's injury. This result has been influenced by the discussion of causation in nondisclosure cases, where the courts have found "causation-in-fact" (*i.e.,* that the nondisclosed fact would have been material had it been disclosed).

c) **"Failure to disclose" cases.** The difficult causation cases arise in the context of a failure to disclose.

(1) In *Shapiro v. Merrill Lynch, Pierce, Fenner & Smith, supra,* those receiving inside information ("tippees") about a company's poor earnings sold their stock; at the same time the plaintiffs were purchasing shares on the stock exchange, without the benefit of the same information. The court held that causation could be established without privity; the proper test in a nondisclosure case is "whether the plaintiff would have been influenced to act differently than he did act if the defendant had disclosed to him the undisclosed fact."

(2) In *Affiliated Ute Citizens v. United States,* 406 U.S. 128 (1972), two bank officers making a market in the restricted securities of the Ute Tribal Development Corporation failed to disclose to Indian sellers that the price they were paying to the sellers was less than could be obtained by the defendants in the secondary market, which they were helping to create. The Court stated that in finding causation, all that is necessary is that the facts

withheld be material in the sense that a reasonable investor "might have considered them important in making his decision about buying or selling the securities."

c. **Remedies.** The rule itself says nothing about any remedies. It is clear, however, that both rescission and damages are available in Rule 10b-5 actions.

1) **Rescission.** A seller can recover her securities, and a buyer can recover the amount she paid for securities. There are limitations (such as waiver, laches, estoppel, etc.) on rescission actions. Or the remedy may just not be available (the defendant purchaser has sold the securities purchased from the plaintiff).

2) **Damages.** The basic formula for damages is to provide restitution—*i.e.,* to restore what the plaintiff has lost. But the formula has been applied differently by different courts.

3) **Unlimited liability.** An unresolved issue is whether a defendant can be held liable for the total amount of damages suffered by all plaintiffs in a Rule 10b-5 case—despite the fact that this amount will far exceed the profit made by the defendant. There is authority that apparently would permit such unlimited damages.

a) **Example.** In an affirmative misrepresentation case, the defendant was a corporate officer who had bought his company's stock on the basis of inside information. He was held liable to the plaintiffs who sued, with no apparent allowance for the fact that he also might later be sued by other plaintiffs who had also sold their stock on the exchange during the same period. If such additional plaintiffs did sue, the defendant's liability could exceed his trading profits many times over. [Mitchell v. Texas Gulf Sulphur Co., *supra*]

b) **Example.** In a nondisclosure case, the Second Circuit did not limit the possible extent of the defendant's liability; although in remanding the case to the district court, it noted that the lower court should inquire into factors that could possibly circumscribe unlimited damages. [Shapiro v. Merrill Lynch, Pierce, Fenner & Smith, *supra*]

c) **Attempts to limit liability.** Courts have attempted to find a rationale for limiting a defendant's liability in a Rule 10b-5 action. For example, one court indicated that in order for Rule 10b-5 liability to exist, there must be "trading causation" between a plaintiff's losses and a defendant's trading on the basis of the undisclosed inside information. [*See* Fridrich v. Bradford, 542 F.2d 307 (6th Cir. 1976), *cert. denied,* 429 U.S. 1053 (1977)]

4) **Punitive damages.** There are no punitive damages under Rule 10b-5.

d. **Trading by insiders and the duty to disclose.**

1) **Introduction.** Obviously, Rule 10b-5 has very broad application to securities transactions. For example, even though Rule 10b-5 does not mention "insiders" specifically, nor specifically require that one person having information not had by another disclose this in a securities transaction, nevertheless the S.E.C. and the courts have used Rule 10b-5 to cover such transactions.

2) **Fiduciary relationship.** The origin of the concept of an "insider" is the idea that when one person occupies a "fiduciary relationship" with another, this fiduciary must disclose relevant, material information to the person for whom she has the responsibility.

3) **Insiders defined.**

a) **The test.** There are two elements that must be shown in order to designate someone an "insider":

(1) The person must have a relationship giving access, directly or indirectly, to information intended to be available only for a business purpose and not for the personal benefit of anyone; and

(2) An inherent unfairness must be present when a party takes advantage of such information, knowing it is unavailable to those with whom she is dealing.

b) **Misleading press releases--**

S.E.C. v. Texas Gulf Sulphur Co., 401 F.2d 833 (2d Cir. 1968), *cert. denied,* 394 U.S. 976 (1969).

Facts. Texas Gulf Sulphur ("TGS") (D) was engaged in exploration and mining of minerals. In November 1963, it drilled a test hole on property near Timmins, Ontario, Canada, and the sample revealed significant deposits of copper, zinc, and silver. Present at the site, among others, were employees Clayton (D) and Holyk (D). TGS then began to acquire rights to the surrounding property (which was completed by March 27, 1964). The assay report of the drilling indicated that the ore discovery could be very significant, and the president of TGS (Stephens, also a defendant) instructed those employees who knew of the discovery to keep it quiet. Additional holes were drilled to track the extent of the ore deposit, and all indicated that the discovery was significant. By April 10, 1964, rumors of the find had reached the New York newspapers. Stephens therefore had two TGS executives (Ds) prepare a news release that was issued on April 12. The release discounted the rumors, indicated that insufficient information was available upon which to evaluate a possible ore discovery, and stated that additional drilling would be required before definite conclusions could be arrived at. In the meantime, more holes were drilled, and the company's analysis of the results was completed by April 16. Between April 12 and April 16 TGS (through company employees, including two additional defendants, Mollison and Darke) gave out two reports that indicated that a discovery had been made, and on April 16 a disclosure was made to representatives of the press that a discovery had been made. A written release concerning the discovery went over a brokerage firm wire service that morning. TGS stock on the New York Stock Exchange went from $17.50 per share on the date of the first test hole, to $32 on April 12, to $37 on April 16, and finally to $58 per share in the middle of May 1964. The S.E.C. (P) brought an action under Rule 10b-5 against employees of TGS who bought stock or calls to buy TGS stock prior to the full disclosure to the public concerning the ore discovery. P also sued TGS for the misleading press release of April 12 and the employees who received options to purchase TGS stock prior to public disclosure (or disclosure to the TGS directors granting the options for that matter). And finally, tippees (of the insiders) who bought TGS stock were also joined as defendants.

Issues.

(i) Is it a violation of Rule 10b-5 for officers, directors, and employees of a corporation, having inside information concerning the probability of a major ore discovery by the corporation, which information has not been disclosed to the public and which if it were disclosed would affect the price of the corporation's securities, to purchase the corporation's securities or to receive options to purchase such securities without public disclosure of the material information?

(ii) May those communicating the inside information to others (who purchase securities based on this information) also be held liable under Rule 10b-5?

(iii) Is it a violation of Rule 10b-5 for TGS to have issued a misleading press release concerning information that could have a material effect on the price of its securities?

Held. (i) Yes. (ii) Yes. (iii) Yes. Case remanded.

- Rule 10b-5 says that anyone trading for his own account in securities of the corporation who has access, directly or indirectly, to information intended only for corporate purposes and not for personal benefit, may not take advantage of such information knowing that it is unavailable to those with whom he is dealing. Either the information must be disclosed to the investing public or trading in or recommending the securities must be discontinued until after such disclosure. This includes "tippees" (those who are told of the material information by corporate insiders).

- Only information that is essentially extraordinary in nature and which is reasonably certain to have a substantial effect on the market price of the security if disclosed need be disclosed. The test is whether a reasonable investor would attach importance to the information in determining his course of action. To make the determination, the probability that the event will occur and the magnitude of the event if it does occur must be balanced. Here, the first public disclosure may have been misleading—the case is remanded to determine if it was such that a "reasonable investor" would have relied on it.

- ♦ If corporate management can show that it was diligent in ascertaining that the information that it published in the press release was the whole truth, and that such information was disseminated in good faith, Rule 10b-5 is not violated. The case is remanded to the trial court for a determination of whether the press release was misleading and, if it was, whether the corporation violated the required standard of care in issuing it so that an S.E.C. injunction will issue against further violations.

- ♦ Before insiders may act, the information must have been effectively disclosed in a manner sufficient to ensure its availability to the investing public. So the director who left the news conference on April 16 to call his broker to purchase securities is liable.

- ♦ Specific intent to defraud need not be shown. Negligent insider conduct is sufficient for liability. Hence, the claim that the news was public when the officer phoned his order the night before the company news conference is not a reasonable belief, and the officer is liable for negligent violation of the Act.

- ♦ Accepting stock options in February 1964 from a company committee and the board, neither of which knew of the information, is a violation by officers who did know.

- ♦ The 1934 Act was meant to promote a free market and protect the investing public. Section 10(b) protects against fraudulent or misleading statements or acts "in connection with" the purchase or sale of securities. This means that any device is proscribed, whatever it might be, that would cause reasonable investors to rely thereon in connection with buying or selling corporate securities. It need not be shown that the party using the device was involved in the purchase or sale.

---

c) **Examples of insiders:**

(1) Controlling shareholders, directors, and officers with "inside" information.

(2) Inside tippers (such as directors and officers) who pass along information to relatives, friends, and business associates (tippees). In *Texas Gulf Sulphur, supra,* these tippers were held liable for the profits made by the tippees, but the question of tippee liability and the liability of

tippees of tippees was not reached (although the court did not hold the tippers liable for profits made by the tippees of tippees).

(3) A broker who receives inside information and uses it to assist her customers in making sales ahead of public disclosure of material facts. [*In the Matter of* Cady, Roberts & Co., 40 S.E.C. 907 (1961)]

d) **Outside printer not an insider--**

Chiarella v. United States, 445 U.S. 222 (1980).

Facts. An employee of a financial printer that had been engaged to print corporate takeover bids was convicted of a violation of section 10(b) of the Securities Exchange Act, based on his purchasing stock in target companies without informing their shareholders of his knowledge of the proposed takeover and on his selling such shares at a profit immediately after takeover attempts were made public.

Issue. Does a person who learns from the confidential documents of one corporation that it is planning an attempt to secure control of a second corporation violate section 10(b) of the Securities Exchange Act of 1934 if he fails to disclose the impending takeover before he trades in the target company's securities?

Held. No. Judgment against petitioner reversed.

- An employee could not be convicted on a theory of failure to disclose his knowledge to shareholders or target companies, as he was under no duty to speak. He had no prior dealings with the shareholders and was not their agent or fiduciary and was not a person in whom sellers had placed their trust and confidence, but dealt with them only through impersonal market transactions.

- Regular access to market information by those who occupy strategic places in the market mechanism does not alone support a duty to disclose and imposition of liability under section 10(b). A duty arises from the relationship between the parties and not merely from one's ability to acquire information because of his position in the market.

- The Court does not decide whether the employee breached a duty to the acquiring corporation since such theory was not submitted to the jury.

Dissent (Burger, C.J.). A person who has misappropriated nonpublic information has an absolute duty to disclose that information or to refrain from trading. The Court's approach unduly minimizes the importance of the petitioner's access to confidential information that the honest investor, no matter how diligently he tried, could not legally obtain. The petitioner knew that the information was unavailable to those with whom he dealt. He took full advantage of this artificial information gap. By any reasonable definition, his trading was inherently unfair.

Comment. In response to *Chiarella*, the S.E.C. adopted Rule 14e-3, discussed in the following case.

e) The misappropriation theory--

United States v. O'Hagan, 521 U.S. 642 (1997).

Facts. O'Hagan (D) was a partner in a law firm retained by Grand Metropolitan ("Grand Met") to represent it in a potential tender offer for the common stock of the Pillsbury Company. D personally did not work on the case. While his law firm was still representing Grand Met, D began buying Pillsbury stock options and common stock. When Grand Met announced its tender offer, the price of Pillsbury stock increased from $39 per share to $60 per share. At that time, D sold all of his Pillsbury stock, making a profit of $4.3 million. The S.E.C. began an investigation, which led to a 57-count indictment against D, including 17 counts of fraudulent trading in connection with a tender offer in violation of section 14(e) and Rule 14e-3(a), and 17 counts of securities fraud in violation of section 10(b) and Rule 10b-5. A jury convicted D on all 57 counts, but the court of appeals reversed all of the convictions. The appellate court held that liability under section 10(b) and Rule 10b-5 could not be grounded on the "misappropriation theory." It also held that Rule 14e-3(a) exceeds the S.E.C.'s rulemaking authority because it contains no breach of fiduciary duty requirement. The Supreme Court granted certiorari.

Issues.

(i) Is a person who trades in securities for personal profit, using confidential information misappropriated in breach of a fiduciary duty to the source of the information, guilty of violating section 10(b) and Rule 10b-5?

(ii) Did the S.E.C. exceed its rulemaking authority by adopting Rule 14e-3(a), which proscribes trading on undisclosed information in the tender offer setting, even in the absence of a duty to disclose?

Held. (i) Yes. (ii) No. Judgment reversed and case remanded.

- The "misappropriation theory" holds that a person commits fraud in connection with a securities transaction, and thereby violates section 10(b) and Rule 10b-5, when he misappropriates confidential information for securities trading purposes, in breach of a duty owed to the source of the information. Instead of premising liability on a fiduciary relationship, the misappropriation theory premises liability on a trader's deception of those who entrusted him with access to confidential information. That is, the trader's duty is not owed to another trader, but to the source of the information.

- A section 10(b) violation requires "deceptive" conduct "in connection with" securities transactions. That is, the misappropriation of information first must involve some deceptive device or connivance. In this case, D's feigning fidelity to the source of the confidential information, while secretly converting the information for personal gain, constitutes deception. If D had disclosed to the source that he planned to trade on this nonpublic information, there would be no deceptive device and thus no 10(b) violation.

- We find that the "in connection with the purchase or sale of a security" requirement is also met in this case. D's fraud was consummated not when he gained the confidential information, but when he used the information to purchase and then sell securities. The securities transaction and the breach of duty to the source of the information thus coincide. This is so even though the person or entity defrauded is not the other party to the transaction. The Act does not require deception of an identifiable individual. It requires only that the deception be "in connection with" a purchase or sale.

- We therefore find that the misappropriation theory can provide the basis for a section 10(b) violation. To hold otherwise would frustrate the congressional purposes of the Act. If such conduct were not held to be a violation, it could have the effect of inhibiting participation in the market.

- Section 14(e) prohibits fraudulent, deceptive, or manipulative acts in connection with a tender offer. For section 14(e) purposes, the S.E.C. is given authority to "by rules and regulations define, and prescribe means reasonably designed to prevent, such acts and practices as are fraudulent, deceptive, or manipulative."

- Under the authority of section 14(e), the S.E.C. promulgated Rule 14e-3(a). Rule 14e-3(a) is violated if an individual trades on the basis of material nonpublic information concerning a pending tender offer that he "knows or has reason to know has been acquired directly or indirectly from an insider of the offeror or issuer, or someone working on their behalf."

- The lower court held that Rule14e-3(a) exceeds the S.E.C.'s rulemaking authority because it applies whether or not the trading in question breaches a fiduciary duty. The court reasoned that the S.E.C. does not have authority to create its own definition of fraud, but only to identify and regulate acts and practices that the law already defines as fraudulent. Thus the rule exceeds the S.E.C.'s authority.

- We disagree. Section 14(e)'s rulemaking authorization gives the S.E.C. latitude to regulate nondeceptive activities as a means of preventing manipulative acts. We therefore find that the S.E.C. may prohibit acts that are not themselves fraudulent under the common law or section 10(b) if the prohibition is "reasonably designed to prevent . . . acts and practices [that] are fraudulent."

Concurrence and dissent (Scalia, J.). The clear language of section 10(b) must be construed to require the manipulation or deception of a ***party*** to a securities transaction.

Concurrence and dissent (Thomas, J, Rehnquist, C.J.). I concur with the Court's finding on the mail fraud convictions. However, the S.E.C.'s interpretation of the "in connection with" requirement of Rule 10b-5 fails to provide a coherent and consistent interpretation of this element of liability. The majority's inability to explain why the theft of information falls under the S.E.C.'s misappropriation theory but the theft of money does not illustrates the problems with the majority's logic.

---

f) **Broker--**

Dirks v. S.E.C., 463 U.S. 646 (1983).

Facts. Dirks (D) was an employee of a broker-dealer firm that specialized in providing investment analysis of insurance companies for institutional investors. He received information from Ronald Secrist, a former officer of Equity Funding (a New York Stock Exchange company), that its assets were vastly overstated since the company was creating false insurance policies. D investigated by interviewing company officers and employees. Some of the employees verified the charge. D discussed this information with some of his clients, who sold the stock, driving the market price down. Finally, the S.E.C. halted trading in the stock. Then the California insurance commissioner investigated and discovered the fraud. Equity Funding entered receivership. The S.E.C. sued D under section 17(a) of the 1933 Act for aiding and abetting his clients that sold their stock based on the inside information. The circuit court affirmed the S.E.C.'s decision against D. The Supreme Court granted certiorari.

Issue. When the insider is not motivated by personal gain, is a person who got the inside information from an insider and who gave it to tippees that traded on the information in violation of Rule 10b-5?

Held. No. Judgment of the circuit court reversed.

- To be an insider, a person must have a fiduciary relationship with the shareholders of the company whose stock is traded.

- The S.E.C.'s position is that a tippee from such an insider inherits the fiduciary duty of the insider if he knows the information is material and nonpublic and if he knows that the insider has a fiduciary duty not to disclose it.

- But a rule such as that suggested by the S.E.C. might inhibit market analysts from doing their work, which is to question corporate insiders and discuss this information with their clients.

- ♦ The motivation of the insider is critical. The test is whether the insider will personally benefit, directly or indirectly, from his disclosure. Absent some such personal gain, there is no breach, and the tippee who takes such information and gives it to those who might trade on it has not breached any duty, since his duty is derivative from the insider's duty. Gain might be monetary, reputational, etc.

Comment. The Court noted that in certain circumstances, such as when corporate information is revealed legitimately to an underwriter, accountant, lawyer, or consultant working for the corporation, these outsiders may become fiduciaries of the shareholders because they have entered into a confidential relationship in the conduct of the business of the corporation and are given access to information solely for corporate purposes.

---

g) Fiduciary or "similar relationship of trust and confidence"--

---

United States v. Chestman, 947 F.2d 551 (2d Cir. 1991), *cert. denied,* 503 U.S. 1004 (1992).

Facts. Ira Waldbaum was the controlling shareholder of Waldbaum, Inc. In 1986, Waldbaum agreed to sell the corporation. He told his sister and his children about the pending sale, and admonished them to keep the news confidential until after the public announcement of the sale. However, Waldbaum's sister told her daughter, Susan, who then told her husband, Keith, about the pending tender offer. Keith told Chestman (D), a stockbroker, that Waldbaum, Inc. was going to be sold for a substantially higher price than market price. D then traded on behalf of himself, several clients, and Keith based on this information. Keith agreed to cooperate with the S.E.C. in their investigation. D was convicted under Rule 10b-5 as an aider and abettor of the misappropriation and as a tippee of the misappropriated information and for mail fraud. D appeals.

Issue. If a wife tells her husband about a pending tender offer for stock in her family's business, and the husband tells his stockbroker who then trades based on the information, has the husband breached a fiduciary or "similar relationship of trust and confidence" sufficient to impose liability for violation of Rule 10b-5 and mail fraud?

Held. No. Convictions reversed.

- ♦ The relationship between Keith and Susan Loeb does not fall within any of the traditional fiduciary relationships, thus, we must determine whether their relationship constitutes a "similar relationship of trust and confidence" sufficient to impose Rule 10b-5 liability.

- ♦ A "similar relationship of trust and confidence" must share the same qualities as a fiduciary relationship. A fiduciary relationship depends on reliance, control, and dominance and exists when confidence is reposed on one side and there is a resulting superiority and influence on the other. A fiduciary relationship involves discretionary authority and dependency: one person depends on the other to serve his interests. Because the fiduciary obtains access to the other person's property to serve the ends of the fiduciary relationship, he becomes duty bound not to appropriate the property for his own use.

- Here, we find that the government presented insufficient evidence to establish a fiduciary relationship or its functional equivalent between Keith Loeb and the Waldbaum company. Keith had not been brought into the family's inner circle whose members discussed confidential business information. Keith was not an employee of Waldbaum and he did not participate in confidential communications regarding the business. The confidential information was gratuitously communicated to him and did not serve the interests of the Waldbaum company. Nor was the relationship characterized by influence and reliance of any sort. A fiduciary duty cannot be imposed unilaterally by entrusting a person with confidential information.

- Nor was there sufficient evidence to establish a fiduciary relationship or its functional equivalent between Keith Loeb and his wife. Kinship alone does not create a fiduciary relationship. Susan admonished Keith not to disclose that Waldbaum was the target of a tender offer. Although they had maintained confidences in the past, there was no evidence of the nature of the confidences, therefore, the jury could not reasonably find that there existed a fiduciary relationship. In the absence of explicit acceptance by Keith of the duty of confidentiality, there is no fiduciary relationship. While acceptance can be implied, it must be implied from a preexisting fiduciary-like relationship between the parties. Susan's disclosure of the information served no business purpose and was unprompted; Keith did not induce her to convey the information. The government did not prove a pattern of sharing business confidences between Keith and Susan.

- Thus, Keith did not owe a fiduciary duty to either Susan or the Waldbaum company, and he did not defraud them by disclosing the news of the tender offer to D. Since Keith is not guilty of fraud, D cannot be held derivatively liable as Keith's tippee or as an aider and abettor. A mail fraud conviction requires a breach of the same fiduciary-like duty, which we have found does not exist here. Therefore, D's convictions must be reversed.

Concurrence. A family member who has received or expects benefits from family control of a corporation, who is in a position to learn confidential corporate information through ordinary family interactions, and who knows that under the circumstances both the corporation and the family desire confidentiality, has a duty not to use such information for personal profit where the use risks disclosure. To hold otherwise would discourage open family communication and would mean that a family-controlled corporation is subject to greater risk of disclosure of confidential information than a publicly-owned corporation. Thus, I would affirm D's convictions.

Concurrence. Judge Winter's proposed familial rule adds an element of uncertainty to this area of the law: it is unclear who would be subject to the duty of confidentiality.

---

4) **Disclosure responsibilities of insiders.** Rule 10b-5 imposes an affirmative duty on insiders to disclose their inside information to those who might reasonably be affected thereby before engaging in securities transactions in which the information would be material. For example, in *Texas Gulf Sulphur, supra,* corporate officers, directors, and key employees knowing of the significant ore discovery were held to a duty to disclose the information before purchasing the company's securities.

5) **Statutory remedies for insider trading.**

a) **Introduction.** During the 1980s, Congress enacted two statutes dealing with insider trading. The first, the Insider Trading Sanctions Act of 1984 ("ITSA"), introduced statutory civil penalties into the law of insider trading. The second, the Insider Trading and Securities Fraud Enforcement Act of 1988 ("ITSFEA"), amended and codified ITSA and added several important new concepts. Neither act defined insider trading; this was left up to the courts.

b) **Civil penalties—section 21A.** The S.E.C. may bring an action in United States district court to seek a civil penalty against any person who trades on inside information or who communicates such information to others. Liability may extend also to persons who control the person who committed the violation. The amount of the penalty may be up to three times the profit gained or loss avoided as a result of the use of the inside information.

(1) Payment of the penalty is to the United States Treasury.

(2) This type of action is in addition to any other action the S.E.C. or the Attorney General may bring.

(3) Informants may receive a percentage of the penalty (up to 10%).

(4) ITSFEA also increased the criminal penalties for willful violation of the Securities Acts or regulations from $100,000 and five years to $1 million and 10 years for individuals, and a fine of up to $2.5 million when a defendant is a person other than a natural person. [*See* ITSFEA §4]

(5) Obviously, section 21A greatly increases the risks of insider trading now that the penalties may far exceed simply a disgorgement of insider trading profits. Note also that many controlling persons (such as employers for their employees) must now establish policies and procedures designed to prevent the misuse of inside information, or suffer the possible consequences of a breach of the law.

c) **Liability to contemporaneous traders—section 20A.** Any party who purchases or sells a security based on inside information may be liable, in an action brought in any court of competent jurisdiction, to any person who contemporaneously purchased or sold the same securities.

(1) The damages are limited to the profit gained or loss avoided by the defendant, less any disgorgement remedy imposed on that same person.

(2) Those communicating the inside information to the person actually doing the trading are also liable.

(3) Liability under this section does not prevent other private rights of action or other public prosecutions.

(4) Prior to enactment of this section, courts differed as to whether private action could be maintained against persons trading on inside information.

3. Section 16—Short-Swing Profits from Insider Transactions.

a. **Basic provisions of section 16.** Section 16 of the 1934 Act is designed to prevent corporate insiders from unfairly using information about their company. The approach used by the statute to accomplish this is to make insiders (i) report their transactions in securities of their companies [SEA §16(a)], and (ii) forfeit to their companies any "profit" resulting from short-term trading (within a period of less than six months) in their company's securities. [SEA §16(b)] (*Note*: In some cases the statute deems a profit to exist when in fact the individual defendant lost money.)

1) **Rationale for section 16.** The rationale for section 16 is that insiders often possess valuable information about their companies, and this information might be used by them to gain an advantage over an "outside" seller or buyer of their companies' securities.

a) **Makes use of inside information difficult.** Section 16(b) makes it more difficult for an insider to use inside information.

For example, an insider may know that her company is going to issue a favorable earnings report next week. She might be certain that the price of her company's stock will rise as soon as the earnings report is made public. If she purchases shares of her company's common stock, however, she will have to wait for at least six months before selling any shares, otherwise she will have to forfeit any profits she earns on the purchase and sale.

b) **Makes short sales by insiders unlawful.** Section 16(c) makes it unlawful for insiders to engage in short sales of their company's equity securities. In other words, an insider may not sell shares she does not own, and then buy the shares for delivery later. (This strategy can be thought of as a "bet against the company"—the short seller sells at today's price, hoping that by the time she has to cover the sale by delivering the securities, the price will have gone down.)

2) **Distinguish Rule 10b-5 "insider trading."** Although both Rule 10b-5 and section 16 are sometimes said to prohibit "insider trading," the provisions operate entirely differently. A Rule 10b-5 case is based on a misrepresentation or failure to disclose. Section 16, on the other hand, is based on the amount of time elapsed between a purchase and sale (or a sale and purchase) of the issuer's securities by an insider. If the amount of time is too short, the insider must give up her "profits," regardless of whether information was misrepresented or withheld. The presence or absence of fraud is irrelevant to a section 16 case.

3) **Limitations of section 16.** Section 16 is not a comprehensive solution to the problem of insider trading. In fact, its narrow focus on short-swing trades makes it oblivious to even the most outrageous intentional frauds, as long as there are no purchases and sales within six months of one another.

a) **Example.** A, an insider of X Corp., has owned 100 shares of X Corp. for three years. A becomes aware that X Corp. is about to suffer a large loss of business. A sells her X Corp. shares, based on her inside information. A has not incurred any liability under section 16 (although she may be liable under Rule 10b-5).

b) **But note.** Rule 10b-5 and section 16(b) can apply to the same transaction. For example, an insider could be liable to the corporation under section 16(b) for profits made on a purchase and sale of securities, and concurrently liable under Rule 10b-5 to the person to whom the securities were sold (assuming some fraud took place).

4) **Companies covered under section 16.** Section 16 applies to all companies with a class of equity security registered under section 12 of the 1934 Act.

5) **Reporting requirements.** Section 16(a) requires any person who beneficially owns more than 10% of a registered class of equity securities, and every officer and director of a "covered" corporation, to file a report or Form 3 with the S.E.C. at the time of attaining such status and a Form 4 and at the end of every month in which she purchases equity securities of that corporation. In addition, any person who was an insider at any time during the issuer's fiscal year must file an annual report on Form 5.

6) **Forfeiture of profits.** Section 16(b) provides that all profits made by any person required to file reports under section 16(a) in the purchase and sale, or sale and purchase of an equity security within a period of less than six months belongs to the corporation.

   a) **Example.** A, an officer of XYZ Corp. (which has its common stock registered under section 12) buys 100 shares of XYZ common stock at $5 per share. Within six months, A sells these shares at $10 per share. A is liable to XYZ for his profit of $5 per share.

   b) **Example.** B, a director of G Corp. (which has its common stock registered under section 12), sells 100 shares of G common stock on June 1, at $10 per share. Two months later, on August 1, B purchases 100 shares of G common stock at $5 per share. B is liable to G Corp. for her profit of $5 per share.

   c) **Rationale.** The rationale for the $5 per share profit is that after making the August 1 purchase, B is in precisely the position she was in before the June 1 sale, except that she has $500 in cash that she didn't have before. In other words, had she not engaged in the two stock transactions, she would have had 100 shares of G common stock on August 2. Having engaged in the transactions, she has 100 shares of G common stock, and $500 in cash, which represents her profit on the transactions (and which is forfeitable to G Corp. under section 16(b)).

b. **Strict liability.** The general rule is that there are no defenses to a section 16(b) action if all elements of the cause of action are present (*i.e.,* an "insider," registered equity securities, and a matching purchase and sale within the required time period). Thus, it makes no difference that the insider cannot be shown to have had access to any inside information, or to have used any inside information in effectuating the matching purchase and sale.

c. **"Insiders" defined.** "Insiders" covered under section 16 are officers and directors of a corporation with a class of equity securities registered under section 12 of the 1934 Act, ***and*** all persons who beneficially own more than 10% of any class of the corporation's equity securities registered under section 12. Courts have generally refused to expand the class of potential defendants beyond the persons described in section 16 (*e.g.,* to other persons who possess the same inside information as officers and directors).

1) **Officers and directors.** Whether a potential defendant was an officer or director at a particular point in time is in most cases readily established through the corporate minute book.

a) **"Officer" defined.** An officer includes an issuer's president, principal financial officer, principal accounting officer, any vice president of the issuer in charge of a principal business unit, division or function (such as sales, administration, or finance), any other officer who performs a policy-making function, or any other person who performs similar policy-making functions for the issuer. [SEA Rule 16a-1(f)]

b) **Timing issues.** Section 16 raises two timing issues with respect to officers and directors: What happens if a person was not an officer or director at the time of the purchase, but becomes one by the time of the sale? And what is the result in the reverse situation; that is, the person was an officer or director at the time of the purchase, but is no longer one at the time of the sale?

(1) **Transaction before person becomes an officer or director.** When a transaction takes place before the person becomes an officer or director of a covered company, then the policy underlying section 16 does not apply: That is, such a person generally has no access to inside information. The S.E.C. adopted this view in 1991, in Rule 16a-2(a): Transactions carried out in the six months prior to the person's becoming an officer or director are not subject to section 16.

(a) **Exception—transaction shortly before going public.** There is one case, however, in which the rule stated immediately above does not apply. The exception is intended to trap transactions by persons who trade shortly before their company goes public. The S.E.C. believes that in general, insiders of companies that are about to go public know about those plans far enough in advance to plan for section 16; in addition, the possibilities for abuse just before the company goes public are greater than they are later on, when a market price has been established for the company's securities. In order to trigger the exception (and thus trigger section 16(a) reporting and section 16(b) liability), the officer or director must have become subject to section 16 solely as the result of the issuer registering a series of securities under section 12.

(2) **Transaction after person ceases being officer or director.** A transaction that takes place after the person ceases to be an officer or director is subject to section 16 only if it takes place within six months of a transaction that happened while the person was an officer or director.

c) **Deputization issue.** Despite its general limitation to named insiders, section 16 may also apply to situations in which an officer or director of A Corp. has been appointed by A to an inside position (such as director) in B Corp. While the person might not engage in any prohibited purchases or sales in B stock for himself, the entity with which he is affiliated (A) may.

2) **More-than-10% shareholder.** Every person who directly or indirectly is the "beneficial owner" of more than 10% of any class of registered equity security is subject to the provisions of section 16.

a) **Beneficial ownership.** In calculating 10% ownership, it is "beneficial ownership" that counts—*i.e.,* whether a person receives the benefit of owning the stock, even if he does not hold record title. The question of beneficial ownership is significant beyond the case of 10% holders; it is equally important in analyzing questions involving officers and directors. For example, if an officer of a covered company is claimed to be required to disgorge profits under section 16(b), then the plaintiff must establish that equity securities of the company beneficially owned by the officer were involved in the challenged transactions.

b) **Family ownership.** As part of a complete overhaul of its rules relating to section 16, the S.E.C. in 1991 provided that an insider is presumed to be the "beneficial owner" of securities held by virtually all relatives, including in-laws and adopted relatives (all of whom are considered to be members of the insider's "immediate family")—but only if the relative "shares the same household" as the insider. [SEA Rules 16a-1(a)(2)(ii)(A); 16a-1(e)] The presumption may be rebutted by the insider.

c) **Securities held in trust.** The S.E.C.'s rules relating to section 16 treatment of securities held in trust were also completely revised in 1991 and again in 1996.

(1) **Trust as "beneficial owner"—section 16(a) reporting.** A trust is subject to section 16(a) reporting only if it is the ***beneficial owner of more than 10% of a registered class of equity securities***. (This is because a trust cannot be an officer or director of the issuer.) Beneficial ownership of more than 10% is determined the same way for trusts as it is for natural persons; *i.e.*, the question is whether the trust has sole or shared voting power with respect to the securities.

(a) **Status of trustees and beneficiaries.** One of the issues that makes dealing with trusts complicated is that trustees and beneficiaries may personally be subject to section 16, quite apart from the trust. This is the case, for example, if the trustee (or beneficiary) is an officer or director of the issuer, or owns more than 10% based on voting power. When this happens, it is important to ***separate the status of the trust from the individual status of the trustee or beneficiary***.

1] **Trustee (personally) as beneficial owner.** Merely being a trustee of a trust does not make the trustee, personally, a beneficial owner of the securities in the trust. However, if the trustee or any member of her immediate family who shares the same household is a beneficiary of the trust, the trustee, personally, is a beneficial owner of the securities held in trust. [SEA Rule 16a-8(b)(2)] This becomes especially important when the trustee is personally subject to section 16, because trust transactions can then be matched with personal transactions to produce profit that must be disgorged under section 16(b).

2] **Beneficiaries as beneficial owners.** Trust beneficiaries almost inevitably are beneficial owners of the securities held in trust, because they have the necessary pecuniary interest in the securities. [*See* SEA Rule 16a-1(a)(2)]

(b) **Trustee and beneficiary reporting requirements—investment control.** A trust that holds more than 10% must report transactions in the issuer's equity securities, and this is done by the trustee on behalf of the trust. However, there are also situations in which the trustee or beneficiaries, personally, must report such transactions.

1] **Trustee reporting requirement.** A trustee must personally report trust transactions over which the trustee had investment control (which is by far the most common case), ***if the trustee also was a beneficial owner of the securities.***

2] **Beneficiary reporting requirement.** Beneficiaries must report trust transactions over which they had (or shared) investment control.

(2) **Liability under section 16(b).** The liability of a trust, trustee, or beneficiary to disgorge profit under section 16(b) follows reporting liability under section 16(a), as described above. [SEA Rule 16a-8(d)] Thus, if a trustee is required to report a transaction on behalf of the trust, the trust will be liable to disgorge any profit. Likewise, if the trustee was required personally to report the transaction (because the trustee was a beneficial owner of the securities held in trust), the trustee will be required personally to disgorge profit. Finally, if the beneficiary is required to report the transaction (because the beneficiary had or shared investment control over the transaction), the beneficiary will be liable to disgorge any profit from the transaction. [SEA Rule 16a-8(d)]

d) **Securities owned by corporation.** Another possibility complicating the question of beneficial ownership under section 16 involves the use of a corporation that owns the securities (rather than direct ownership, or ownership by a trust). When is an officer, director, or 10% holder of an issuer the beneficial owner of the issuer's securities if the securities are owned of record by a corporation of which the individual is a shareholder?

(1) **S.E.C. General Counsel opinion.** In 1938, the General Counsel of the S.E.C. opined that a shareholder of a corporation is considered the beneficial owner of securities held of record by the corporation only if the corporation "merely provides a medium through which [the shareholder] invest[s], or trade[s] in securities." [S.E.C. Rel. No. 34-1965 (1938)]

(2) **Opinion not always followed.** The General Counsel's opinion has not always been followed by the courts, however. Thus, in a case in which A, a more-than-10% owner of M, a family corporation, also owned a large block of shares in B, another corporation, A was held individually liable to disgorge 19% of B's profits from short-swing trades in M stock. [Marquette Cement Manufacturing Co. v. Andreas, 239 F. Supp. 962 (S.D.N.Y. 1965)]

(3) **Rule 14a-8 safe harbor.** Finally, with respect to corporations, the S.E.C. has provided a safe harbor rule that states that a shareholder is not liable for transactions by the corporation if: (i) the shareholder is not a controlling shareholder, and (ii) the shareholder neither shares nor has sole investment control over the corporation's transaction. This safe harbor is non-exclusive, and a shareholder not meeting its requirements remains free to argue purely on the basis of the S.E.C.'s General Counsel opinion, *supra*.

3) **Timing of ownership.** Although officers and directors need ***not*** be such at the time of both purchase and sale, the language of the statute indicates that 10% shareholders can only be liable when such ownership exists both at the time of purchase and at the time of sale.

a) **Example.** A owns no stock in X corporation. On March 3, A buys X corporation common shares (which are registered under the 1934 Act) in an amount sufficient to make A an 11% shareholder. On May 1 (less than six months later), A sells all the X corporation common shares. *Result:* Although A must report the May 1 sale under section 16(a), A is ***not*** liable to disgorge any profit under section 16(b).

b) **Example.** A owns 12% of a registered equity security, sells 3% on Monday, and sells the remaining 9% on Tuesday. A can only be held liable for his profits from the sale of the first 3% since at this point he owned 10%; thereafter, at the time he sold the remaining 9%, he did not own 10%. [Reliance Electric Co. v. Emerson Electric Co., 404 U.S. 418 (1972)]

c) **Limited applicability of section 16(b).** Thus, it is clear that if the 10% owner is careful, he may structure his purchases and sales so as to limit the applicability of section 16(b). For example, a person could buy over 10% in a series of separate purchases and only those acquired ***after*** he reached 10% could be matched with subsequent sales under section 16(b).

4) **All equity security transactions regulated.** To qualify as an "insider" by virtue of stock ownership, a person must beneficially own more than 10% of some class of ***registered*** equity security. But once qualified as an "insider" (either by owning more than 10% of a registered equity security, or by being an officer or director of a company with a class of registered equity security), purchases and sales of any equity security of the issuer—whether or not it also is registered—may give rise to liability.

d. **Elements of a section 16(b) cause of action.** The following elements must be shown to sustain a cause of action under section 16(b):

1) **Transactions involving equity securities.** The transaction(s) for which the plaintiff seeks to hold the defendant liable must involve an "equity security." The 1934 Act defines "equity security" as "any stock or similar security; or any security convertible, with or without consideration, into such security"; as well as certain "acquisition rights" to such securities; and "any other security which the Commission shall deem to be of a similar nature and consider necessary or appropriate . . . to treat as an equity security." [SEA §3(a)(11)]

2) **Purchase and sale requirement.** To establish liability under section 16(b), there must be a matching purchase and sale, or sale and purchase. The general rule is that for the purposes of section 16(b), a "purchase" occurs when the purchaser incurs an irrevocable liability to take and pay for the stock; and a "sale" occurs when the seller incurs an irrevocable liability to deliver and accept payment for the stock. Although these rules are easily stated, there are several types of stock transactions where it may not be clear if a "purchase" or "sale" has actually occurred. Many of these transactions involve the exchange of stock either for property or for other stock.

3) **Time requirement.** For section 16(b) to apply, the matching purchase and sale must occur within a period of less than six months.

a) **Special problems.** Although the specific date on which a purchase or sale occurred is generally a matter of record, in some transactions, it may be difficult to determine, such as when shares are to be delivered as part of a purchase price based on some contingent future events.

e. **Damages.** Generally, the measure of damages in a section 16(b) action is the "profit realized" in the matching transactions, which is the difference between the purchase price and the sale price.

1) **Any purchase or sale.** Section 16(b) may be applied to any matched purchase and sale or sale and purchase if the matched transactions occur within a period of less than six months.

a) **Example.** A, a director, buys 100 shares of XYZ stock on June 1 for $10 per share. On July 1, A sells the stock for $9 per share; on August 1, she buys 100 shares for $8 per share; and on September 1, she sells the stock for $7 per share. In three months she has lost $300, but she is still liable under section 16(b) since the $9 sale can be matched with $8 purchases.

2) **Profit maximized.** Whatever matching of purchase and sale transactions that will produce the maximum profit is the one used. For example, if 100 shares are purchased at $1 per share and 100 at $2 per share, and six months later 100 shares are sold at $10 per share, the profit is $9 per share.

4. **Judicial and Statutory Development of Liability for Securities Fraud.**

a. **Preliminary merger negotiations--**

Basic Inc. v. Levinson, 485 U.S. 224 (1988).

Facts. Officers and directors of Basic Inc., including Ds, opened merger discussions with Combustion Engineering in September 1976. During 1977 and 1978, Basic denied three times that it was conducting merger negotiations. On December 18, 1978, it halted trading on the New York Stock Exchange, saying it had been approached. On December 19, 1978, it announced that the board had approved Combustion's $46 per share tender offer. Levinson and others (Ps) are a class of shareholders who sold their stock after Basic's 1977 statement and before the trading halt on December 18, 1978. They sued under Rule 10b-5. The district court, on the basis of a "fraud on the market theory," adopted a rebuttable presumption of reliance by members of the class. On a motion for summary judgment, the district court ruled for Ds, holding that at the time of the first announcement in 1977, no negotiations were actually going on, and that the negotiations conducted at the time of the second and third announcements were not destined with reasonable certainty to become a merger agreement. The court of appeals affirmed the holding about reliance, but reversed the summary judgment. It held that preliminary merger discussions could be material. Furthermore, it held that once a statement is made denying the existence of discussions, then even discussions that might otherwise have been immaterial can be material. The Supreme Court granted certiorari.

Issues.

(i) Is the standard used to determine whether preliminary merger negotiations must be disclosed a materiality standard under Rule 10b-5?

(ii) Is it appropriate to use a rebuttable presumption of reliance for all members of a class on the basis that there has been a fraud on the market?

Held. (i) Yes. (ii) Yes. Case remanded.

- The *TSC Industries* test is the test of materiality for Rule 10b-5 cases; that is, a fact is material if there is a substantial likelihood that a reasonable shareholder would consider it important.

- With contingent events like mergers (that may or may not happen), the probability that the merger will occur and the magnitude of the possible event are looked at. All relevant facts bearing on these two issues should be considered.

- An absolute rule (such as the one requiring that a preliminary agreement be arrived at before negotiations are material), while convenient, is not in accord with the *TSC Industries* test. Likewise, the circuit court was wrong also. If a fact is immaterial, it makes no difference that Ds made misrepresentations about it.

- Thus, the case must be remanded to consider whether the lower court's grant of summary judgment for Ds was appropriate.

- Reliance is an element of a Rule 10b-5 cause of action. It provides a causal connection between a defendant's misrepresentation and a plaintiff's injury. But this causal connection can be proved in a number of ways. In the case of face-to-face negotiations, the issue is whether the buyer subjectively considered the seller's representations. In the case of a securities market, the dissemination or withholding of information by the issuer affects the price of the stock in the market, and investors rely on the market price as a reflection of the stock's value.

- The presumption of reliance in this situation assists courts to manage a situation where direct proof of reliance would be unwieldy. The presumption serves to allocate the burden of proof to defendants in situations where the plaintiffs have relied on the integrity of the markets, which Rule 10b-5 was enacted to protect. The presumption is supported by common sense. Most investors rely on market integrity in buying and selling securities.

- Ds can rebut the presumption. First, Ds could show that misrepresentation or omission did not distort the market price (for example, Ds could show that market makers knew the real facts and set prices based on these facts, despite any misrepresentations that might have been made). Or Ds could show that an individual plaintiff sold his shares for reasons other than the market price, knowing that Ds had probably misrepresented the status of merger negotiations.

Dissent (White, O'Connor, JJ.) (as to the fraud-on-the-market theory).

- The fraud-on-the-market theory should not be applied in this case.
- The fraud-on-the-market theory is an economic doctrine, not a doctrine based on traditional legal fraud principles. If Rule 10b-5 is to be changed, Congress should do it.
- It is not clear that investors rely on the "integrity" of the markets (*i.e.,* on the price of a stock reflecting its value).
- In rejecting the original version of section 18 of the Securities Exchange Act, Congress rejected a liability provision that allowed an investor recovery based solely on the fact that the price of the security bought or sold was affected by a misrepresentation. Congress altered section 18 to include a specific reliance requirement.
- The fraud-on-the-market theory is in opposition to the fundamental policy of disclosure, which is based on the idea of investors looking out for themselves by reading and relying on publicly disclosed information.
- This is a bad case in which to apply the fraud-on-the-market theory. Ps' sales occurred over a 14-month period. At the time the period began, Basic's stock sold for $20 per share; when it ended, the stock sold for $30 per share, so all Ps made money. Also, Basic did not withhold information to defraud anyone. And no one connected with Basic was trading in its securities. Finally, some Ps bought stock after Ds' first false statement in 1977, disbelieving the statement. They then made a profit, and can still recover under the fraud-on-the-market theory. These Ps are speculators. Their judgment comes from other, innocent shareholders who held the stock.

---

b. When class action does not allege fraud or misrepresentation--

---

MDCM Holdings, Inc. v. Credit Suisse First Boston Corporation, 216 F. Supp. 2d 251 (S.D.N.Y. 2002).

Facts. Mortgage.com entered into an underwriting agreement with Credit Suisse First Boston Corporation (D) under which D was to handle its initial public stock offering

("IPO"). Mortgage.com sold over seven million shares of common stock to D for $7.44 per share, which was exactly 7% less than the public offering price of $8 per share. D's compensation was the 7% price difference, which amounted to over $4 million. Two weeks after the IPO, Mortgage.com's stock had almost doubled in value. Mortgage.com, now known as MDCM Holdings, and other companies who had used D to underwrite their IPOs (Ps) filed a class action suit alleging several state law claims. Ps alleged that D breached the underwriting contract by not selling the IPO shares to the public but directing them to favored customers, and that D required purchasers to pay them a price higher than that provided in the prospectus, thereby unjustly enriching D. In addition to breach of contract, Ps alleged that D violated implied covenants of good faith and fair dealing, as well as fiduciary duties of loyalty and due care. D moved to dismiss the complaint, arguing that Ps' state law claims are barred by the Uniform Standards Act.

Issue. Is Ps' action barred by the Uniform Standards Act?

Held. No. Motion to dismiss denied.

- Congress created the Uniform Standards Act to stop attempts by class action attorneys to circumvent the Private Securities Litigation Reform Act of 1995 ("Reform Act"). The Reform Act contained heightened procedural and substantive standards for private securities suits in federal courts with the goal of stopping meritless and abusive lawsuits. When Congress determined that attorneys were filing suit in state court in order to get around the heightened requirements of the Reform Act, it enacted the Uniform Standards Act. This Act precludes "covered class actions" based on state law when they allege an "untrue statement or omission of material fact in connection with the purchase or sale of a covered security."

- In this case, Ps' complaint does not allege any misrepresentations or omissions. Ps allege breach of contract. Thus, they need only prove that D did not satisfy the requirements set forth in the underwriting agreement. The contract claims do not involve or require allegations of misrepresentation or omissions, and thus are not barred by the Uniform Standards Act.

XIV. INDEMNIFICATION AND INSURANCE

A. INDEMNIFICATION OF OFFICERS AND DIRECTORS

Statutes in most states govern the extent to which the corporation may properly indemnify its directors and officers for expenses incurred in defending suits against them for conduct undertaken in their official capacity. These statutes apply to derivative suits and direct actions by the corporation, its shareholders, or third parties (*i.e.,* the state for criminal violation, the S.E.C. for security law violations, or an injured party for a tort).

1. **Statute as the Basis for Indemnification.** Most states provide that the state statute is the exclusive basis on which indemnification is permitted. A few states, however, allow the matter to be regulated by the articles or bylaws or shareholder agreement.

2. **When the Defendant Wins.** As long as the director or officer wins on the merits, there is generally no problem; most states allow the corporation to reimburse the defendant for reasonable attorneys' fees and expenses.

    a. **Rationale.** The rationale is that public policy favors indemnification when the director or officer is vindicated, since it encourages people to serve in these capacities, to resist unfounded charges against them, and thus to preserve the corporate image. Moreover, it discourages minority shareholders from filing frivolous derivative suits, knowing that if they lose, the defendant's expenses will be paid from the corporation.

3. **When the Defendant Settles or Loses.** The statutes vary significantly as to the extent to which indemnification is permitted when the officer or director loses the lawsuit against him, or the suit is settled by his paying or incurring liability to pay. Many statutes distinguish between third-party suits and derivative suits.

    a. **Third-party suits.** When the suit against the director or officer is by an outsider (*i.e.,* the state in a criminal action or an injured party in a tort action), the statutes generally permit indemnification both for litigation expenses and also for whatever civil or criminal liabilities are incurred (monies paid out in settlement, judgment, or fines) ***provided*** the directors or shareholders determine that he "acted in good faith, for a purpose which he reasonably believed to be in the best interests of the corporation, and (where a criminal action was involved) that he had no reason to believe that his action was unlawful." [N.Y. Bus. Corp. Law §723]

b. **Derivative suits.** When the suit against the director or officer is a derivative action, charging him with wrongdoing to the corporation, the statutes in most states are much stricter.

1) **Suit settled.** When the derivative suit is settled prior to judgment, many statutes permit indemnification of the officer or director for his litigation expenses, including attorneys' fees, provided (i) the settlement was made with court approval and (ii) the court finds that "his conduct fairly and equitably merits such indemnity." [Cal. Corp. Code §830(a)]

2) **Judgment against defendant.** When a director or officer is adjudged to have breached duty to the corporation in a derivative suit, most statutes prohibit indemnification by the corporation, and this applies both as to his litigation expenses and any liability imposed upon him. [Cal. Corp. Code §830]

4. **Must Indemnify on Successful Counts--**

Merritt-Chapman & Scott Corp. v. Wolfson, 321 A.2d 138 (Del. 1974).

Facts. Wolfson, Gerbert, Kosow, and Staub (Ps) were agents of Merritt-Chapman (D) and participated in a plan to cause D to secretly purchase hundreds of thousands of shares of its own common stock in violation of the federal securities laws. All of the Ps were criminally charged and after lengthy trials, appeals, and retrials, Wolfson pleaded nolo contendere to filing false annual reports and received a $10,000 fine and an 18-month suspended sentence (all other counts against him were dropped). Gerbert agreed not to appeal his conviction of perjury before the S.E.C. and received a $2,000 fine and an 18-month suspended sentence (the other charges were dropped). All charges were dropped against Kosow and Staub. Ps all moved for indemnification under state law from D for their legal costs in defending those counts on which their defense was successful. Both Ps and D move for summary judgment.

Issue. May agents of a corporation receive indemnification for legal costs in defending those counts on which they were successful even if they were convicted on other counts of the same indictment?

Held. Yes. D must indemnify Ps for defense costs on the successful counts.

- Under state law corporate agents may be indemnified on those counts for which their defense is successful even if they are not completely successful on all counts. "Successful" is not being convicted, even if success comes by having a charge dropped for practical reasons.

- But the company's bylaws provided for indemnification ***except*** when the defendant is judged or it is determined that the defendant was derelict in performance of his duty, in which case the corporation could determine whether to indemnify. As to the counts not dropped but not carried to a final judgment of conviction against Wolfson and Gerbert, under state law D could determine whether to indemnify, since the conviction established their dereliction as to the counts not dropped.

---

5. Technical Requirements of a Liability Policy--

McCullough v. Fidelity & Deposit Co., 2 F.3d 110 (5th Cir. 1993).

Facts. Fidelity (D) issued director and officer liability policies to four affiliate banks and three subsidiaries of one of the banks. The policies required that for claims to be covered, the insured had to give certain notice during the policy period. In addition, claims could be covered after lapse of the policies if, during the policy term, the insured gave notice "of any act, error, or omission which may subsequently give rise to a claim . . . for a specified wrongful act." The banks were having financial difficulties; D was aware of this fact through financial reports. Also, the banks gave D its 1984 annual report, which had a footnote that referred to a cease and desist order to the banks from the Office of the Comptroller of the Currency. In September 1985, D gave notice that it was cancelling the policies on October 9, 1985. Shortly thereafter, the banks went into receivership with the Federal Deposit Insurance Corporation ("FDIC"), which sued the banks and its officers and directors for making improper loans. D denied coverage of the officers and directors under the policies. The FDIC filed a declaratory judgment action seeking a determination that D should provide coverage since it had received proper notice before the policies lapsed. The trial court granted summary judgment for D; the FDIC appeals.

Issue. If an insured only generally informs its insurer of a cease and desist order and of declining financial conditions, has the insured given sufficient notice of potential claims during the policy period?

Held. No. Judgment affirmed.

- This type of "claims made" policy requires that the insured give notice of ***specified*** wrongful acts.
- Notice of a cease and desist order and of a deteriorating financial condition are not sufficient notice of specified, wrongful acts by the officers or directors.

B. INSURANCE AGAINST DERIVATIVE SUIT LIABILITY

A number of states have statutes that authorize a corporation to purchase and maintain insurance (i) to protect the corporation against liability to its directors and officers for indemnification when otherwise authorized by law (above) and (ii) to protect the directors and officers against any liability arising out of their service to the corporation, and against the expense of defending suits asserting such liability. (Sometimes, but not always, the directors and officers pay a portion of the insurance premium.)

XV. TAKEOVERS

A. PROXY FIGHTS

A proxy contest typically results from a fight between management and other shareholders for control of the company. Most often the insurgent shareholders will have acquired a substantial position in the company and either (i) want to control the company through the election of a majority of the directors or (ii) will have proposed a merger or tendered the shares of the company, and management seeks to avoid a loss of control by a proxy fight, fighting off the tender offer, or merging with a third company.

1. In the first situation (proxy fight), management will solicit the shareholders for proxies to elect their slate of directors, and the insurgents will solicit the shareholders for proxies to elect their slate of directors.

2. In the second situation (a defensive merger), the insurgents will be attempting to get the shareholders to approve the tender offer, while management will be soliciting proxies from the shareholders to approve the defensive merger into a third company.

3. The expenses for a proxy battle in a major corporation can be very substantial. A major issue always concerns who can be reimbursed for these expenses.

   a. Normally courts hold that if management is successful in the proxy contest, it can recover its expenses from the corporation. The limitation is that the expenses must have been incurred in "good faith" for the benefit of the corporation.

   b. Furthermore, in a contest over "policy," as compared to a purely personal power contest, directors (***current management***) have the right to make reasonable and proper expenditures, subject to the scrutiny of the courts when duly challenged, for the purpose of persuading shareholders of the correctness of their position and soliciting their support for policies that the directors believe, in good faith, are in the best interests of the corporation. There is no obligation on the corporation to reimburse the successful outside contestants. But the shareholders may vote to reimburse such contestants for the reasonable and bona fide expenses incurred by them. [*See* Rosenfeld v. Fairchild Engine & Airplane, 128 N.E.2d 291 (N.Y. 1955)]

B. TENDER OFFERS

1. **Introduction.** A tender offer is an offer by a corporation (the tendering corporation) to purchase the securities of another corporation (the tendered corporation), which offer is made directly to the shareholders of the tendered

corporation. This offer may be made either in cash or in the stock of the tendering corporation. The offer may be made with or without the knowledge and/or cooperation of the tendered corporation's management.

2. **Federal Regulation of Tender Offers.**

   a. **Jurisdiction to regulate.** Jurisdiction of the federal government to regulate tender offers is based on their effect on interstate commerce.

   b. **Overview of the Securities Exchange Act of 1934 provisions.** The following sections of the 1934 Act apply to tender offers:

      1) **Reporting requirement.** Any person who has acquired beneficial ownership in excess of 2% of a class of equity security registered with the S.E.C. under section 12 of the Act within a 12-month period, and who thereby or otherwise owns more than 5% of that class of security, must file an information statement with the S.E.C., sending copies to the issuer of the security and to any exchanges where the security is traded.

      2) **Disclosure requirement.** Section 14(d) regulates the making of tender offers. Under this section, the party who makes a tender offer must make an appropriate disclosure to the tendered company, the S.E.C., and exchanges where the security of the tendered company that is registered under section 12 of the 1934 Act is traded.

      3) **Antifraud provision.** Section 14(e) is an antifraud provision that makes it unlawful for any party making a tender offer or defending against one to make untrue statements concerning material facts, or to omit to state material facts, or to engage in any fraudulent, deceptive, or manipulative acts or practices in connection with any tender offer.

3. **Private Action for Injunctions.** A plaintiff who is injured by violation of the tender offer rules may, as an alternative to an action for damages, sue for an injunction.

   a. **Preliminary injunctions.** A plaintiff seeking a preliminary injunction against the defendant tender offeror must meet the burden of showing either (i) probable success if the case were to go to trial on the merits and the possibility of irreparable harm if the injunction is not issued, or (ii) the existence of serious questions concerning material misrepresentations or omissions by the offeror and a balance of hardships in the plaintiff's favor. [General Host Corp. v. Triumph American, Inc., 359 F. Supp. 749 (E.D. Wis. 1973)]

b. **Permanent injunctions.** Before the courts will permanently enjoin the making of a tender offer, a plaintiff must show that it will suffer irreparable injury as a result of the defendant's violation of the tender offer rules.

4. **Antifraud Provision.** Plaintiffs that have standing to sue may bring an action for damages under section 14(e) of the 1934 Act.

5. **State Regulation--**

CTS Corp. v. Dynamics Corp. of America, 481 U.S. 69 (1987).

Facts. Indiana passed the Control Shares Acquisitions Act, which applied to businesses incorporated in Indiana that have: (i) 100 or more shareholders; (ii) their principal place of business, their principal office, or substantial assets within Indiana; and (iii) either: (a) more than 10% of their shareholders resident in Indiana; (b) more than 10% of their shares owned by Indiana residents; or (c) 10,000 shareholders resident in Indiana. An entity acquires "control shares" in such a corporation whenever it acquires voting power to or above 20%, 33.3%, or 50%. Voting power of these acquired shares is only granted on petition and approval of a majority vote of all disinterested shareholders of each class of stock. The acquirer can request a meeting for such a vote within 50 days; if voting power is not granted, the corporation ***may*** buy back the stock, or if no petition calling for a vote is asked for, the corporation can buy back the stock.

Dynamics owned 9.6% of CTS Corporation, an Indiana corporation. CTS elected to be governed by the new Act. Dynamics tendered one million shares of CTS, which would bring its interest to 27.5%. Dynamics sued, alleging that the Act violated the Commerce Clause and was preempted by the Williams Act. The district court agreed with Dynamics; the circuit court affirmed. Dynamics appeals.

Issues.

(i) Does the federal Williams Act preempt Indiana's state law?

(ii) Does the state law violate the Commerce Clause?

Held. (i) No. (ii) No. Judgment reversed.

♦ The state law is consistent with the intent of the Williams Act—it protects the shareholders against both management and the tender offeror. Neither contending party gets an advantage; it does not impose an indefinite delay on tender offers; it does not impose a government official's view of fairness on the buyer and selling shareholders. The shareholders can evaluate the fairness of the proposed terms.

♦ If the tender offeror fears an adverse shareholder vote, it can make a conditional offer, accepting shares on condition that the shares receive the voting rights within a certain time period.

- The Williams Act does not preempt all state regulation of tender offers, or state laws that limit or delay the free exercise of power after a tender offer (example: staggering the terms of the members of the board of directors).

- The state law does not discriminate against interstate commerce by imposing a greater burden on out-of-state offerors than Indiana offerors.

- The law does not adversely affect interstate commerce by subjecting activities to inconsistent regulations of more than one state. It applies only to corporations incorporated in Indiana.

- It is an accepted practice for states to regulate the corporations it creates. Thus, it is appropriate for the state to regulate the rights that are acquired by purchasing the shares of the corporation in order to promote stable relationships among the parties involved in the state's corporations.

- It is not for this Court to decide, or the intent of the Commerce Clause to promote, any specific economic theory— *i.e.,* whether tender offers are good or bad.

- There is no conflict with the provisions or purposes of the Williams Act.

Concurrence (Scalia, J.). If the law does not discriminate against interstate commerce or risk inconsistent regulation, then it does not offend the Commerce Clause. It is irrelevant whether it protects the shareholders of an Indiana corporation.

Dissent (White, Blackmun, Stevens, JJ.). The law undermines the policy of the Williams Act by preventing minority shareholders in some cases from acting in their best interests by selling their stock. Thus, the law directly inhibits interstate commerce (*i.e.,* the interstate market in securities).

C. DEFENSIVE TACTICS

Most managements of companies that are tendered, under the threat of losing their jobs, attempt to fight the takeover attempt. There are several ways of doing so:

1. **Advance Provisions.** Management will normally structure the corporation so as to make a takeover as difficult as possible; *i.e.,* staggering the election of directors so it is more difficult to gain control of the board.

2. **Persuasion of the Shareholders.** Management may attempt to persuade the shareholders not to tender their shares. Management must file certain information with the S.E.C. before opposing a tender offer; and anything said by management is subject to the antifraud provision of section 14(e) of the 1934 Act.

3. **Litigation.** Management may begin litigation, alleging that something done by the tender offeror is improper. This is often successful in stopping a tender offer, because litigation is time consuming, and market conditions can change so that financing is difficult to get.

4. **Merge with Another Company.** The tendered company's management may find a third company to merge with that is more sympathetic with management (*i.e.,* will allow them to keep their jobs).

5. **Purchase Its Own Shares.**

   a. **Introduction.** The management of the tendered company may attempt to have the corporation (or its pension plan, etc.) purchase enough of its own shares on the open market to prevent control from going to another company.

   b. **Federal law.** There are no outright prohibitions in the federal securities laws on the issuer purchasing its own shares.

      1) **Tender offer rules.** As a matter of fact, such an offer is exempt from the provisions of section 13(d) and 14(d) of the 1934 act (discussed *supra*). However, such an offer would be subject to the antifraud provision of section 14(e).

      2) **General liability provisions.** It would also be subject to other general liability provisions in the securities law. *See* the discussion *infra* of section 10(b) and Rule 10b-5 of the 1934 Act.

      3) **S.E.C. rules.** The S.E.C. has, however, adopted a series of rules to regulate such purchases.

   c. **Application of state law.** State corporation law also governs a corporation's purchase of its own shares.

      1) **Introduction.** Corporate law permits the corporation the right to purchase its own shares. Several legitimate reasons for doing so exist: Management may have an excess of funds and wish to use them this way rather than to pay dividends (believing that the company's earnings per share will be increased in this way), or, because of certain provisions in a class of securities (such as limitations on increases in debt), management may wish to retire the issue. There are also several illegitimate reasons for wanting to purchase the stock—management's wish to maintain control of the company to protect their jobs when an outside company wishes to buy control.

2) **Defensive takeover plans--**

Moran v. Household International, Inc., 500 A.2d 1346 (Del. 1985).

Facts. In August 1984, the board of Household International (Ds) adopted a plan providing for shareholders to receive rights to purchase Household preferred stock under certain conditions. If a company tenders 30% or more of Household's stock, then each shareholder gets a right, for each share owned, to purchase one-hundredth of a preferred share for $100. These rights are redeemable by the board for $.50 per right. If a company acquires 20% or more of Household's stock, nonredeemable rights are issued. If a merger occurs and rights have not been redeemed, the holder can pay $100 and get $200 of the acquiring company's common stock. The proposal was adopted because of concern about possible takeover attempts. One director, Moran (P), had discussed with the board the possibility of his heading a leveraged buyout of the company. Household's law firm and brokerage firm recommended the defensive plan. After adoption of the plan, P sued. The trial court upheld the plan as a legitimate exercise of the directors' business judgment. P appeals.

Issue. Was the adoption of the defensive takeover plan done as a proper exercise of business judgment by the board of directors?

Held. Yes. Judgment affirmed.

♦ The first question is whether the directors had the authority to adopt such a plan.

> Provisions of state law allow the issuance of rights to purchase stock and the issuance of preferred stock. Just because they are usually issued as part of a financing plan and not in connection with a defensive plan to a takeover does not make them invalid.
>
> The rights and preferred stock are not sham securities. They are issued on triggering events and can be bought and sold.
>
> The statute allows issuance of rights to purchase the issuer's own shares, not the shares of another corporation. But in the issuance of shares it is traditional to provide for antidilution (the right to purchase the shares of another, acquiring corporation) so as to preserve the right of purchase in the event of a merger.
>
> The provision that requires that notice of intention to make a tender offer be given is not proof that the state is in favor of no other regulation. Little state regulation does not prohibit private corporations from taking whatever fair defensive measures they feel are appropriate.
>
> The rights plan is not unconstitutional as a burden on interstate commerce. Here the corporation, a private party, and not the state, enacted the plan.

The board also has authority to issue the rights plan because it is in charge of the business of Household.

- The board has not usurped the shareholders' right to receive tender offers. Other approval defensive plans limit this right more than the plan adopted.

  There are many ways around the plan: tender Household stock with the conditions that the board redeem the rights first, tender and solicit consents to remove the board and redeem the rights, etc.

  Also, the board, if faced with a tender and request to redeem the rights, cannot arbitrarily reject it. They have fiduciary standards in reviewing such an offer.

  The rights plan results in less of a structural change in the corporation than do many other defensive plans (*i.e.,* there is no increased corporate debt, no change in the market price of stock, no dilution in earnings per share, etc.).

- The mere acquisition of the right to vote 20% or more of the common stock does not trigger the rights plan. But owning 20% or more does. This limits groups that want to wage a proxy contest from acquiring more than 20%. This impact on the ability to wage such contests is minimal.

- In application of the business judgment rule to adoption of defensive takeover plans, the burden should be shifted from those attacking the plan to the directors adopting it to show that they had reasonable grounds for believing that a danger to corporate policy and effectiveness existed. They must show good faith and a reasonable factual investigation to prove this. They must also show that the action they took is reasonable in relation to the threat posed. It helps if a majority of the directors approving the action were outside directors.

  After showing these things, the burden of proof shifts back to the plaintiff.

  There is no allegation here of bad faith.

  There is no allegation of taking the action to entrench their positions; the board feared threats of two-tier tender offers.

  The board's decision was an informed one; they were not grossly negligent in researching the facts. They knew what was happening in the marketplace, lawyers advised them, etc.

  The plan adopted was reasonable in relationship to the threat.

3) Defensive measures must be reasonable and proportionate--

Mentor Graphics Corporation v. Quickturn Design Systems, Inc., 728 A.2d 25 (Del. Ch. 1998).

Facts. Quickturn Design Systems, Inc. (D) and Mentor Graphics Corporation (P) were both computer technology concerns. P and D had been involved in several patent actions that ultimately resulted in P being barred from competing with D in the United States electronic emulation market. P began exploring the possibility of acquiring D and thereby ending the remaining patent litigation and its consequences. When D's stock began to decline in price, P announced an unsolicited cash tender offer for all outstanding shares of D at a price reflecting a 50% premium. D's board met three times to discuss the tender offer, but ultimately concluded that it was inadequate. D's board then adopted two defensive measures in response to the hostile takeover bid. First, the board amended D's bylaws, which permitted stockholders holding 10% or more of D's stock to call a special meeting. The amendment provided that if a special meeting were requested, D would fix the date, time, and place for the meeting, and that the meeting must take place no less than 90 days nor more than 100 days after the shareholder request. Second, the board amended D's shareholder rights plan by adding a Deferred Redemption Provision under which no newly elected board could redeem the rights plan for six months after taking office if the purpose of the redemption was to facilitate a transaction with an "interested person" (a person who proposed, nominated, or supported the election of the new directors to the board). The combined effect of the two provisions would be to delay P's acquisition of D for at least nine months. P filed suit seeking a declaratory judgment that D's takeover defenses are invalid, and an injunction to force D to dismantle those defenses.

Issue. Was D's Deferred Redemption Provision a valid takeover defense?

Held. No.

- We find that D's bylaw amendment was valid. The only remaining issue is the validity of the Deferred Redemption Provision ("DRP"). Decisions made by a board of directors are normally subject to the business judgment form of review, which is a presumption that the directors acted on an informed basis, in good faith, and in the honest belief that the action was in the best interest of the corporation. However, when a corporation takes an action to defend against a hostile takeover bid, the board's actions are subject to enhanced judicial scrutiny to ensure that the directors are not simply acting in their own interests.

- For the board's actions to be entitled to business judgment rule protection, the board must establish that it had reasonable grounds to believe that the hostile bid constituted a threat to corporate policy and effectiveness, and that the defensive measures it adopted were proportionate, *i.e.*, reasonable, in relation to the threat.

- D's board was concerned that shareholders, in ignorance of D's true value, would accept P's inadequate offer, and elect a new board that would prematurely sell the company before the new board could adequately inform itself of the company's fair value. The Delaware Supreme Court has held that recognition of the risk that shareholders will mistakenly accept an underpriced offer is a cognizable threat. We therefore find that D's board reasonably perceived a cognizable threat. However, we find that the response to that threat was disproportionate.

- The board's justification for adopting the DRP was to force any newly elected board to take sufficient time to become familiar with Quickturn and its value, and provide shareholders time to consider alternatives. However, the evidence shows that the DRP, as written, would create a six-month delay only if the newly elected board sought to sell the company to an "interested person." Under the terms of the DRP, the newly elected board could sell the company to anyone other than P on its very first day in office. Thus, the terms of the DRP cannot be reconciled with the board's stated purpose for adopting it, and therefore, the board cannot carry its burden to show that the DRP was reasonable in response to the perceived threat.

- In addition, the board cannot show that the time period selected (six months) was reasonable. D's amended bylaw would already impose a delay of 90 to 100 days, purportedly to give shareholders time to make an informed decision about how to vote on any tender offer. D cannot explain why shareholders would need an additional six months in which to adequately inform themselves of the company's value.

Comment. On appeal, the Delaware Supreme Court affirmed this decision, but on broader grounds. The Court held that the DRP enacted by D's board would impermissibly deprive any newly elected board of both its statutory authority to manage the corporation under section 141(a) of the Delaware corporations law, and its concomitant fiduciary duty pursuant to that mandate. Section 141(a) requires that any limitations on the board's authority be set out in the certificate of incorporation. D's certificate contained no limiting provision. However, the DRP would nonetheless restrict the board's power in an area of fundamental importance to the shareholders—negotiating a possible sale of the corporation. The Court found the DRP invalid because it conflicts with section 141(a), which confers on any newly elected board of directors full power to manage and direct the business and affairs of the corporation. [*See* Quickturn Design Systems, Inc. v. Shapiro, 721 A.2d 1281 (Del. 1998)]

---

4) Shareholder's rights plans--

International Brotherhood of Teamsters v. Fleming Companies, 975 P.2d 907 (Okla. 1999).

Facts. The International Brotherhood of Teamsters (P) owned 65 shares of Fleming Companies, Inc. (D). D's board of directors implemented a shareholder's rights plan that would give the board authority to adopt and implement discriminatory shareholder rights as an anti-takeover mechanism. Such plans typically become effective in the event of certain contingencies, such as when a certain percentage of shares is accumulated by a single shareholder, possibly signaling an impending takeover contest. P argued that the plan was simply an attempt by D's board of directors to entrench themselves in the event of a takeover, and proposed an amendment to the company's bylaws that would require any rights plan implemented by the board to be put to a vote by the shareholders. D refused to acknowledge the proposal, stating that under Oklahoma law, the issue was not one for shareholder review. P filed suit in federal court. The district court held for P and D appealed. The Tenth Circuit Court of Appeals certified the question to the Oklahoma Supreme Court.

Issue. Does Oklahoma law give the board of directors exclusive authority to create shareholder rights plans?

Held. No.

- D argued that Oklahoma statutes give the board of directors exclusive authority to develop and implement rights plans through language stating "every corporation may create and issue . . . rights or options entitling the holders thereof to purchase from the corporation any shares of its capital stock of any class or classes, such rights or options to be evidenced by or in such instrument or instruments as shall be approved by the board of directors." D contends that the word "corporations" as used in the statute actually means "board of directors." However, we note that throughout the rest of the statute, both terms are used distinctly. We can find no reason why our legislature would not have used the term "board of directors" in the above passage if that is in fact what was intended.

- Clearly, individual shareholders' degree of control in corporate governance is limited. However, the authority of the board of directors is not completely without shareholder oversight, even in large publicly held corporations. The nature of a shareholder rights plan is essentially that of a stock option plan, and there is ample authority supporting shareholder ratification of stock option plans. We find nothing in the Oklahoma General Corporation Act or existing case law that would indicate that shareholder rights plans are somehow exempt from shareholder approval.

- Our holding here does not suggest that all shareholder rights plans ***must*** be submitted to shareholder approval. Instead we find that shareholders ***may*** restrict the authority of the board of directors to implement shareholder rights plans by proceeding through the proper channels of corporate governance.

Comment. Note that a number of states have enacted legislation, typically called shareholders rights plans endorsement statutes, which give the board of directors explicit authority to create and implement rights plans to protect the company from takeover. In the *Fleming* case, no such statute existed in Oklahoma.

D. INTERNAL OVERTHROW

There are several ways in which an internal change may be made in the management of the corporation.

1. **Change Made by a Major Shareholder.** When one person, or a group, controls a majority of the stock, they may change directors and management by following state corporate law procedures.

2. **Change Made by the Directors.** When a corporation gets into serious financial trouble, or does not perform up to the expectations of the board of directors, the directors may pressure the president to resign, or perhaps fire him.

3. **Cooperation with Insurgents.** Sometimes management may attempt to come to peaceful terms with the insurgents and attempt to include them in the decisionmaking process of the corporation. This does not always work.

XVI. CORPORATE BOOKS AND RECORDS

A. TYPES OF BOOKS AND RECORDS

The books and records of a corporation fall into four basic categories: (i) shareholder lists; (ii) minutes of board meetings, shareholders' meetings, board committees, and officer committees; (iii) financial records, such as books of account and monthly, quarterly, and annual period summaries; and (iv) business documents, such as contracts, correspondence, and office memoranda.

B. COMMON LAW

At common law, a shareholder acting for a proper purpose has a right to "inspect" (examine) the corporate books and records at reasonable times. The shareholder has the burden of alleging and proving proper purpose.

C. STATUTES

In most states today, shareholder inspection rights are affected by statutes. Many of these statutes apply only to certain kinds of shareholders, such as those who are record holders of at least 5% of the corporation's stock, or who have been record holders for at least six months. [*See* N.Y. Bus. Corp. Law §624] The statutes are normally interpreted to preserve the proper purpose test, but to place on the corporation the burden of proving that the shareholder's purpose is improper. Those statutes that are limited to only certain shareholders, or only certain books and records, are usually interpreted to supplement the common law, so that a suit for inspection that does not fall within the statute can still be brought under the common law.

1. **Kind of Record Sought.** The burden of proof under a statute may be affected by the ***kind*** of corporate record sought. For example, the Delaware statute provides that when inspection is sought of shareholder lists, the burden is on the corporation to prove that the information is being sought for an improper purpose; for other corporate records, the burden is on the shareholder to prove proper purpose. [*See* Del. Gen. Corp. Law §220(c)]

D. PROPER VS. IMPROPER PURPOSES

In determining what constitutes a proper or improper purpose, the basic test is whether the shareholder is seeking inspection to protect his interest as a shareholder, or is acting primarily for another purpose, such as furthering his interest as a potential business rival or as a litigant.

1. **Multiple Purposes.** As long as the primary purpose is a proper one, the fact that the shareholder has an improper secondary purpose usually will not defeat the claim.

2. **Proxy Fights.** Inspection of a shareholder list to enable a shareholder to make a takeover bid or engage in a proxy contest with management is normally considered a proper purpose, since it is reasonably related to the interest of the shareholder.

3. **Other Purposes.** Among other purposes the courts have recognized as proper for exercising the inspection right are the following: (i) to determine whether the corporation is being properly managed or whether there has been managerial misconduct, at least if the shareholder alleges some specific concerns; (ii) to determine the corporation's financial condition; and (iii) to determine the value of the shareholder's stock.

4. **Social or Political Interests.** Several cases have held that a shareholder is not entitled to inspect corporate records solely for the purpose of advancing political or social views, as contrasted with economic or financial interests in the corporation.

   a. **Example.** Shareholder bought 100 shares in H Corp., a Delaware corporation, for the sole purpose of giving himself a voice in H's affairs so that he could persuade H to cease producing munitions. Shareholder then demanded access to the shareholder list and all corporate records dealing with weapons and munitions manufacture, for the purpose of communicating with other shareholders to elect a new board of directors who would represent his viewpoint. The Minnesota court denied inspection. It construed the Delaware statute to require a proper purpose germane to the applicant's interest as a shareholder and held that inspection that is sought solely to persuade the company to adopt a shareholder's social and political concerns, irrespective of any economic benefit to the shareholder or the corporation, did not meet this standard. [*See* State *ex rel.* Pillsbury v. Honeywell, Inc., 191 N.W.2d 406 (Minn. 1971)]

   b. **But note.** A subsequent Delaware case held that the desire to solicit proxies for a slate of directors in opposition to management is a purpose reasonably related to the shareholder's interest as a shareholder; that any further or secondary purpose in seeking the list is irrelevant; and that insofar as *Pillsbury* is inconsistent with these rules, it is inconsistent with the Delaware statute as properly applied. [*See* Credit Bureau Reports, Inc. v. Credit Bureau of St. Paul, Inc., 290 A.2d 691 (Del. 1972)] It is not clear, however, whether these rules are applicable to more than the shareholder list.

E. MANDATORY DISCLOSURE OF INFORMATION

In contrast to the law governing the shareholder's inspection right, which puts the initiative on the individual shareholder, various federal and state statutes require corporations to make affirmative disclosure of certain information.

1. **1934 Act.** Extensive disclosure requirements are imposed on corporations whose stock is registered under section 12 of the 1934 Act.

   a. **Annual and periodic reports.** Such corporations must file with the S.E.C., and any securities exchange on which the stock is listed, periodic reports disclosing their financial condition and certain types of material events. These reports are open to inspection by the public.

   b. **Proxy rules.** Under the federal proxy rules, corporations whose stock is registered under section 12 must annually disclose certain information to shareholders, such as the compensation of the five highest paid officers, the compensation of officers and directors as a group, details on the operation of stock option and pension plans, and transactions with insiders during the previous year involving amounts in excess of a certain amount.

2. **State Statutes.** State laws vary greatly as to the amount of information that must be provided by corporations incorporated in the jurisdiction.

   a. **Report to state.** Most states require corporations incorporated in the jurisdiction to file an annual report with an appropriate state officer, such as the secretary of state, providing at least certain minimal information—*e.g.,* the names and addresses of its directors and officers, the address of its principal business office, its principal business activity, and the name and address of its agent for the service of process upon the corporation. [RMBCA §16.22]

   b. **Report to shareholders.** In addition, some states require corporations to send an annual report to shareholders containing financial statements. For example, under the Model Act, a corporation must furnish its shareholders with annual financial statements that include a balance sheet, an income statement, and a statement of changes in shareholders' equity. If financial statements are prepared for the corporation on the basis of generally accepted accounting principles, the annual financial statements furnished to the shareholders must also be prepared on that basis. If the annual financial statements are reported on by a public accountant, the accountant's report must accompany them. If not, the statements must be accompanied by a statement of the president or the person responsible for the corporation's accounting records: (i) stating his reasonable belief whether the statements were prepared on the basis of generally accepted accounting principles and, if not, describing the basis of preparation; and (ii) describing any respects in which the statements were not prepared on the basis of accounting consistent with the statements prepared for the preceding year.

F. SHAREHOLDERS' INSPECTION RIGHTS LITIGATION

1. Evidentiary Burden and Scope of Inspection--

Thomas & Betts Corporation v. Leviton Manufacturing Company, Inc., 681 A.2d 1026 (Del. 1996).

Facts. Thomas & Betts Corporation (P) and Leviton Manufacturing Company (D) were engaged in the manufacture of electronic components. The companies were not in direct competition because D focused on residential markets only. However, P had for years been interested in either acquiring D or engaging in some type of joint venture. D had never expressed interest in either possibility. P decided to seek a minority position in D in order to eventually force a sale of the company to P without the knowledge of D's owner, Harold Leviton. P began negotiating to purchase the shares of Thomas Blumberg and his wife. Blumberg was D's former Group Vice President and owned 29.1% of D's outstanding shares. Ultimately, P paid Blumberg $50 million for his shares. When informed of the sale, Harold Leviton refused to establish an amicable relationship with P, and remained obstinate in his opposition to P's ownership position. After months of failed negotiations, P served D with a formal demand seeking inspection of corporate documents, including shareholder lists, minutes of corporate meetings, audited financial statements, tax returns, organizational charts, and documents relating to D's lease of real estate or equipment. P's stated purpose for its request was to investigate possible waste and mismanagement, and to assist in P's valuation of its shares. D formally refused P's inspection demand and P filed suit seeking to compel inspection of D's books and records. The trial court found that the evidence indicated that P's demand was not motivated by its stated purpose of investigating mismanagement, but by P's desire to gain leverage in its efforts to acquire D. However, the court found that P was entitled to limited inspection of certain documents so that it could value its shares. P appealed the decision, arguing that the trial court applied an incorrect evidentiary burden, and that the court abused its discretion in limiting the scope of P's inspection. D did not cross-appeal.

Issues.

(i) Did the trial court err in subjecting P to a higher than normal evidentiary burden under the circumstances?

(ii) Did the trial court abuse its discretion in limiting the scope of P's inspection?

Held. (i) No. (ii) No. Judgment affirmed.

♦ P's claims of mismanagement are based on D's purportedly substandard performance, the company's failure to pay dividends, and D's poor cash flow and higher than average expenses. P also alleged misconduct, arguing that D paid for the Leviton family's personal expenses, that D was overcompensating its officers and directors, and that D's lease agreements with members of the Leviton family are self-dealing transactions. The trial court found that these claims were so lacking in evidentiary support that inspection could not be justified. P argues that, in so finding, the trial court incorrectly subjected P to a higher evidentiary standard.

- While investigation of waste and mismanagement is a proper purpose for a books and records inspection, a mere statement of this purpose is not sufficient. P bears the burden of providing specific and credible allegations sufficient to warrant a suspicion of waste or mismanagement. P is not required to prove by a preponderance of the evidence that waste and mismanagement are actually occurring.

- The trial court stated that in a case such as this, where substantial evidence indicates that P's motives for the inspection are improper, a "greater than normal evidentiary burden is required." While we agree with P that as a general standard, this articulation of P's burden is unclear and could be interpreted as an unduly difficult obstacle for shareholders seeking to investigate mismanagement, this is not a typical case. This case does not involve a typical uninformed shareholder attempting to protect his investment. P acquired shares of D with the acknowledged purpose of acquiring the company. When efforts to force a friendly transfer of control failed, P suddenly filed an inspection demand alleging mismanagement. P's admitted acquisition motives cast serious doubt on the genuineness of its claim that it needs these documents to investigate waste and mismanagement. In such a case, a higher evidentiary standard is required.

- We also note that the trial court's decision did not turn solely on its conclusion that P failed to meet a heightened evidentiary burden. The decision rested, in large part, on the court's determination that P's witnesses were not credible. We are required to show deference to the trial court's credibility assessments.

- We further find that the trial court did not abuse its discretion in limiting the scope of P's inspection. The plain language of section 220 of the Delaware corporations law states that "[t]he Court may, in its discretion, prescribe any limitations or conditions with reference to the inspection." The trial court has wide latitude in this determination and must ensure that the interests of the corporation are harmonized with those of the inspecting shareholder. In this case, the trial court found P's primary purpose for inspection is at odds with the interests of the corporation. Therefore, it was entirely appropriate for the court to limit P's inspection to those documents essential to its valuation purpose.

---

2. Documents Reasonably Related to Shareholder's Proper Purpose--

Saito v. McKesson HBOC, Inc., 806 A.2d 113 (Del. 2002).

Facts. Saito (P) was a shareholder of McKesson HBOC, Inc. P demanded access to certain corporate books and records because he wanted to investigate McKesson's apparent failure to learn of HBOC's accounting irregularities until several months after the two companies merged to become McKesson HBOC, Inc. The Court of Chancery found that although P had a proper purpose for his request, he was barred from bringing a derivative suit or compelling inspection rights because he had not been a shareholder of McKesson or HBOC at the time of the merger. He owned stock in the newly merged company. The court further denied P access to documents related to the merger that the corporation obtained from financial and accounting advisors on the ground that P could not use section 220 to develop potential claims against third parties. Finally, the court would not permit P to access any HBOC documents because he was never a shareholder of HBOC. P appeals.

Issues.

(i) Is P barred from inspecting records about the merger because he was not a shareholder at the time of the merger?

(ii) Is P barred from inspecting records prepared by third parties?

(iii) May P, a shareholder of the parent corporation, inspect the books of a subsidiary corporation?

Held. (i) No. (ii) No. (iii) No. Judgment affirmed in part, reversed in part, and remanded in part.

- ♦ The Court of Chancery properly stated that stockholders who bring derivative suits must allege that they were stockholders at the time of the alleged wrong. However, the court went on to hold that P was therefore limited to examining the conduct of McKesson and McKesson HBOC's boards following the negotiation and public announcement of the merger agreement. We disagree. Even when a stockholder's only purpose is to gather information for a derivative suit, the date of his stock purchase should not be used as an automatic cut-off date. If the activities that occurred before the merger date are reasonably related to the stockholder's interest as a stockholder, then he should be given access to records necessary to an understanding of those activities. This portion of the court's decision is reversed.

- ♦ The Chancery Court also denied P access to documents prepared by third parties. The source of the documents should not control a stockholder's right to inspection. The issue is whether the documents are necessary and essential to the stockholder's proper purpose. In this case, P's proper purpose is to investigate McKesson and McKesson HBOC's failure to discover HBOC's accounting irregularities. The reports of financial and accounting advisors would clearly be critical to P's investigation. This part of the decision is remanded to determine whether the court meant a blanket exclusion of these documents, which would be improper.

- ♦ Finally, we affirm the court's decision with respect to the HBOC documents. P is a shareholder of McKesson HBOC, the parent company. Stockholders of a parent corporation are generally not entitled to inspect a subsidiary's books and records. However, we note that this rule does not apply to any relevant documents that HBOC gave to McKesson before the merger, or to McKesson HBOC after the merger, as P would need these documents in order to understand what the company's directors knew and why they failed to recognize HBOC's accounting irregularities.

---

3. Types of Records Sought--

Parsons v. Jefferson-Pilot Corp., 426 S.E.2d 685 (N.C. 1993).

Facts. Louise Parsons (P) owned 300,000 shares of Jefferson (D) stock, worth several million dollars. She sent a written request to D for a list of the beneficial owners of its stock and for the right to inspect certain accounting records to determine if there had been mismanagement. D refused the first request on the basis that it did not keep a list of beneficial owners, and the second request was not within the allowed scope of a North Carolina statute. P then asked for the records of compensation paid to officers, board members, and their families. D refused. P sought a preliminary injunction granting access to the information. The trial court held that D was required to allow P to inspect records of board and shareholder actions, but denied that D had to supply P with a list of beneficial owners. The appellate court affirmed the decision not requiring D to produce the shareholder list, but reversed the ruling that D had to supply records of director and shareholder meetings. The case was remanded to the trial court to determine whether the director and shareholder meeting records were directly related to P's purpose. The state supreme court granted discretionary review.

Issue. Do common law shareholder inspection rights still exist when North Carolina has enacted a statute on the matter?

Held. Yes. Judgment affirmed in part and reversed in part. Case remanded.

- ♦ Section 55-16-02(b) gives shareholders the right to inspect corporate accounting records, with proper notice, but denies such right to shareholders of a public corporation (*i.e.,* ones registered under the Securities Exchange Act of 1934). But section 55-16-02(e)(2) states that courts may decide to compel production of corporate records. The legislative commentary to this section indicates that this section was meant to keep all common law shareholder rights in place, and expand these rights in other sections of the statute. We hold that this was the legislative intent. Thus, shareholders may make reasonable inspections of accounting records of public corporations for proper purposes.

- ♦ P also seeks a list of the beneficial owners of D's stock who do not object to the release of their names. To put this list together would require that D get these names from brokers and others in whose name the stock appears. It does not have such a list at this time and it should not be required to get such a list.

However, if it did have such a list and was using it to communicate with shareholders, it would probably be required to give it to a shareholder with a proper purpose.

♦ Section 55-16-02(c)(2) requires that a shareholder describe with reasonable particularity the information being sought. What constitutes sufficient particularity depends on the situation. Here, P sought records of the final actions taken by the board or committees of the board, the minutes of shareholder meetings, and records of actions of shareholders taken without meetings. P was dissatisfied with the return on her investment, and was seeking to determine whether D was being mismanaged. Since P had no more particular information at her disposal, she could not have described the desired records with any more particularity. D should understand what records P wants to see. Thus, P's request was stated with sufficient particularity.